Chicago Public Library
D1030730

The World of
King Arthur

The World of KING ARTHUR

CHRISTOPHER SNYDER

Original illustrations by Samuel Valentino

With 262 illustrations, 64 in color

To the Lord of lords, the King of kings

Author's note

Ten years ago two college students and their history professor collaborated on a book about King Arthur. Stealing a line from Chaucer, they called the book *In th'olde dayes of the Kyng Arthur*, and hoped that it would serve for fans of the Arthurian legends as an introduction to the history of 'Dark Age' Britain. The next year it was used as the textbook for a team-taught history course called 'King Arthur and the Dark Ages', whose large enrollment was only slightly swelled by friends recruited by the young authors. Both the book and the course proved to be terrific learning experiences that launched, respectively, the academic and artistic careers of the author and illustrator of the present volume. For this they wish to thank their inspiring history professor, Dr W.R. McLeod, for giving them their first professional opportunity.

It is my good fortune to have the opportunity to collaborate on a second Arthurian project with Samuel Valentino. Mr and Mrs Donald E. Snyder and Dr Virginia Valentino gave their love and support in the making of our first Arthur book, as did Renée Baird Snyder in the making of the second. Financial support was given graciously by Emory University and Marymount University. Thanks to the staff of Thames & Hudson, especially Peter Warner and Colin Ridler, and to the following individuals who have read and commented on the manuscript: Bonnie Wheeler, Jeremy Adams, Norris Lacy, Peter Field, Simon James, Lillian Bisson, Karen Waters, W.R. McLeod, and V.B. McLeod. Lastly, in producing this book we honour the memory of a man whose editorial contributions helped shape its predecessor: Professor Donovan H. Bond, *requiescat in pace*.

Half-title: King Arthur, thirteenth-century sculpture, possibly from a group of the Nine Worthies. Germanisches Nationalmuseum, Nuremberg. Title-page: King Arthur, detail from a group of the Five Worthies with Attendant Figures, south Netherlandish tapestry, c.1400–1410. The Metropolitan Museum of Art, The Cloisters Collection, Munsey Fund, 1932 (32.130.3a). Photograph © 1985 The Metropolitan Museum of Art.

First published in hardcover in the United States of America in 2000 by Thames & Hudson Inc., 500 Fifth Avenue, New York, New York 10110

Library of Congress Catalog Card Number 99-69560
ISBN 0-500-05104-6

Printed and bound in Slovenia by Mladinska Knjiga

CONTENTS

IV

THE CHRONICLES OF THE BRITONS

V

THE LEGENDS OF THE BRITONS

VI

MONARCHY, CHIVALRY AND THE RETURN OF ARTHUR

VII

THE QUEST FOR CAMELOT

VIII

CONCLUSION: AN AGE OF ARTHUR

THE STORY OF ARTHUR

LIONEL
GAWAIN

I

INTRODUCTION: WHO WAS ARTHUR?

In th'olde dayes of the Kyng Arthour,
Of which the Britons speken greet honour,
Al was this land fulfild of fairye.
The elf-queene with her joly compaignye
Daunced ful ofte in many a grene mede.
This was the olde opinion, as I rede . . .

Geoffrey Chaucer, *The Canterbury Tales*

THUS BEGINS THE famous fourteenth-century tale of the Wife of Bath. Geoffrey Chaucer, like many great writers before and after him, chose to write about Britain in the time of the fabled King Arthur, when the green and pleasant land of the Britons was filled with knights and dancing fairies. This magical age, the 'brief, shining moment' of Camelot that inspired Chaucer and Malory, Tennyson and Steinbeck, was Britain in the fifth and sixth centuries AD. Although a somewhat obscure historical period, dismissed by many as the 'Dark Ages', this era gave birth not only to the legends of Arthur and Merlin but also to the very real St Patrick.

'I speke of manye hundred yeres ago,' explains the Wife of Bath. 'But now kan no man se none elves mo.' Like the good Wife, I shall here speak of a time many hundreds of years ago (fifteen hundred, to be exact), a time for which historical facts – like elves – have proven quite elusive to modern observers. Thus an air of mystery is lent to the origins of Arthur, appropriate for a ruler whose death in the legends is also enigmatic. But while we cannot answer the ultimate questions about Arthur, we can achieve a better understanding of the historical period which produced, if not the king himself, then the people who believed in him, who sang songs and wrote stories about him, and of the succeeding eras when Arthur became a symbol of Christian rulership, national monarchy and romantic nostalgia.

The Holy Grail appearing before Arthur and the Knights of the Round Table – an illustration from a fifteenth-century French manuscript of the romance Lancelot.

Arthur, Myth and Reality

WHO WAS ARTHUR? Well, to begin with, there was not one Arthur, but many. There was an historical Arthur, or, if you prefer, a folkloric or mythological Arthur who came to be mistaken for a living person. There was a literary Arthur, indeed several, and an Arthur portrayed in almost every other artistic medium. There was, and is, a 'figure' of Arthur made up of all these elements, who has made a very real impact on history because he has made a very deep impression in the hearts of so many men and women, for more than a thousand years.

The myth of Arthur and Camelot is one of the most influential in the western tradition. Like all myths it contains truths, though not usually literal ones. The myth begins with the premise that Arthur was a king; not just any king, but an exemplary Christian monarch who displayed both martial and political virtues. The facts are that we do not have records specifically calling Arthur a king until later in the development of his legend, and that the first history in which he appears calls him simply *dux bellorum*, 'leader of battles'. The truth greater than the facts is that Arthur was considered to be a king by most medieval monarchs, who sought to imitate him and even to bring him into their genealogies. To them, Arthur was one of the three great Christian Kings to be celebrated as being among the Nine Worthies (p. 132).

A Victorian image of Arthur. Photograph by Julia Margaret Cameron for an edition of Tennyson's Idylls of the King *(1874).*

The myth continues with the specifics that Arthur was ruler of Britain – 'King of the Britons' – residing in his many towered castle, Camelot, sometime in the European Middle Ages. Historians who believe in Arthur's existence do indeed see him as some kind of ruler or military official in Britain, though they debate how widespread was his authority and, especially, his dates (estimates have ranged from the second to the seventh centuries AD). As for Camelot, most scholars believe it to have been the invention of a twelfth-century French poet. Archaeologists who have sought Arthur's residence present us with hillforts and military encampments that hardly resemble later medieval castles.

Another component of the myth is that Arthur had a magical helper named Merlin. Like Arthur, Merlin has many guises. He is prophet, poet, wildman and wizard. Some even claim that he was a Celtic Druid. Facts are few, but there does seem to be evidence of an early medieval figure named Myrddin who was known for his prophetic verse. If he lived, however, it may have been a century later than the historical Arthur, and much of his tradition only became attached to Arthur in the twelfth century and later.

Arthur also had a beautiful wife, Guinevere, and a mighty champion named Lancelot. Unfortunately, neither name appears in connection with Arthur's until the twelfth century. Guinevere first appears in a pseudo-history, as a noble Roman lady who wed Arthur but later betrayed him in an affair with his nephew, Mordred. Lancelot is introduced in a French romance (though some argue for older, Celtic roots) as the daring young knight who rescues

(Right) An image of Arthur worthy of an emperor. This bronze statue of the king graces the tomb of Maximilian I (Holy Roman Emperor, 1459–1519) in the Hofkirche at Innsbruck, Austria.

A late medieval vision of Camelot, as a many towered castle, appears in this illustration of Arthur and his knights returning home, from a late-fifteenth-century Flemish manuscript, the romance Guiron le Courtois.

(Above) The tragic love triangle. Lancelot (Franco Nero), Arthur (Richard Harris) and Guinevere (Vanessa Redgrave) in a scene from the 1967 film Camelot.

(Right) Merlin as the old magician or wizard in an illustration by Trevor Stubley for T.H. White's The Book of Merlyn, *published posthumously in 1977.*

a kidnapped Guinevere and later becomes her lover. The Arthur–Guinevere–Lancelot love-triangle soon became one of the most seductive aspects of the myth.

Arthur is said to have formed and presided over a gathering of fighting-men known as the Knights of the Round Table. The table itself can still be seen hanging in the Great Hall at Winchester Castle (p. 134). Though Arthur's Dark-Age warriors may have worn mail armour, knights as we know them do not appear until the very end of the first millennium AD. The massive Winchester table could have served a, rather snug, company of twenty-six knights, but experts believe it was constructed much later, probably in the fourteenth century, and repainted by Henry VIII so that his countenance could be given to its depiction of an enthroned Arthur.

Artist's representation of a British warrior from the 'Arthurian' period (c.400–600). This 'knight' would have fought with sword and spear (possibly on horseback), protected by a helmet, a leather or mail coat, and a round shield bearing a Christian symbol.

These Knights of the Round Table, according to the myth, went in search of a mysterious object known as the Holy Grail. The first poem describing this object, however, was left unfinished, allowing subsequent continuators to supply their own version of the Grail. In some stories it is the chalice (or a dish) from the Last Supper, containing the Blood of Christ and the mysteries of the Holy Trinity. The young Sir Galahad accomplishes its quest. In other versions it is a magic stone, and Perceval serves as the questing hero. Many scholars see in the Grail Quest elements of pagan Celtic tales. Modern novelists use the quest as a metaphor for psychological epiphanies.

Finally, goes the myth, the Round Table collapsed through treason and betrayal, and Arthur, mortally wounded, was carried off to the Isle of Avalon, where he will be healed and one day return to rule over Britain. Early records tell of the deaths of Arthur and 'Medraut' at the Battle of Camlann in the mid-sixth century, but do not describe the circumstances, nor locate Camlann. Avalon was later identified as Glastonbury, whose Tor was indeed occupied and surrounded by marsh in the early Middle Ages. In the twelfth century, the monks of Glastonbury Abbey claimed to have excavated the grave of Arthur and Guinevere, which was marked by an inscribed lead cross. Though archaeologists have proven that the excavation did take place, the cross (now lost) bore an inscription which was later than sixth-century. Many accuse the monks of constructing a hoax in order to increase pilgrimage revenue.

It is easy to be cynical about many aspects of the Arthurian myth. It is, after all, both idyllic and idealistic, a utopian dream for romantics and sentimental fools. Such 'fools' have included Edmund Spenser, Alfred Tennyson, Winston Churchill, John Steinbeck and John F. Kennedy, not to mention half the British monarchy. I, too, am a fortunate fool ensnared by this myth, but Arthur's spell has led me to serious academic pursuits as well as to enjoyment of fantasy novels. The world of King Arthur is a diverse and pluralistic place, encompassing history, literature, art and politics. No single area gives us the full picture of Camelot, but we can move chronologically through the development of this enduring and endearing myth.

Is this the Isle of Avalon? Glastonbury Tor, conspicuous across the Somerset Levels, was once surrounded by marsh and has shown signs of occupation in the Brittonic Age.

(Above) Artist's impression of the Holy Grail as golden chalice. Such a cup, in medieval Christian liturgy, would have been used to serve the Eucharist wine. But this is just one vision of the Grail.

Classical, Celtic, Christian and medieval elements come together in Victorian Arthuriana. The Knights of the Round Table Summoned to the Quest by the Strange Damsel, *tapestry by Morris & Company (c.1890). Figures by Edward Burne-Jones, chairs and other accessories designed by William Morris.*

Sources of Evidence

(Right) Enamelled mount from the base of a hanging-bowl found at Sutton Hoo, in Suffolk. On stylistic grounds, it would seem that the item was manufactured by Britons, even though it was found in a seventh-century Anglian burial, but ethnicity is notoriously hard to determine from artifacts alone.

EXPLORING THE WORLD of King Arthur means tackling a diverse collection of evidence. Written histories, pottery sherds, verse romances, local place-names and modern films may all have something to add to the Arthurian myth. There are also many disciplines involved and different methods of approaching the evidence. An historian and a folklorist, for example, might handle a piece of early medieval literature in very different ways, even if both were trying to answer similar questions about Arthur. It is, moreover, important, in studying Arthur, to understand the type of evidence being used as well as how a particular writer is using it.

History

Professional historians study the past for different reasons, and there are many schools of historical thought. But all historians are taught to place the greatest value on primary sources – that is, written evidence produced by eyewitnesses or at least contemporary witnesses to the events. These can come in many forms – chronicles, formal histories, inscriptions. Unfortunately, we do not have any reliable written source that can claim to be an eyewitness account of Arthur's reign, and contemporary chronicles and inscriptions are quite scarce in Britain during the fifth and sixth centuries AD.

Sherds of so-called 'Tintagel ware' pottery. These are fragments of fine red bowls and amphoras (ceramic containers used to transport, among other things, wine and olive oil) manufactured in the Mediterranean. Such items have been found at Tintagel (p. 41) and other high status insular sites, attesting to long distance trade in late fifth- and sixth- century Britain.

Any written evidence not contemporary with the events is considered a secondary source. Proponents of an historical Arthur often use poems and chronicles written as much as six centuries after the time Arthur is thought to have lived. This makes many academic historians wary of the whole quest for Arthur. These late sources, however, can be treated as primary sources for the period in which they were composed, therefore telling us something about the way a particular age or group of people viewed Arthur.

There are also rules for the proper handling of historical evidence. Historians seldom take their sources at face value. An author's background (gender, faith, nationality, profession) may colour the way he or she portrays events. While this holds true for modern as well as ancient authors, Arthurian writers, it seems, have been particularly influenced by their own personal interests or those of their patrons. One must always remember that objectivity (which many believe is impossible for even the modern historian) was not a priority for most ancient and medieval chroniclers.

Archaeology

Archaeology is often considered an objective, scientifically accurate way of answering questions about the past. There would, surely, no longer be any controversy if we just dug up Arthur's bones? Archaeologists would be the first to refute this. While scientific methods are used for excavating, analyzing and dating finds, archaeologists of the Roman and medieval periods have traditionally been influenced by the humanities and usually match their evidence against historical sources. This is lessening, as archaeology matures as an independent discipline, but it is certainly still in evidence for the excavations of many 'Arthurian' sites.

It is seldom the case that a team of excavators unearths a royal grave with concrete identification. Even at Sutton Hoo, the most famous early medieval royal burial in Britain, experts still debate identity and purpose. If graves are found they are usually simple, anonymous burials. Hair, skin, wood, clothing and even bones disintegrate rapidly in the British climate. But coins and pottery survive, and remain our most important means of dating fifth- and sixth-century sites. Anyone seeking the splendour of a pharaoh's treasure in 'Arthurian' Britain is likely to be disappointed. Modern archaeology more often tells us about processes and practices than pomp and personality.

(Above) Reconstruction drawing by Caroline Fleming of an Anglian king wearing artifacts from Sutton Hoo, Suffolk. Few early medieval graves were as richly furnished as this pagan ship burial, and most Christian Britons are archaeologically invisible.

Arthur's Stone, Cefn-y-Bryn, Gower, West Glamorgan. One of several prehistoric megaliths so named – the folkloric Arthur has left his mark throughout Britain.

From holy texts to hyper-text: (above, left) Arthur pulling the sword from the stone, as narrated in illustrations from a Flemish manuscript c.1290; and (right) a multitude of options confront visitors of this commercial website, which promotes Arthurian tourism. (Below) King Arthur's Footprint, Tintagel, Cornwall. This folkloric feature may have been used in ancient king-making rituals.

Literature

Both historians and archaeologists use literary evidence to help them reconstruct the past. But the modern literary critic is not only interested in historical questions. The form, structure, metre and imagery may be more important in their analysis of an Arthurian poem than determining whether or not Arthur existed. Some literary critics ask questions about a writer's background, others consider such questions irrelevant. Some like to look for comparisons with, and allusions to, other literary works, while others see literary creations as isolated and independent. The literary criticism of an Arthurian work may be completely subjective and idiosyncratic, or the critic may be following a recognizable school of thought (Deconstructivist and Post-colonial, Marxist, Feminist, Jungian, and so on).

The definition of 'text' has also broadened. Latin chronicles, vernacular poetry and modern novels have now been joined by manuscript illustrations, comic books and films. All these types of evidence can be 'read' and can tell us something about the way a society, or an individual author, interpreted the Arthurian myth.

Mythology and folklore

Many literary scholars have read medieval Arthurian literature with an eye to its mythological roots. Both classical and Celtic myths have shaped the way later authors characterized Arthurian figures (Gawain, for example, has characteristics of a sun deity) as well as having provided plots and motifs (the quest for the Holy Grail is only the most obvious example). These critics would say that the true power of the Arthurian myth comes from its incorporation of universal themes or archetypes – the hero on the quest, the sacrificial king – which can be found in many of the world's mythologies. Arthur's existence as an historical person may, in this camp, be viewed as irrelevant.

Others would say that Arthur's existence is indeed relevant, not as an historical figure, but as a figure of folklore. We can better understand a society by exploring the heroes and villains it creates not consciously but corporately: if dozens of megaliths and mountaintops bear Arthur's name, he must have been seen as an important part of the heritage of a particular group of people. Since the names of Arthur, Merlin and Gawain can literally be seen in dozens of places throughout Britain and Brittany (see Gazetteer), the importance of this myth to the Britons and their descendants cannot be easily dismissed.

An Outline History

TO ACHIEVE AN understanding of the historical dimension of the Arthurian myth one cannot simply begin in the fifth century AD, when Arthur is thought by many to have lived. Rather, to understand those 'olde dayes' of which Chaucer spoke we must search further back into the earliest recorded history of the British Isles. Arthur's Britons, unlike their modern counterparts, were the direct cultural heirs of two peoples: the Celts and the Romans. While neither group was homogeneous or genetically a 'race', they did produce vigorous cultures which dominated the European Iron Age for over one thousand years and altered the physical, linguistic and artistic landscape of Britain.

By the late fourth century AD a third powerful force was shaping Britain: Christianity. While its British origins are obscure, Christianity had risen from being a minor eastern sect to become the official religion of the Roman Empire. In the fifth century the British Church produced the heresiarch Pelagius and the missionary Patrick, and in the next century its scholars and missionaries would spark the great Age of the Saints in the Celtic churches.

The Britons of the fifth and sixth centuries were, then, a hybrid of Celtic, Roman and Christian influences. Not surprisingly, all three have left their imprint on the Arthurian legends. But the Britons were not alone. The fifth century was the great Age of Migrations, as Huns, Goths and other displaced peoples followed their military leaders westwards across central Europe. The Britons, already threatened by 'barbarians' from Ireland and Scotland, invited small groups of Germanic mercenaries to cross the English Channel and help in the defence of the island. The mercenaries soon turned against those who had hired them and invited greater numbers of their people to cross the Channel. Such are the shadowy beginnings of the *adventus Saxonum*, the Anglo-Saxon settlement of Britain, which turned into a centuries-long struggle for control of the island, a struggle in which British victories came to be attributed to a warrior named Arthur.

The Anglo-Saxons eventually won the struggle, but as the Britons fell from political prominence they took heart in a heroic national past which came to feature Arthur as a 'once and future' redeemer. The Arthurian myth then passed into early medieval literature, which is a mixed bag of Latin chronicles, bardic poetry and Christian hagiography. The elusive Arthur appears in one account as a Christian warrior, in the next as a tyrannical monarch. Annals record his victories and his death, yet magic surrounds his martial feats and mystery envelops his grave. By the twelfth century the details of Arthur's career were filled in by an inventive clerk named Geoffrey of Monmouth, and soon after that French and German writers began producing chivalric romances centring around the famous monarch and his court, called Camelot.

The first of these romances, written by the French poet Chrétien de Troyes in the late twelfth century, introduced such themes as the

Artist's representation of the historical St Patrick. The revered British bishop, and apostle to the Irish, has left us rare first-hand accounts of life in fifth-century Britain and Ireland.

(Right) An Arthur for American audiences. Mark Twain's dark satire transformed into a Hollywood musical, A Connecticut Yankee in King Arthur's Court *(1949), starring Bing Crosby and Rhonda Fleming.*

John Evan Thomas, *Group of the Death of Tewdric, King of Gwent, at the Moment of Victory over the Saxons near Tintern Abbey (1849). Early insular history and legend were kept alive by bards at the courts of medieval Welsh princes.*

quest for the Holy Grail and Lancelot's adulterous affair with Guinevere. In the early thirteenth century a German poet, Gottfried von Strassburg, made famous a story of another affair, that of Tristan and Isolde, which came to be attached to the Arthurian tradition. The first English Arthurian poem to reach this level of literary achievement was *Sir Gawain and the Green Knight*, written by an anonymous poet around the year 1400. As the Middle Ages came to a close in the fifteenth century, another Englishman, Sir Thomas Malory, composed what most critics recognize as the most ambitious and influential of all Arthurian works, *Le Morte d'Arthur*. One scholar at the court of Henry VIII observed that Malory's *Morte d'Arthur* 'was received into the prince's chamber' when 'God's Bible was banished [from] the court'.

The Arthurian legends were never merely entertainment, however. By the late twelfth century Arthur, the symbol of British resistance against the English (the Anglo-Saxons), was adopted by the Norman conquerors of the English. The Angevin-Norman Plantagenet dynasty in the succeeding two centuries provided great patronage to Arthurian writers, and even claimed to have excavated the graves of Arthur and Guinevere at Glastonbury. They helped gain recognition for Arthur throughout Europe as the ideal Christian monarch, and launched his career as a new kind of national symbol for England. This he was for the Tudors, who traced their Welsh descent from Arthur and showed visiting dignitaries his Round Table hanging in

The adventures of Sir Lancelot (including battling a dragon and rescuing a maiden from a bath of boiling water) are narrated in this woodcut from Lancelot du Lac *(1488).*

the royal city of Winchester, and this he remained for writers such as Edmund Spenser (1552–99) and Alfred Tennyson (1809–92).

The nineteenth century saw a particular fascination with the Arthurian myth. In Britain, poems by Tennyson and Sir Walter Scott celebrated Arthur and his knights, as did many of the paintings of the Pre-Raphaelites, and several new editions of the *Morte d'Arthur* were published. In America, humourist Mark Twain's novel placed *A Connecticut Yankee in King Arthur's Court*. The next century saw Arthur make his mark in such new media as comic books, film and television. And we continue to witness a veritable explosion of Arthuriana, with sightings of the Once and Future King at tourist attractions, on the Internet, and even in academe.

Many readers of this book will be looking for an answer to the essential question: did Arthur really exist? The centuries-long quest for the historical Arthur began with those twelfth-century sceptics who saw little truth in the tales then being told about Arthur. The last two centuries have seen several formidable scholars enter the fray, and writers have turned to such disciplines as archaeology and linguistics to help make their case or, indeed, to tear down the theories of others.

For many, however, finding the historical Arthur can only diminish the legendary figure. Whether a stoical Roman general or a beleaguered Celtic warlord, such a person will never compare to the noble king depicted by Geoffrey of Monmouth, by Malory, or even by

Aubrey Beardsley, 'The Lady of the Lake Telleth Arthur of the Sword Excalibur' (1893–94). An illustration for a late Victorian edition of Malory's Le Morte d'Arthur.

T.H. White. With such a reader I can sympathize, and indeed it is not my goal to unearth the 'real Arthur'. Rather, I hope to show for all those interested in Arthur that there was a very real and vibrant historical era at the beginning of his story. Whether he existed or not, this period would produce the stuff of legends, legends that would become the basis of one of the most important and lasting literary traditions in the West.

Furthermore, the fact that people from the Middle Ages onwards have believed in Arthur, and that writers and kings have used that belief to their advantage, means that his impact on history has surpassed that of a mere historical being. Yet history informs this story, and must be neither ignored nor misused in discussing Arthur. As I am certain the Wife of Bath would have said, every good story begins with an historical setting.

AD100 200 300 400 500 600 700 --------- 1100

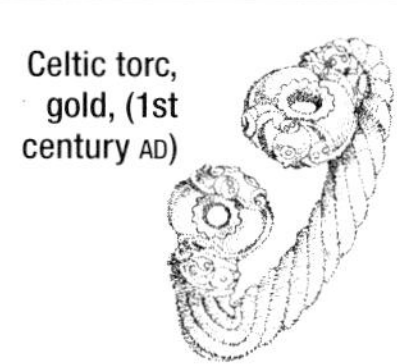
Celtic torc, gold, (1st century AD)

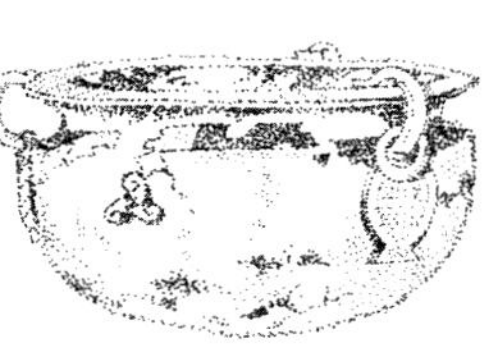
Bronze hanging-bowl (5th or 6th century)

Pictish warrior gravestone inscription (8th century)

Detail from archivolt of Modena Cathedral (*c.*1120)

BRITAIN AND IRELAND

- Claudius invades Britain (43)
- Revolt of Boudica (60/61)
- Construction of Hadrian's Wall begins (122)
- Lucius Artorius Castus commanded Sarmatian cavalry in Britain (175)
- Picts, Saxons, Scots and Atacotti harass Britain (364)
- Magnus Maximus declared emperor (383)
- Stilicho withdraws troops from Britain (401 or 402)
- Election of usurpers Marcus, Gratian and Constantine III (406–7)
- Britain devastated by Saxon incursions (408 or 410)
- Britons revolt from Roman Empire (409)
- St Germanus of Auxerre sent to Britain (429)
- Britons ask Agitius for aid against barbarians
- Patrick's mission in Ireland
- *Superbus tyrannus* invites Saxon mercenaries to Britain
- Ambrosius Aurelianus leads British forces against the Saxons
- Battle of Mount Badon and birth of Gildas (*c.*485)
- Entry for Battle of Badon in *Annales Cambriae* (518)
- Gildas's *De Excidio Britanniae* (*c.*529)
- Entry for the Battle of Camlann in *Annales Cambriae* (539)
- Battle of Arderydd, in which Myrddin goes mad (*c.*573)
- Battle of Dyrham (577)
- Battle of Catraeth (*c.*590)
- St Augustine arrives at Canterbury and the death of St Columba at Iona (597)
- Aneirin composes *Y Gododdin*
- St Kentigern's mission in Strathclyde
- Kingdom of the Gododdin destroyed (638)
- Bede completes his *Ecclesiastical History* (731)
- Harleian manuscript produced, containing *Historia Brittonum* and *Annales Cambriae*
- *Culhwch ac Olwen* is written down
- Geoffrey of Monmouth's *History of the Kings of Britain* (*c.*1136–38)
- Geoffrey of Monmouth's *Life of Merlin* (*c.*1150)

FRANCE

- Witnesses in Gaul observe that part of Britain has fallen to the Saxons (*c.*441)
- Wace's *Roman de Brut* (*c.*1155
- Chrétien de Troyes writes five Arthurian romances (*c.*1170–91)

GERMANY

REST OF WORLD

- Visigoths sack Rome; Honorius urges cities of Britain to see to their own defence (410)
- Archivolt of Modena Cathedral (*c.*1120)

The timeline above is intended to help readers visualize the temporal span of the significant figures, historical events and creative works mentioned in this book. At the same time, it reveals how these elements may have influenced one another. Also evident from such a chart is the remarkable longevity of the Arthurian myth.

The chronology is less precise in its early medieval phase than in later eras. While the historical and mythological roots of Arthuriana stretch back into antiquity, most scholars have considered the fifth and sixth centuries (shaded above) to be the most formative. For some, this is because the historical Arthur may actually have lived in this period – thus it is often known collo-

1200 1300 1400 1500----1800 1900 2000

The Sword in the Stone, from a medieval manuscript illumination

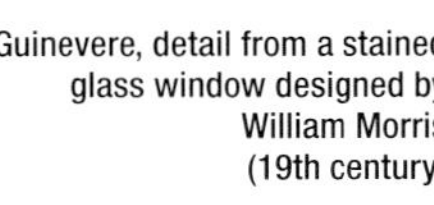
Guinevere, detail from a stained glass window designed by William Morris (19th century)

Prince Valiant, created by Hal Foster in 1937

- Layamon's *Brut*
- *Sir Gawain and the Green Knight*
- Thomas Malory's *Le Morte d'Arthur* (1470)
- Edmund Spenser writes *The Faerie Queene* (1590–96)
- Alfred Tennyson's *Idylls of the King*
- T.H. White's *The Sword in the Stone* (1938)
- Rosemary Sutcliff's *Sword at Sunset* (1963)
- Leslie Alcock's excavations at Cadbury 'Camelot' (1966–70)
- *Monty Python and the Holy Grail* (1975)
- John Boorman's *Excalibur* (1981)
- Geoffrey Ashe's *Discovery of King Arthur* (1985)

- Robert de Boron's *Merlin*
- The anonymous *Perlesvaus*
- French Vulgate cycle (1215–35)
- Post-Vulgate cycle (1230–40)
- Joseph Bédier's *Le Roman de Tristan et Iseut* (1900)
- Founding of the International Arthurian Society (1949)

- Hartmann von Aue's *Erec* and *Iwein*
- Ulrich von Zatzikhoven's *Lanzelet*
- Wolfram von Eschenbach's *Parzifal* (1210)
- Gottfried von Strassburg's *Tristan* (1210)
- Richard Wagner's *Tristan und Isolde* (1865)
- Richard Wagner's *Parsifal* (1882)

- Old Norse *Tristrams Saga*
- Dante's *Inferno* (*c.*1310)
- Ariosto's *Orlando Furioso* (1516)
- Mark Twain's *A Connecticut Yankee in King Arthur's Court* (1889)
- Hal Foster's *Prince Valiant* appears in American newspapers
- *Camelot* opens on Broadway (1960)
- Marion Zimmer Bradley's *The Mists of Avalon* (1982)
- The NBC-TV mini-series *Merlin* (1998)

quially as 'The Age of Arthur'; for others, because these years provided the personal names, battles and heroic ethos which form the heart of the Arthurian legends.

Lastly, the timeline illustrates the spatial dimension of the Arthurian tradition. From being a wholly insular figure in the early Middle Ages, Arthur came to 'conquer' much of continental Europe by the early modern period and, beginning in the nineteenth century, to capture the attention of America as well. While never entirely shedding its guise as a national British myth, Arthuriana in the twenty-first century is certainly a trans-Atlantic, if not international, phenomenon.

II
BACKGROUND: BRITONS AND ROMANS

The island of Britain lies virtually at the end of the world, towards the west and north-west. . . . Ever since it was first inhabited, Britain has been ungratefully rebelling, stiff-necked and haughty, now against God, now against its own countrymen, sometimes even against kings from abroad.

Gildas, *De Excidio Britanniae*

THE EARLY HISTORY of the British Isles is a story of invasion, migration and cultural change. It involves a number of different peoples speaking Celtic, Romance and Germanic tongues who, at one moment could be engaged in peaceful trade and, at the next, violent struggle for control of the island. Military invasions – Roman, Anglo-Saxon, Viking, Norman – dominate the written histories of early Britain, but tell only part of the story. Assimilation and cultural exchange between the 'civilized' and the 'barbarian' have, until recently, received less attention. But Arthur's Britain is the product of both, and his Britons are the heirs of two great, and often contrasting, ancient European cultures: Celtic and Roman. Both of these cultures emerged from prehistoric Europe to create civilizations which would expand and eventually encompass much of the British Isles, providing the languages and myths which form the basis of the Arthurian legends.

Statue of Queen Boudica on her war chariot by Thomas Thornycroft, erected in 1902 on the Thames Embankment in London. Boudica serves as a powerful symbol of the native Britons' revolt against the Roman Empire.

PREHISTORIC BRITAIN

Stonehenge has several associations with Merlin and the legendary history of the Britons. According to Geoffrey of Monmouth, the stones were brought from Africa to Ireland by giants who arranged them in a circular dance formation, and Merlin later reassembled them in Britain (see box, below).

SOME HAVE TRACED Arthur's roots all the way back to prehistoric Britain. By definition, this is the period before written records appeared either in or about the island. All that we have to help us understand these prehistoric Britons are their material remains and a variety of place-names and myths that seem to predate written records. Archaeology, anthropology and folklore are more appropriate tools than history in elucidating the dawn of Arthur's world.

The earliest inhabitants of Britain probably spoke a non-Indo-European language. In the Neolithic period (c.4000–c.2000 BC) they practised settled agriculture and built megalithic tombs and henge monuments, of which Stonehenge (above) is only the most famous. Though not originally, many of these tombs and monuments came to be associated with Arthur (see Gazetteer on p. 180). Moreover, the ceremonies that – it has been conjectured – took place at these sites have been seen by some scholars as underlying much of the Arthurian myth.

As stone technology began to give way to bronze, we can see that the inhabitants of Britain shared many cultural traits with northern Europeans across the Channel. These included styles of pottery and metalwork as well as the construction of large defended hilltop settlements commonly called 'hillforts', several of which were reused in the years associated with the historical Arthur (p. 42). One explanation for these developments is that invasion and migration had taken place, with the culture of the conquerors supplanting that of the conquered. Another is that trade and kinship ties between Britain and the Continent had resulted in a cultural exchange. Indeed, both may have occurred.

At some unknown point in the late Neolithic or Early Bronze Age an Indo-European language, or languages, became dominant in Britain. Linguists in the sixteenth century were the first to identify this language as 'Celtic', for it was related to the Gaulish language spoken by the people of central France whom Julius Caesar called *Celtae* (see chart on opposing page). We cannot identify one single group of migrating or invading Celtic-speakers; the linguistic transformation may have been prolonged, with many Celtic and non-Indo-European tongues coexisting. But, by the beginning of the British Iron Age (c.600 BC), we can discern cohesive groups of Celtic-speakers and warlike chiefdoms building hillforts and competing with their neighbours. The language and warrior elitism of these Britons constitute their legacy to the world of Arthur.

MERLIN AND STONEHENGE

Geoffrey of Monmouth (p. 80), in his History of the Kings of Britain *(1136), narrates the story of the creation of Stonehenge, attributing it to Merlin. The British king, Aurelius Ambrosius, wanted to erect a monument for fallen Britons, and asked the advice of Merlin, who promised that he could retrieve the so-called Giants' Ring from Ireland and reassemble it on Salisbury Plain. Merlin accomplished this miraculous feat, but with engineering skills rather than magic (shown here in this fourteenth-century French manuscript illustration).*

Far-fetched theories about Stonehenge abound – involving everything from Druids to UFOs – and many questions remain unanswered. But it seems that Geoffrey was not too far from the truth when he described the stones being transported from afar and erected with technical ingenuity. Some of the massive bluestones were brought from the Preseli

mountains in Wales, and erected with a fairly sophisticated array of Neolithic and early Bronze Age instruments. Moreover, Stonehenge did contain some cremation burials and the erection of the monument may indeed have been initiated by a powerful chieftain. Stonehenge was constructed, however, over a long span of time – c.3100–c.1100 BC – well before either Druids or knights trod on Britain's soil.

The Celts live beyond the Pillars of Hercules [the Straits of Gibraltar], next to the Cynesians who are the most westerly people of Europe.

Herodotus, *The Histories*

ANCIENT PEOPLES are as well known to us from myths and stereotypes as they are from the 'facts' of history and archaeology. This is certainly true of the Iron Age Britons, commonly called 'Celts', whose vigorous culture (or cultures) survived Roman occupation and Germanic settlement to become the basis for much of the Arthurian tradition. While archaeologists now debate whether there was ever an identifiably 'Celtic' culture in the British Isles, Herodotus and other classical writers believed the Celts to be a culturally distinct barbarian people occupying much of northwestern Europe. The Britons, moreover, shared the stereotypical barbarian characteristics that Greek and Roman authors applied to the *Celtae* and other Gauls, just as they shared similar languages (see chart, below), religious beliefs and material cultures.

Classical writers, however, never applied the terms *Celtae* or *Keltoi* to the ancient Britons, nor is it likely that the Britons ever used the label themselves. Early Greek explorers, in the sixth century BC, described Britain as 'the isle of the *Albiones*', though Prettania, or Brettania, soon afterwards became the preferred name. We do not know if these names meant anything to the Iron Age Britons (though *Priteni* and the element *Alb-* are both found in the vernacular of the early Middle Ages); farmers, mostly, they identified themselves with the family-based 'tribes' emerging, under powerful chieftains, on the first coins and in the literature of the period.

European 'Celtic' cultures have traditionally been divided by archaeologists into two periods, Hallstatt (*c.*1200–*c.*475 BC) and La Tène (*c.*500 BC to the Roman conquests), so named from important excavations at the Austrian and Swiss sites of these names. Hillforts and weaponry from royal tombs have come to define Hallstatt culture, which spanned the Bronze and Iron Ages and probably included non-Celtic-speakers. La Tène culture, defined particularly by curvilinear and stylized art (usually seen in its metalwork), is more closely associated with Celtic-speakers, to whom classical sources ascribe great migration and conquests in the fourth century BC. Both Britain and Ireland received some elements of La Tène culture and developed some of its most celebrated and defining products, particularly jewelry and weapons.

Moreover, La Tène culture did not disappear from the British Isles as it did in other areas conquered by the Romans. Ireland and the Scottish Highlands and Islands were never conquered by Rome, and their Iron Age inhabitants continued to develop 'Celtic' styles and forms throughout the Middle Ages. But even such areas as southern Scotland, Wales and Cornwall, where Rome maintained a presence for 400 years, were able to preserve some elements of their Iron Age past into the post-Roman period. The important question is, which of these elements survived to influence Arthur (if, indeed, he was an historical figure) and the depiction of Arthur and his knights in the earliest forms of the legend?

Caesar and the Britons

The early Britons left no writings, apart from a few names on their coins. We can reconstruct their culture only through archaeology, the classical authors and in medieval vernacular literature (especially Irish) that shows little classical or Christian influence.

Julius Caesar is, without doubt, the most important of the classical observers. During his conquest of northwestern Gaul, he recorded that the natives were receiving help from a people called the Britons who lived across the Channel. Indeed, the island had served as a place of refuge for various leaders of the Belgae, a network of related tribes which extended from northern Gaul to southeastern Britain. The mineral

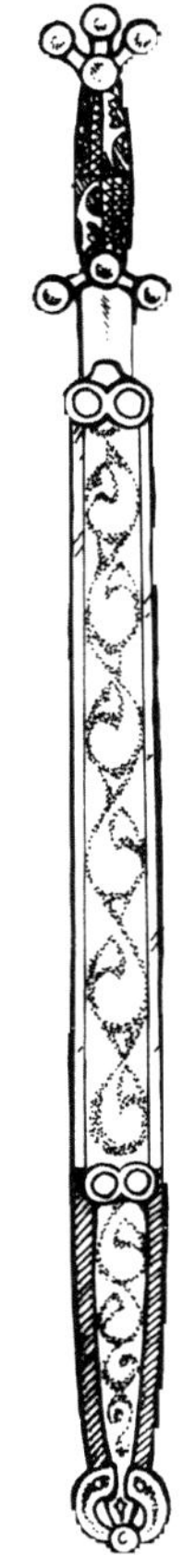

(Above) Iron Age British sword, showing curvilinear designs. (Below) By the Iron Age, the Celtic languages were already splitting into two major groups.

THE CELTIC LANGUAGES

Extinct | **Modern**

- Common Celtic
  - Gallo-Brittonic
    - Gaulish
    - Pictish?
    - British (Brittonic)
      - Cumbric
      - Cornish (P-Celtic)
      - Welsh (P-Celtic)
      - Breton (P-Celtic)
  - Common Gaelic (Goidelic)
    - Modern Irish (Q-Celtic)
    - Scottish Gaelic (Q-Celtic)
    - Manx (Q-Celtic)

Julius Caesar, general and statesman. In his writings, Caesar gives us some of the earliest and most detailed descriptions of the ancient Britons.

wealth of Britain, together with the unprecedented prestige that conquest of the island would bring him, led Caesar to launch two exploratory expeditions in 55 and 54 BC. While far from conquering the island, Caesar did win some minor skirmishes and forced some of the tribes to give him hostages and tribute.

More importantly, these expeditions opened up the island to Roman observers and, ultimately, to Roman influence. Caesar recorded details of British geography and his own personal observations of the military, political and religious life of the Britons. Caesar observed that the Britons were very much like the Gauls in their way of living and fighting. Archaeology has confirmed that, through trade and kinship, the Britons were developing along similar lines as the Gauls. This includes the appearance in both Britain and the Continent of proto-towns, the apparent result of emerging centralized states. In southeastern Britain examples can be seen at St Albans, Silchester and Winchester, all of which would later become important Roman towns (Winchester being, additionally, a royal burg and candidate for Arthur's Camelot).

It was British warfare and politics that most interested Caesar. Archaeologists have observed a more densely settled agrarian landscape in the late pre-Roman Iron Age and an increase in hillforts and objects of war. Sometimes covering hundreds of acres and surrounded by timber walls and towers, British hillforts were used as places of refuge in war, but gradually became marketplaces and housed artisans and the warrior-aristocracy. Bold and reckless, the typical Celtic warrior went into battle wearing little more than woollen trousers (as do most horse-based cultures), decorated tunics and long capes. Sometimes they fought wearing nothing but body tattoos (sacred and protective symbols) and the gold torcs which signified nobility. A few wore chain-mail armour (probably a Celtic invention c.300 BC); most had long shields and iron-headed spears. According to Caesar, chariots brought British warriors to the battlefield, and there is both written and physical evidence for the Britons continuing to use chariots in the post-Roman period (p. 49). Ancient writers often commented on the remarkable physical appearance of Celtic warriors, depicting them as fair-haired giants with long hair (sometimes spiked with lime) and swooping moustaches. This is how Arthur's 'knights' appear in early works such as *Culhwch and Olwen* (p. 96).

Society in the late pre-Roman Iron Age

As hillforts grew larger in the Iron Age and the economy prospered, British society became more stratified. At the top was the tribal chieftain or king (*rí* or *rix*). In some Celtic societies the king was elected, for life, by the nobility. The one most able to rule was elected, and women could, and did, become tribal leaders and command armies. (Queens in both early Irish and Arthurian legends wield more power than one might expect.) Below the king was an aristocracy of birth and accomplishment, which included the warrior class and the priestly class, known as the Druids. Next was a class of freemen that included farmers, blacksmiths and artisans. At the bottom was a mass of labourers, serfs and slaves. Slavery was endemic throughout the ancient world, but among the Celts it was primarily a by-product of war.

Celtic-speaking peoples have always held family loyalty in great esteem, and this is reflected in the clan feuds throughout the Arthurian legends. The ancient Celts lived in large extended families or clans, grouped with other families in the tribe (*túath* in Irish) which

THE HUNT OF THE WILD BOAR

The boar was a powerful, sometimes divine, symbol in Celtic lands. Throughout the Welsh Arthurian tradition there are references to Arthur hunting a giant wild boar. Usually identified as Twrch Trwyth (corresponding to the king of the boars, Torc Triath, of Irish myths), it is said to have been a king whom God transformed into a boar because of his sins. In Culhwch and Olwen *(p. 96), Arthur's men are charged with retrieving the comb and shears from between Twrch's ears. They succeed, but the boar disappears into the sea. This boar figurine (right) dates from the Gallo-Roman period.*

DRUIDS IN BRITAIN

Druids were the priests of Iron Age Gaul and Britain, though they performed many other functions in the tribe and occasionally wielded princely powers. Druids also came to be associated with human sacrifice, a practice that both repulsed and fascinated Roman observers such as Julius Caesar. The Lindow Man (right), whose well-preserved body was found in Cheshire, England, in 1984, appears to have been a sacrificial victim. His ritualistic three-fold killing (from blows to the head, a slit throat and strangulation) has parallels in Irish myth and the legend of Myrddin (p. 95).

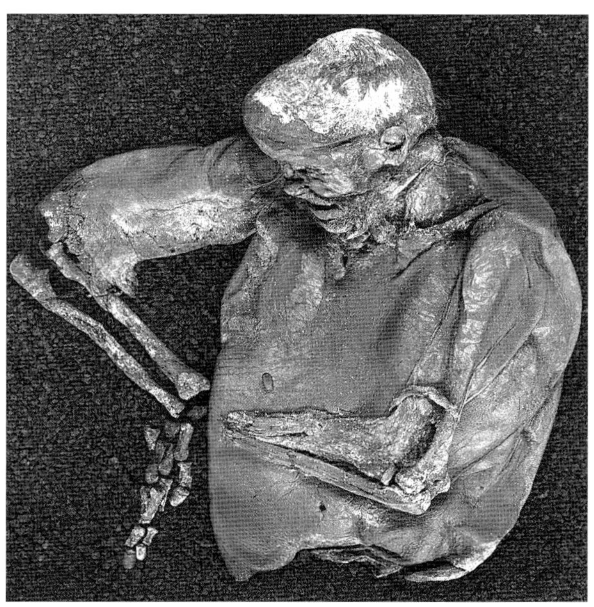

was ruled by a king and a general assembly. The children of the nobility were educated by the Druids, as Caesar observed in both Britain and Gaul. In the greater households there were also bards, who were trained to memorize the laws, customs, genealogy and history of the tribe and recited these in the form of songs. Merlin is often depicted as a bard or even as performing Druidic functions (see box, above), such as the education and advising of the young King Arthur.

Druids presided over religious ceremonies in Gaul and Britain, which were often held in sacred groves or on mountaintops. Samhain and Beltaine, fertility festivals which became Halloween and May Day, were the most important holy days. The Celts worshipped a multitude of gods and goddesses, most of whom were only local or regional deities. While there was no unified Celtic pantheon, some widely worshipped Celtic gods include Lugh, 'shining light'; Cernunnos, 'the horned one'; and Epona, a horse goddess. There were also divine triads, three-in-one deities such as the *matres* (mothers), of whom the Irish Mórrígan is the most famous and is, perhaps, reflected in the Morgan le Fay of Arthurian tales. A Celtic Otherworld (in Irish Tír na n-Óc or Land of Youth), is also featured in many early Arthurian poems and is quite likely to have been the basis for the Isle of Avalon.

An Iron Age British warrior and his wife, in a painting by Peter Connolly. Some evidence suggests that the iron sword was actually worn on the warrior's back in parts of Britain.

The Roman Conquest of Britain

So the Romans slaughtered many of the treasonable, keeping a few as slaves so that the land should not be completely deserted. . . . They were to make the name of Roman servitude cling to the soil . . . so that the island should not be rated as Britannia but as Romania, and all its bronze, silver and gold should be stamped with the image of Caesar.

Gildas, *De Excidio Britanniae*

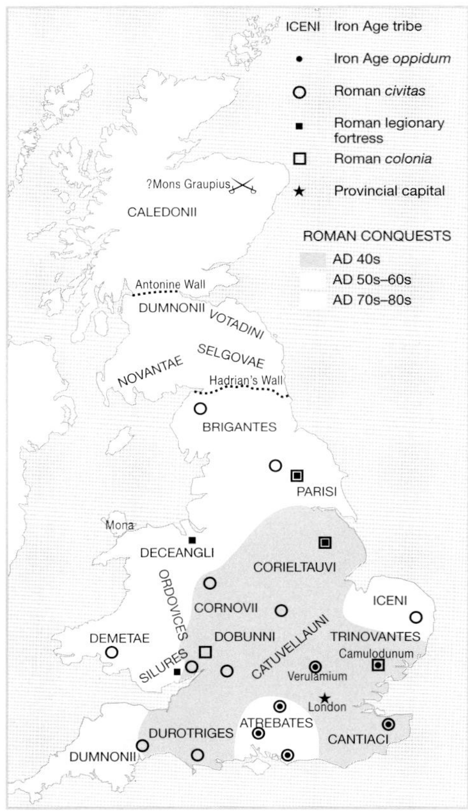

The peoples of Iron Age Britain and the Roman conquest. In the late Iron Age, both native coinage and proto-towns (which scholars call oppida*) began to appear in central southern Britain. This region was developing into a strong state and was thus the target of the Roman conquest of* AD *43. While the first Roman settlements were fortresses and veterans' colonies (*coloniae*), Roman administration of the conquered tribes was usually based on a Mediterranean-style town (*civitas*) often created from a native* oppidum.

Bronze head of the emperor Claudius, found in the River Alde, Suffolk. The head was torn from a public statue, possibly during the revolt of Boudica.

THE ROMAN CONQUEST of Britain has traditionally been seen as a landmark event in the history of the island. Characterization of this event has ranged from Gildas's portrait of brutality to the modern romanticizing of Roman ruins. While today's historians and archaeologists debate the extent of Romanization in Britain, it is appropriate for us to ask what impact 400 years of Roman rule had on shaping Britain's most enduring legend. The most obvious answer is Latin, the language of the Romans which was adopted by the Britons to chronicle the deeds of Arthur. But there are other, more subtle, influences which can be discerned from the history and archaeology of the Roman period.

The Claudian Conquest

In the years following Caesar's expeditions the Britons began importing Roman goods on a large scale and adopted the Mediterranean practice of minting coins bearing images of their deities and rulers. Britons also travelled to the Continent, with some nobles going to Rome to air grievances or promise friendship. But, since Caesar's first landing in 55 BC, the Romans had intended to add Britain to their possessions, and only civil war and unstable emperors prevented a full-scale invasion. This materialized in AD 43 under the emperor Claudius. Sending ahead the general Aulus Plautius with an invasion force of some 40,000 troops, Claudius himself arrived after most of the southern Britons had been subdued (or bribed), proceeding to awe the natives with a display of war elephants trumpeting his victory.

Caratacus and Boudica

Britannia then became the westernmost province of the Roman Empire, with the captured British stronghold of Colchester (Camulodunum) its first capital. Many British chieftains were happy to accept client status. Others vowed to resist the Roman occupation, and were led by the prince Caratacus. From the mountains of Wales, Caratacus harassed the Romans for nine years as they tried to expand their holdings westward. His guerrilla tactics at first proved successful, but in a pitched battle in AD 51 he was defeated and taken to Rome in chains.

More serious for Roman rule in Britain was the revolt of the Iceni in AD 61, led by Queen Boudica. Widow of the Roman ally Prasutagus, Boudica was publicly flogged by slaves of the emperor Nero who had come to confiscate her lands after her husband's death. Even worse, the proud queen was forced to watch as Roman soldiers raped her two young daughters. The enraged Britons held a council and chose Boudica as their leader as they plotted revenge on the Romans. Colchester, London and St Albans (Verulamium) fell to Boudica's warriors before Suetonius Paulinus, the military governor, could return from Wales – where he had wiped out the Druids on Anglesey (Mona) – to face the Britons in a pitched battle.

Caught between high ground defended by the Romans and their own wagons arranged in a semi-circle behind them, laden with supplies and civilians, the massive army of Britons had no means of retreat when the battle turned against them. Paulinus's disciplined troops cut them down, with as many as 200,000 British casualties including the queen and her daughters. Not satisfied with simply punishing the rebels, Paulinus systematically exterminated all natives in the area, until the emperor recalled him. At South Cadbury hillfort (Cadbury 'Camelot' as it is also known) archaeologists have uncovered bodies, weapons and signs of destruction by fire which have been attributed to Paulinus's campaign.

The Romanization of Britain

With a new governor, things began to settle down in Britain. But while most of the south was pacified, extreme northern and western Britain remained independent and hostile regions. The vigorous governor Gnaeus Julius Agricola went on the offensive towards the end of the first century. According to his biography, written by his son-in-law, Tacitus, Agricola subdued the Welsh tribes, then turned his army northward, marching all the way up to the Highlands of Scotland. At Mons Graupius in AD 84, Agricola defeated a confederation of northerners called the Caledonians. He even turned his glance westward, commenting that with two legions he could bring Ireland under Roman control!

But Agricola had insufficient troops to hold even the Scottish territories, and so was forced to retreat to the south leaving only slight traces of the Roman military establishment in the north. Neither Ireland nor Scotland was brought under Roman control, though the army of the emperor Hadrian did succeed in building a remarkable defensive network stretching from coast to coast in northern Britain. Hadrian's Wall stands today as a visible reminder of Roman military and engineering achievement in Britain, but also of Rome's inability to complete the conquest of northern Britain. This would prove crucial later in the independent Britons' struggle against the barbarians, depicted vividly by Gildas (pp. 69–70) and in Arthurian legend.

Scholars now debate the extent of Romanization in Britain. A common view has been that the Britons 'did what they were told by the Romans because it represented progress'; that is, they came into the cities and became passive receptacles of Latin culture. The material evidence suggests a more complex interchange of ideas and tastes: the impressive Roman mosaics which survive from British villas display classical and Christian motifs while utilizing Celtic interlace border designs and an abstract, native perception of the human form. On the other hand, written sources throughout the Roman Empire reveal a consistently negative portrayal of Britons as crude, isolated barbarians who 'never advanced to exalted toga-wearing status'.

If we look at Roman political administration in Britain we discover a mixed bag. The province was divided into some twenty city-states, or *civitates*, corresponding roughly to pre-existing tribal entities. Mediterranean-style cities were established for both military veterans and non-Roman provincials. Each of these towns acted as an administrative centre for the city-state, and was governed by a council of 100 aristocrats headed by two elected magistrates. In both Gaul and Britain, the native nobility participated in these councils and held offices. St Patrick's father was one of these decurions, or town-councillors, whose decision to hire Saxon mercenaries for protection in the early fifth century (p. 38) began the wars for which Arthur was to become famous.

Maiden Castle, near Dorchester, one of the largest and best defended hillforts in Iron Age Britain. After being captured by the Romans its defences were dismantled and it became a temple site.

A stretch of Hadrian's Wall, near the fort at Housesteads, Northumberland.

The Coming of Christianity

A male water-gorgon adorns the pediment of the Temple of Sulis Minerva, Bath, showing the conflation of Roman and native deities.

'THAT MOST CHRISTIAN king Arthur' is a phrase heard often in the medieval and later versions of the Arthurian legends. The advent of Christianity in Britain, though little understood by scholars, made possible the traditions of monarchs who championed the Faith, from Arthur to Alfred to Mary Tudor. But of all Britain's Christian monarchs, it is Arthur who has become the most celebrated Christian king. Is there an historical basis to this? Or could the historical Arthur have been pagan rather than a follower of Christ?

The religions of Roman Britain

Religion in Roman Britain was syncretistic: instead of destroying native shrines and temples, the Romans encouraged their use and even constructed Mediterranean-style facilities for such sites – the most famous example is the complex at Bath. Local deities were given Latin names, or else a dual identity like the god Sulis Minerva worshipped at Bath. Rome's famous tolerance of different religions was not extended, however, to Druids and Christians. The Druids were singled out in attacks by the Roman military because they instigated rebellion. After the destruction of their sanctuary on Anglesey, we hear no more of Druids in Roman Britain. This does not mean, however, that they simply disappeared from Britain. We can expect them to have survived beyond Hadrian's Wall, as they did in Ireland. Even in Romanized Gaul aristocrats continued to bear Druidic names and recalled Druids in their lineage well into the fourth century, and several of these later Druids were renowned teachers and orators.

The Constantinian Chi-Rho, *one of the early symbols of Roman Christianity. The Greek letters* Chi *and* Rho *were combined to denote the word* Christos.

Like the Druids and the Jews, the early Christians suffered persecution because Roman officials saw in them a potential political threat. Thus Christianity remained an underground, mostly eastern, urban phenomenon until the third century AD. No one knows for sure when Christianity came to Britain. Medieval legends speak of early Christian apostles such as Joseph of Arimathea bringing the gospel (and, in his case, the Holy Grail!) to Britain in the first century AD. While military and trade contacts between Britain and the Middle East do not make this impossible, it is more likely that the first Christians arrived, unnoticed, in Britain in the late second century.

The early church

Christianity remained small and materially modest in Britain until the fourth century, when the Great Persecutions finally ended and a Christian champion was found in the person of the emperor Constantine the Great. Constantine passed legislation in 313 enforcing tolerance and restoring property to Christians, and the emperor went on to encourage the construction of basilical churches throughout the Empire. While Italy and the eastern Mediterranean have produced magnificent examples of such structures, archaeologists have only proposed a few candidates for Britain, such as the small basilicas at Silchester and Colchester. Other artifacts from Britain, chiefly mosaics and silver utensils, bear Christian symbols such as the *Chi-Rho* and attest to the wealth of some British Christians.

For Britain, as elsewhere in the Empire, early Christianity was mainly an urban phenomenon. Only with the advent of monasticism in the fifth century and subsequent missionary work did the Faith spread into the countryside and among barbarian settlers in Britain. A fifth- or sixth-century British Arthur would almost certainly have been Christian, but his religion may have retained many elements of native devotion.

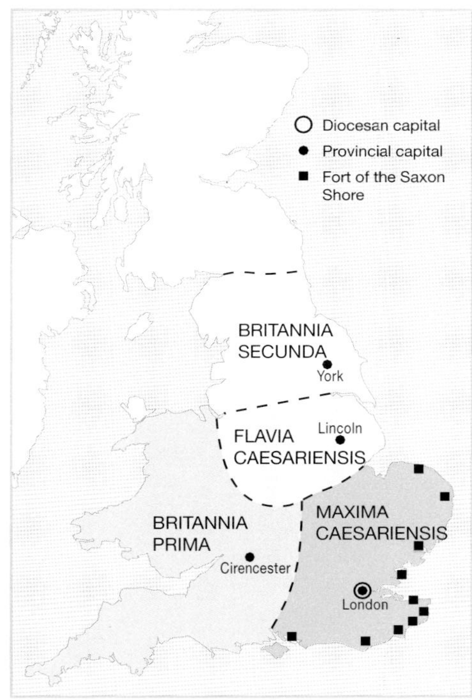

(Left) Late Roman civil and military reorganization in Britain. When the emperor Diocletian's administrative reforms reached Britain, they resulted in the island province being reorganized into a diocese consisting of four provinces (it had briefly been reorganized into two provinces in the third century). We know that a fifth province was added in the late fourth century and named (or renamed) Valentia, but scholars are uncertain of its location. Further reorganization occurred along the frontiers in the fourth century, including the formal establishment of a defence system for the southeast coast, the Saxon Shore (see box, below).

AN UNDERSTANDING OF the particular events of Late Roman Britain is crucial to anyone interested in the fifth- and sixth-century dimension of the Arthurian legends. Of course, an historical Arthur living in this period would have reacted to and been shaped by these events. But even if there was no such person, those who crafted his legend were responding to the crises of this period, crises that determined the political and cultural fate of the island.

The second half of the Roman occupation of Britain was marked by political and military turmoil. Yet Britain continued to follow Roman innovations, one such reform being the emperor Diocletian's (r. 284–304) creation of the 'Diocese of the Britains'. Consisting of four provinces (see map, above), each had a capital city and a civilian governor answerable to the *vicarius* (chief administrator of the diocese) in London. Subsequent innovations included the creation of three new high military commands in Britain: the *dux Britanniarum*, who commanded the garrison troops (*limitanei*) along Hadrian's Wall; the *comes litoris Saxonici*, who probably commanded troops along both the southeast coast (the so-called 'Saxon Shore') and the northwest coast of Britain; and the *comes Britanniarum*, commander of the more mobile field army (*comitatenses*). The Count of the Saxon Shore remains the most enigmatic of these posts, for it is debated whether *litus Saxonicum* means the shore was attacked *by* Saxons or settled *with* Saxons. Some have theorized that the historical Arthur held one of these commands (pp. 149–50).

These military innovations were the work of Constantine I, who was proclaimed emperor at York in 306 and reigned until 337. In around 315 he took the title *Britannicus Maximus* – Geoffrey of Monmouth (p. 80) depicts him as a British emperor – and he supported new military construction in Britain. The material evidence (villa construction and renovation, new mosaics, road repairs) suggests that Britain enjoyed prosperity under Constantine's rule, which saw the end of the Christian persecutions and the rise in status of provincial bishops.

THE SAXON SHORE

*The so-called Saxon Shore (*litoris Saxonici*) is actually a reorganization of an older Roman defence system that served the British fleet (the* classis Britannica*). This reorganization, in the late third century, was most likely a response to Frankish and Saxon piracy in the English Channel. Ten forts were employed to protect the southeast coast, from the Wash to Portsmouth Harbour, and several survived into the post-Roman period. The high walls and corner towers of Burgh Castle, seen here, later converted by the Normans into a motte-and-bailey castle, still stand majestically today in rural Norfolk.*

Statue of the emperor Constantine the Great, in Rome. Raised to the purple in Britain, this champion of Christianity looms large in the legendary history of the island. The name Constantine became quite popular among Britons and appears frequently in the Arthurian legends.

The 'barbarian conspiracy'

The historian Ammianus Marcellinus records that in 364 Britain was being constantly harassed by four peoples: Picts, Saxons, Scots and Attacotti. We do not know what the Roman response was to these attacks, but Ammianus gives a detailed account of a more serious threat, in 367, that he calls the 'barbarian conspiracy'. News reached the emperor Valentinian (r. 364–75) that several groups of barbarians had conspired to launch a joint attack: Picts, Attacotti and Scots devastated much of Britain, while Franks and Saxons ravaged the coast of Gaul. In return for promises of booty, the frontier spies had abandoned their duty and had, allegedly, allied themselves with the barbarians. Desertions from the army were numerous, and armed thugs roamed the land unchecked.

The presence of Franks and Saxons on the coast of Gaul may have delayed the news from Britain, and thus the Roman response. But in 368 Count Theodosius, father of the future emperor of the same name, was sent to Britain to deal with the crisis. He landed at Richborough and advanced with his army to London, cutting down the bands of marauders who were laden with booty – even pursuing them on the seas. After putting down rebellion and insurrection among the British troops, Theodosius reorganized the recovered lands into a fifth British province, Valentia.

Ammianus also tells us that Theodosius 'restored the cities and forts' in the British provinces. One new area of construction took place on Britain's northeastern coastline, where a series of well-fortified watch-towers were built at this time to warn nearby forts of seaborne Pictish raids. Similar stations built on the northwest coast had gone out of service in the second century, but there is archaeological evidence that some of the Cumbrian coastal forts were also rebuilt at this time to protect against raids coming around the other side of the Wall.

Magnus Maximus

One of Count Theodosius's lieutenants in Britain was a soldier from the Hispanic provinces named Magnus Maximus. Maximus was sent to Britain in the early 380s to organize defences. He is credited with a victory over the Picts and Scots in the north in 382, and a year later his British troops declared him emperor of the west. The usurpation began with Maximus taking his army into Gaul, where he defeated and killed the young emperor Gratian (r. 375–83). He certainly did not take all of Britain's troops with him, but he may specifically have removed the Welsh garrisons, for he is remembered as a benevolent ruler in the medieval Welsh poem *The Dream of Macsen Wledig* and is incorporated into at least one Welsh royal dynasty.

Maximus established his court at Trier and was baptized, securing the blessings of the Church and the western frontier at the same time. It was not until five years later, after Maximus had crossed the Alps and occupied the imperial city of Milan, that the eastern emperor Theodosius (r. 379–95) made a move against his rival. Maximus was defeated twice in Pannonia and was finally seized and beheaded at Aquileia in 388. The effect Maximus's bid for power had on Britain and the western provinces is unclear. Gildas portrays it as disastrous for them, while later medieval legend maintains that Maximus's

(Right) The description 'Saxon Shore' first appears in a Late Roman list of offices called the Notitia Dignitatum. This illustration, from a late medieval copy of the Notitia, shows the British forts under the command of the Count of the Saxon Shore.

British troops stayed on the Continent after his death and founded Brittany – 'Lesser Britain' – in the Gallic province of Armorica.

Barbarians and towns

The last Roman coins that appear in Britain in large numbers date to around 402, when Britain was again stripped of her troops by the Roman general Stilicho, to be used in fighting against barbarians elsewhere in the Empire. Yet barbarian attacks on Britain continued throughout the first decade of the fifth century. Who, then, was left to fight these raiders, to protect the cities, and how were the defenders paid?

One solution was to turn to allies and mercenaries, who appear, throughout the Late Roman world, as *laeti* or *foederati*. *Laeti* were barbarian warriors who were recruited to serve in the Roman army as irregular soldiers (particularly as cavalry and in other specialized units) under Roman commanders. The *foederati* were whole groups of barbarians who were invited inside the frontiers of the Empire, and given supplies (*annona*, *epimenia*) and land in exchange for fighting against hostile invaders. This was an attempt to strengthen the frontiers and, eventually, official federate status was extended to such groups as the Visigoths and the Ostrogoths.

Archaeologists developed the theory that Germanic mercenaries began to be used extensively in Britain during the calamities of the fourth century, in particular to man city garrisons and protect rural estates. Inscriptions and the *Notitia Dignitatum* (an official record of military posts in the Empire) show that Germanic units were commonly part of the regular army stationed in Britain, while Ammianus records the transfer of an Alamannic king to Britain in 372 where he was given the rank of tribune. But the belt-buckles and other military items once thought to identify Germanic soldiers in Britain have now been shown to have been a part of the larger Late Roman provincial style adopted by both soldiers and civilians. Only in the fifth century, when obviously Germanic weaponry and cemeteries begin to appear, does it seem likely that the Britons were hiring large groups of continental *foederati*.

Another theory that has gained in popularity is that, by about 350, the cities of Britain had been reduced to mere villages and all signs of urban life had disappeared. This is based mainly on archaeological evidence, which shows a lack of expenditure on urban public buildings in the fourth century. What we do see is military construction in and around the cities: ditches were widened and external towers were added to the city walls to provide fighting platforms, which could also support catapults and *ballistae*. These improvements, most commonly attributed to Theodosius, actually helped the towns to outlive the forts, which were constantly being stripped of manpower.

A Late Roman bastion at York, now in the gardens of the Yorkshire Museum. Constantine I sponsored the construction of stronger defences for the town (a former legionary base) that saw his elevation. The surviving Roman bastion was later incorporated into an Anglian tower.

Whether or not directly inspired by crisis, some radical changes in the structure of Roman Britain did occur in the late fourth century. The decline of the large *civitas*-capitals led to the emergence of small towns (*pagi*) and the decentralization of the economy to the periphery. The small towns in turn came under the control of local magnates, or *possessores*, who owned villas nearby and who turned increasingly to these small towns as markets for their goods. The cities 'were no longer principally economic foci but rather defended centres for their districts'. The powerful curial families increasingly spent their wealth on their own properties and pursuits rather than on their communities, perhaps leading to what appears in the archaeological record as the rapid collapse of orderly urban life in Britain after 400.

We thus see, in the fourth century, many signs of the emergence of a new type of landed elite. These men no longer depended on the Roman government for advancement, and no longer saw the cities as the exclusive means to display their wealth and power. They turned increasingly to patron-client relationships to build a loyal body of supporters, with which they eventually seized control of their districts. In the fifth century they stepped out of the shadows to take the reins of government in independent Britain. Whether called tyrant or king, these were the men – cultural heirs to both the Iron Age chieftains and the Roman magistrates – who ruled Britain in the Age of Arthur.

Gold coin of Magnus Maximus, who seized imperial power in the west from 383–88. Maximus, a military man from Roman Spain who had served in Britain twice, was cast as a British emperor in the medieval legends of Wales and Brittany.

The Isle of the Mighty

EARLY GREEK explorers called it Albion and Prettania, while the Romans knew it as Britannia. But the Welsh bards called it *Ynys y Cewri*, the Isle of the Mighty, and sang of its mighty heroes and heroines. The legendary history of Britain is an ancient mixture of vernacular and classical traditions later included in such medieval works as the *Historia Brittonum* and Geoffrey of Monmouth's *History of the Kings of Britain*. It begins with the Trojan Brutus, whose westward wandering landed him on the island where he expelled its giant inhabitants and began a new race – the Britons, named after Brutus – who would dominate Britain for a thousand years. Brutus's sons founded the kingdoms of Albany (Scotland), Logres (England), Cambria (Wales) and Cornwall. A few British kings, such as Leir and Cymbelin, were powerful enough to hold sway over the entire island, but eventually the Romans – just like the Britons descended from a Trojan – came to power in Britain. Some Roman emperors, most notably Constantine the Great and Magnus Maximus, were remembered as Britons themselves.

In the fifth century, another British Constantine ruled the island until he was murdered and replaced by Vortigern, the unfortunate tyrant who invited the Saxons to Britain as mercenaries. The Saxon leaders Hengist and Horsa turned on Vortigern and the Britons, while Constantine's avenging son Ambrosius trapped the beleaguered tyrant in his fortress and saw him killed (right). Ambrosius enjoyed a short but respected reign and was succeeded by his brother, Uther Pendragon ('Chief Dragon'), the father of King Arthur.

Vortigern perishes in his tower, illustration from an edition of Peter of Langtoft's Chronicle *(1307).*

III
THE AGE OF ARTHUR (AD 400–600)

At that time the English increased their numbers and grew in Britain. . . . Then Arthur fought against them in those days, together with the kings of the Britons; but he was their leader in battle.

Nennius (attrib.), *Historia Brittonum*

THE HISTORICAL NARRATIVE for Roman Britain comes to a dramatic halt in AD 410, for in that year the island was formally cut off from imperial protection and became increasingly alienated from the distant chroniclers who were concerned more with the impending fall of Rome itself. Likewise, as payment ceased to reach the remnants of the imperial army stationed along the British frontier, coinage became extremely scarce in the archaeological record and we are left without this important means of dating new structures and settlements. The tumultuous events of 406–10 – the last in Britain to be detailed by imperial historians – resulted in a new, independent Britain faced with the overwhelming task of defending its citizens and cities from barbarian invasions. Because he is the most famous of the British defenders, the period has come to be known as the Age of Arthur.

There is, of course, much scepticism over whether or not Arthur was an historical figure living at this time, and whether, therefore, we should be naming a period of history after him. Archaeologists prefer to use the label sub-Roman Britain for the fifth and sixth centuries, noting declining standards in Roman-style pottery and architecture. I have suggested an alternative, the Brittonic Age, to emphasize the unique contributions of the Britons who formed the majority of the island's population in this period and who left us the only contemporary written records. But whether or not Arthur existed, for many people this period will always be the Age of Arthur. If it were not for the particular political, military and cultural traditions of the era we would never have known the Arthurian saga in its many forms.

Aerial view of 'Tintagel Island', a rocky promontory in Cornwall which saw much activity in the Brittonic Age (c.400–600). Later tradition identified this scenic spot as Arthur's birthplace.

Tyrants and the End of Roman Britain

Movements of peoples into the Roman Empire in the early fifth century. Any map of the so-called 'barbarian' invasions is bound to be confusing and even misleading. This complex and still little understood process included the movements of whole peoples following military kings, as well as smaller groups of warriors and their warlords. At this point, Britain saw mostly small groups of raiders, and itself sent colonists across the Channel to Brittany.

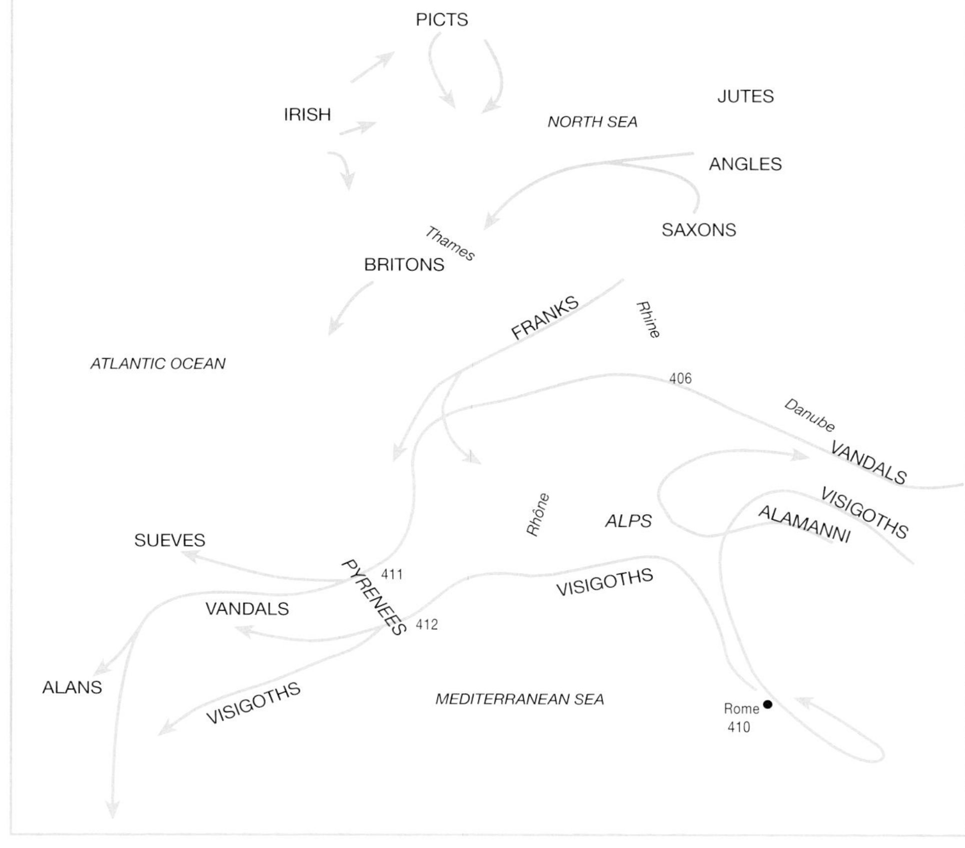

Silver siliqua of Constantine III, proclaimed emperor by the Roman troops in Britain in 407. Later medieval chroniclers would make him the grandfather of King Arthur.

Britain is a province fertile with tyrants.
St Jerome, *Letters*

AS JEROME and other Roman writers attest, Britain had a particular reputation for producing 'tyrants' in the fourth and fifth centuries. Military and political crises elsewhere in the Empire created the conditions for imperial usurpers to emerge throughout the west. Britain not only had a seemingly greater supply of these men, it continued to be dominated by them even after Roman rule ended in the island c.410. These tyrants certainly left their imprint on the Age of Arthur.

Constantine III

In 398, after a successful war against the Picts in Scotland, *magister militum* Stilicho began withdrawing troops from Britain. Though Britain was not left completely unprotected against barbarian attack, its security was more than ever tied to the precarious defence of the western provinces which centered around Gaul. Disaster struck on the last day of December 406, when barbarian Alans, Vandals and Sueves crossed the frozen Rhine and overran the provinces of Gaul. The invasion of Gaul terrorized the troops in Britain, who, fearing that the barbarians would cross the Channel next, responded by electing their own emperors to solve the frontier problems.

The first to be elected was a soldier named Marcus, but he was soon put to death when he failed to please the soldiery. Their second choice is more interesting. He was a civilian, probably a city official, named Gratian. The soldiers bestowed upon him the imperial garb – purple robe and crown – and 'formed a bodyguard for him as they would an emperor'. But the result of this usurpation was the same: failing to please his supporters, Gratian was killed after four months.

The third candidate proved to be longer lived. Constantine – who became Constantine III – was chosen from the ranks of the military solely, we are told, on the basis of his name. He followed the example of another usurper, Magnus Maximus, by taking British troops across to Gaul to secure the western frontier. After establishing himself there he bestowed upon his eldest son, Constans, the title of Caesar and sent him to Spain with a British general named Gerontius. After initial successes, disaster struck both father and son. Gerontius threw his support behind another usurper and incited the barbarians in Gaul to revolt against Constantine. Deprived of his Spanish troops, Constantine allowed more barbarians to make unrestricted incursions in both Gaul and Spain. Seeing the western defences faltering, other 'barbarians from beyond the Rhine' – most likely Saxons – attacked the coasts of Britain and Gaul. By 411 Constantine, Constans and Gerontius were all murdered and thus eliminated as threats to the rule of the legitimate emperor Honorius (r. 395–423).

British independence

Contemporary written sources are unequivocal in their judgment of Constantine and his ilk: they were tyrants whose actions (and those of their barbarian allies) had a disastrous impact on the Roman provinces of Britain, Gaul and Spain. Yet Constantine and Constans were remembered as tragic heroes in Geoffrey of Monmouth's *History*, where they are Arthur's grandfather and uncle respectively, and Gerontius lived on in the Welsh name Geraint (one of Arthur's knights) and in the famous oratorio by Edward Elgar.

Constantine's actions in Gaul did, seemingly, leave Britain defenceless against a devastating attack by the Saxons in 408 or 410. According to the Byzantine historian, Zosimus,

> [Constantine] allowed the barbarians over the Rhine to make unrestricted incursions. They reduced the inhabitants of Britain and some of the Gallic peoples to such straits that they revolted from the Roman empire, no longer submitted to Roman law, and reverted to their native customs. The Britons, therefore, armed themselves and ran many risks to ensure their own safety and free their cities from the attacking barbarians. The whole of Armorica [modern Brittany] and other Gallic provinces, in imitation of the Britons, freed themselves in the same way, by expelling the Roman magistrates and establishing the government they wanted.

The actions taken by the Britons and Armoricans in successfully freeing themselves from the Empire were revolutionary, and unprecedented in the annals of Roman history. The emperor Honorius was somewhat distracted in 410 – he had just murdered Stilicho, Constantine was threatening to invade Italy, and Alaric's Visigoths were sacking Rome – and therefore could not come to the Britons' aid. Instead, he granted them official permission to defend themselves in the so-called Rescript of Honorius, as described by Zosimus: 'Honorius sent letters to the cities in Britain, urging them to fend for themselves.'

Another Byzantine historian, Procopius, tells us that, after the usurpation of Constantine, 'the Romans were no longer able to recover Britain, which from that time on continued to be ruled by tyrants'. Who were these enigmatic 'tyrants', and were they responsible for Britain's revolt against Rome? The picture is not fully clear, but it does seem that the urban aristocracy lay behind some of the events of 408–10 and were the first successors to imperial rule. These *possessores* simply took charge of the defence of their cities, but must have appeared, from a distant perspective, to be illegitimate tyrants. Local people probably perceived them as 'lord', in something of the later feudal sense of the term, and their vernacular title – *tigernos* or *tiern*, recalling the Latin *tyrannus* – became a synonym for 'prince' in Brittany and Wales. Clerical writers such as Patrick and Gildas withheld from them the more respectable title *rex* (king) but to their supporters and dependants they were probably viewed as such.

Stilicho, on the wing of an ivory diptych dated c.400. The son of a Vandal serving in the Roman army, Stilicho rose brilliantly through the military ranks, eventually serving as regent to the boy emperor Honorius and as Master of the Soldiers. For a time he was the most powerful figure in the western Empire.

The Departure of the Romans, from a fourteenth-century English manuscript.

The Historical Evidence

(Above) St Patrick depicted on a slab from Faughart churchyard, Co. Louth. The legitimate writings of Patrick are primary historical evidence for Britain and Ireland in the fifth century.

IT IS IMPOSSIBLE to write a narrative history of Britain in the two centuries after Roman rule. The only datable references to Britain in contemporary documents are the two visits of St Germanus of Auxerre to the island to fight Pelagianism in 429 and *c.*445 (see box on opposing page), and a Gallic chronicle entry for the year 441 stating that at least a portion of the island had 'passed into the power of the Saxons'. The next securely datable events in British history begin with St Augustine's arrival in Kent in 597. In order to say more than this about the Brittonic Age, historians are forced to deal with a lot of 'unhistorical' material that is devoid of dates, and often of personal or place-names.

Fortunately, at least we have the perspectives of two 'insiders' from the fifth and sixth centuries. These are Patrick, a Briton who became the most famous (and arguably the most successful) Christian missionary in Ireland, and Gildas, also a Briton and a member of the clergy (both p. 68). They adhered to a new 'providential' approach to writing history that would inspire many of Britain's medieval historians, including the early chroniclers of Arthur's battles.

Gildas claimed that the Scots and, especially, the Picts were causing such a serious threat to Britain that a council was convened and its members, together with the 'proud tyrant' (*superbus tyrannus*), elected to hire Saxon mercenaries to defend the eastern portion of the island. (Gildas uses the technical military language associated with the hiring of *foederati.*) The Saxons, however, showed little loyalty, defeating British forces and plundering the towns until a Romano-Briton named Ambrosius Aurelianus assumed military leadership. Thereafter, victories were traded by both sides until the siege of Badon Hill, traditionally dated *c.*500, which took place in the year of Gildas's birth.

The Britons emerged from Badon victorious, but soon fell into civil war and corruption. Gildas attacks five contemporary British rulers – Constantine of Dumnonia, Aurelius Caninus, Vortipor of the Demetae, Cuneglasus and Maglocunus (see map on p. 68) – for swearing false oaths, acting as corrupt judges and entertaining flatterers and murderers at their courts (not to mention their own sins, which ranged from adultery to regicide). The British secular clergy are

Original illustration of Vortigern, 'the proud tyrant', arguing before the British council in favour of hiring Saxon mercenaries.

little better in Gildas's eyes – greed, gluttony and simony weigh them down – while only the monks (probably few in Gildas's day) are worthy of praise. Interspersed among these attacks, and throughout his writings, are more mundane details about diet, dress and entertainment in sixth-century Britain.

Gildas and Patrick are our two most important sources of information for the Brittonic Age. There are, nevertheless, a few other sources which because, for the most part, they were written down later must be used cautiously as evidence for the fifth and sixth centuries. These include the earliest British vernacular bardic poetry, such as those verses attributed to Aneirin and Taliesin (both p. 92); Bede's *Ecclesiastical History of the English Peoples* (p. 46), written in the eighth century but which draws on much earlier material (including Gildas); the *Anglo-Saxon Chronicle* – English monastic annals composed in the ninth century and later; the *Annales Cambriae* (p. 72) and the *Historia Brittonum* (p. 76), both the products of Welsh monasteries in the eighth and ninth centuries. There is also a vast body of Welsh genealogies and lives of the saints. These works all draw on written records or oral traditions from the fifth and sixth centuries, but untangling these bits of information has proved to be both difficult and dangerous.

Illuminated initial 'B' from a manuscript of Bede's Ecclesiastical History of the English Peoples.

ST GERMANUS AND PELAGIANISM IN BRITAIN

In the early fifth century the Christian theologians of the Roman Empire were debating the nature of Grace as opposed to Free Will. St Augustine of Hippo (354–430), a north African bishop, argued that human salvation depended on the unwarranted Grace given mysteriously by God. He was opposed by Pelagius, a British scholar, who stressed man's Free Will in salvation. After a period of bitter Church politics, Pelagianism was condemned as a heresy and Pelagius was driven from the Empire.

Pelagianism and semi-Pelagianism, however, continued to thrive in Gaul and Britain. To combat these beliefs Pope Celestine sent to Britain the bishop of Auxerre, a former soldier named Germanus. The biographer of Germanus records the saint's debates with the splendidly attired British Pelagians, as well as the healing miracles that he performed. Even more miraculous was the Allelujah! Victory, in which Germanus directed a British army to shout 'Allelujah!' to frighten off a band of marauding Picts and Saxons.

THE LITERARY EVIDENCE available sometimes provides names for persons and places in the Brittonic Age, but more often we must deal with the clues present in both the political and ecclesiastical terminology employed by the writers. These clues are also present in the epigraphic evidence for Roman and sub-Roman Britain. The corpus of Roman inscriptions from Britain – mostly inscribed on stone but also occasionally on metal plaques, pottery and writing tablets – can tell us something of both the public and private lives of Britons in the twilight years of the Roman occupation. While much of this evidence comes from the military (from, for example, soldiers' tombstones), it tells us something of the religions prevalent in Roman Britain, the ethnic origins of the soldiery, and even which foodstuffs (such as the ever-present *cervisa*, a Celtic beer) were shipped to the frontier.

Christianity, of course, became a significant presence in all of the western provinces by the end of the fourth century. Some Christianized Britons, perhaps inspired by their Gallic counterparts, began commemorating their dead in the fifth century through inscribed memorial stones. Most of the surviving examples come from Wales and the southwest, with a few instances in southern towns and in Scotland. These inscriptions are usually in Latin and are occasionally accompanied by the short-lived Irish alphabet known as Ogam (left). This epigraphic evidence from the fifth and sixth centuries has revealed a multitude of personal names (of the famous and the obscure), various terms for rulers (*rex, protector, magistratus*) and the clergy, and at least one profession (a *medicus*). While dating these inscriptions can be difficult, much more can be made of this evidence for early medieval British society than has hitherto been attempted.

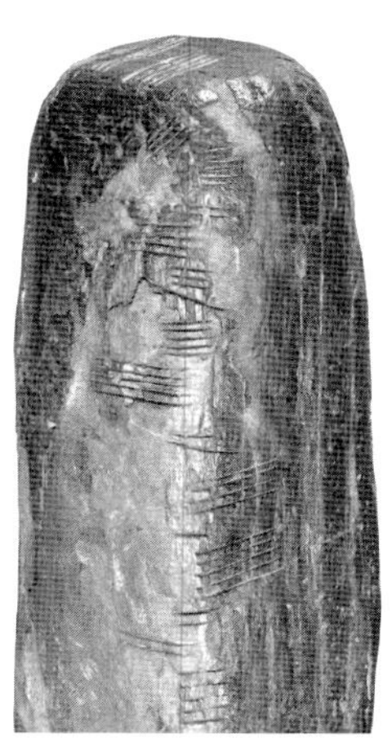

The Ogam alphabet (above) consists of groups of horizontal and diagonal lines carved on the vertical edge of a stone or piece of wood. It appears first, perhaps in the fourth century, when the Irish came into contact with Roman letters. Later Irish settlers carried it to western Britain. This example is from Ballaqueeney, Isle of Man.

THE ARTHUR STONE?

In the summer of 1998, an excavation team from the University of Glasgow uncovered an inscribed stone at Tintagel that ignited Arthurian enthusiasm worldwide. The stone, which had been broken and re-used as part of a drain cover, has a small, lightly incised inscription in Latin (with some primitive Irish and British elements) which reads PATER/COLI AVI FICIT/ARTOGNOV. Professor Charles Thomas has suggested the translation 'Artognou, father of a descendent of Coll, has had (this) made/built/constructed'. The stone can be securely dated to the sub-Roman period (fifth or sixth century) because of its letter forms and its association with 'Tintagel ware' (imported pottery).

What has caused so much stir is that the British name represented by the Latin ARTOGNOV is Arthnou, which contains the same Celtic element – art *or* arth*, meaning 'bear' – as does the name Arthur (p. 149). This does not prove an historical Arthur with connections to Tintagel. It does, however, favour the interpretation that Tintagel was a secular, high-status (probably royal) site with a surprising level of literacy associated with non-clerical activity. The incised cross above the letters makes it likely that Arthnou was Christian.*

THE MATERIAL CULTURE of the Britons is increasingly being revealed through the medium of archaeology. At first used merely to supplement the written sources, archaeological evidence is now often taking centre-stage. The maturation of scientific archaeology has even led some adherents to ignore the problematic written sources and treat the fifth and sixth centuries AD as a 'prehistoric' era, which has freed them to construct new socio-political models devoid of names and dates. More common, however, is the archaeological survey that attempts to answer the questions posed by the written sources and to come up with historical, or at least quasi-historical, explanations for the Brittonic Age.

While Roman urban archaeology has long been pursued enthusiastically in Britain, Dark Age archaeology has been just that – dark. But excavations in the last fifty years have shed new light on both the post-Roman phases of many Roman towns and the rural fortified settlements – 'hillforts' – and monasteries. If not exactly spectacular in their artifactual assemblage, these excavations have revealed impressive structures and provided the insight that Britain was anything but isolated and culturally impoverished in the fifth and sixth centuries.

Tintagel

The first, and perhaps most important, discovery came in the 1930s with Ralegh Radford's excavations at Tintagel, Cornwall. Beyond the inner ward of Tintagel's Norman castle, he uncovered the remains of several small rectangular structures of stone and slate, and thousands of sherds of imported Mediterranean pottery, then termed 'Tintagel ware'. Much of the pottery came from wine and oil containers datable from the fifth to the seventh centuries, leading Radford to interpret this settlement as a Celtic monastery. Subse-

N
Tintagel 'Island'
wells
garden
well
medieval chapel
path
path
cove
remains of the Norman castle
iron gate
Merlin's Cave
path
excavated features
0 100 m
0 300 feet

(Above) Plan of Tintagel 'Island', showing features excavated by C.A. Ralegh Radford in the 1930s. While Radford's dating of these stone structures to the sub-Roman period is now controversial, a turf fire in 1983 revealed the debris of dozens of smaller, turf-walled huts associated with sub-Roman imported pottery.

Stone foundations of buildings at Tintagel, reconstructed in the 1930s. Recent excavations have uncovered smaller hut-foundations just below these buildings.

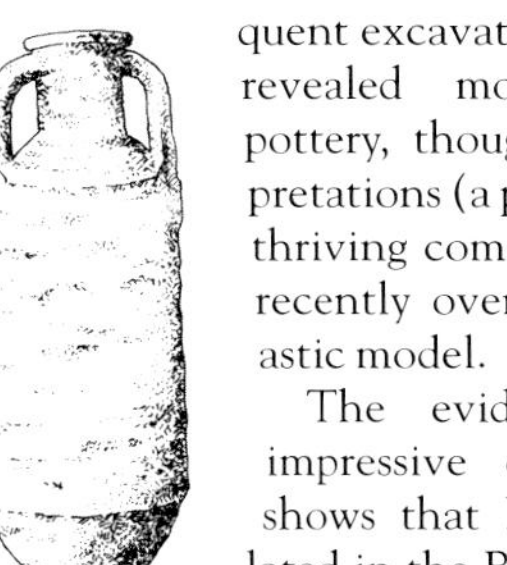

Drawings of imported pottery found at Tintagel: a fine red bowl (above) and an amphora (right), used to transport oil and wine.

quent excavations at Tintagel have revealed more structures and pottery, though alternative interpretations (a princely stronghold, a thriving commercial centre) have recently overshadowed the monastic model.

The evidence of Tintagel's impressive commercial activity shows that Britain was not isolated in the Brittonic Age. On the contrary, Britain seems to have opened up new trade relations with Gaul, North Africa and the eastern Mediterranean where British commodities (most likely tin and slaves) were exchanged for luxury goods. 'Tintagel ware' soon began to be identified at other sites, and new excavations turned up more examples, along with imported glass and jewelry. The defended hilltop settlement at Dinas Powys, near Cardiff, while quite small compared with Tintagel and the sub-Roman hillforts, yielded an abundance of these imports. Leslie Alcock's excavations there in the 1950s also revealed evidence of a thriving native metalworking industry, perhaps controlled by local rulers who exchanged goods for military services.

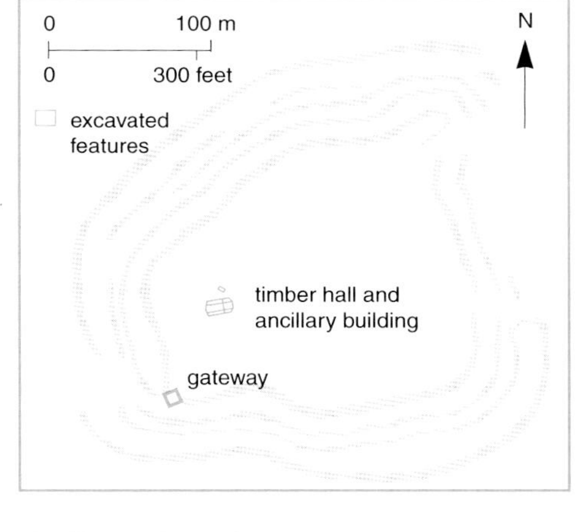

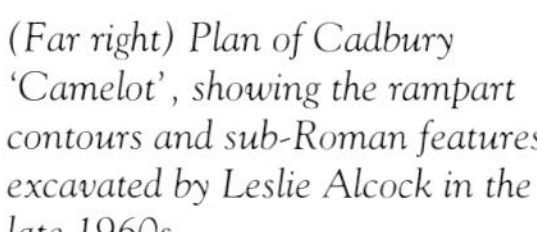

(Far right) Plan of Cadbury 'Camelot', showing the rampart contours and sub-Roman features excavated by Leslie Alcock in the late 1960s.

Cadbury 'Camelot'

It was Alcock who directed the much publicized excavations at South Cadbury hillfort in the late 1960s. Claimed by Tudor antiquarians to be King Arthur's 'Camelot', this massive hillfort rises 500 ft (150m) above the Somerset plains, its steep sides defended by five massive ramparts enclosing a plateau (see plan, above) of about 18 acres (7ha). South Cadbury revealed a long sequence of activity, from the Neolithic to the Late Saxon periods. Extensive fortifications – including stone walls with timber fighting-platforms and a sophisticated timber gateway – were made in the fifth century, when a large feasting hall dominated the plateau. Once again, excavators found an abundance of imported pottery along with Late Roman

Native hillforts were not the only form of defence for the Britons. Recent excavation along Hadrian's Wall has revealed much fifth- and sixth-century evidence, including new timber structures built at the Wall forts. At Birdoswald, for example, timber 'halls' (right) replaced two Roman granaries, while at South Shields a new gateway was constructed. Once thought to have been abandoned after 410, it now appears that the forts and villages along Hadrian's Wall continued to be used to defend local civilian populations in the Brittonic Age. This may have been the case as well for the Saxon Shore forts in the southeast. Both Richborough (below left) and Portchester (below right) show signs of lingering occupation, their walls providing shelter for churches.

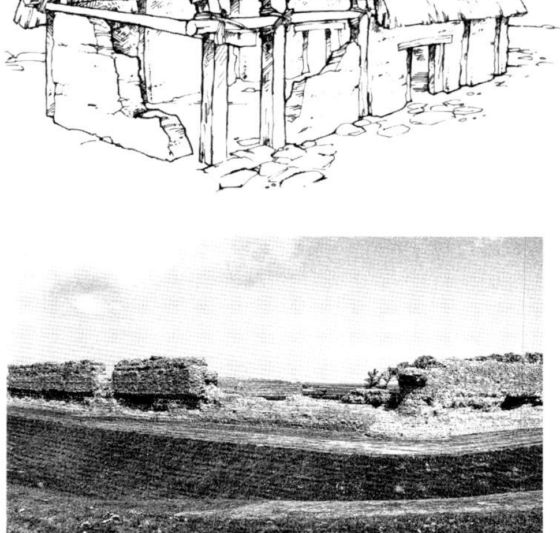

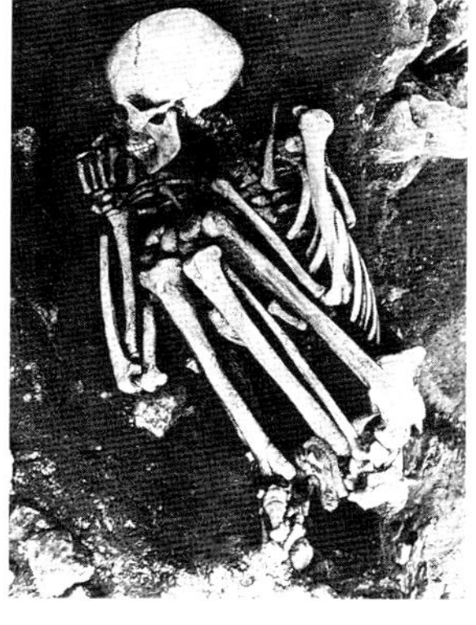

Excavations at South Cadbury (far left) revealed a long history of occupation. This skeleton (left), found in a pit behind the ramparts, was a late Iron Age inhabitant of the hillfort.

coins and Saxon brooches. While the much hoped-for clues to the existence of Arthur were not found there, Alcock did reveal a significant post-Roman settlement that was perhaps the residence of a major British ruler.

Glastonbury

Not far west of South Cadbury is Glastonbury, long the focal point of Arthurian and early Christian tradition in Somerset. The two features that have received the most attention there are the Abbey, one of Britain's most magnificent pre-Reformation religious houses, and Glastonbury Tor, an enigmatic terraced hill rising high above the Somerset Levels (see plan, right). The Tor has yielded strong evidence for sub-Roman occupation, but neither area has been fully excavated and little archaeological work has been done since the 1960s.

Some thirty years earlier, Radford's excavations at the Abbey were aimed at discovering the earliest religious activity on the site. An ancient cemetery of slab-lined graves was found near the remains of a timber structure, thought to be the original church of St Mary. Along with this small wattled building were found post-holes, interpreted as the remains of wattled oratories, and the entire area was bounded on the east by a great bank and ditch thought to be a monastic *vallum*. Though no dating evidence was found at the Abbey, these features lay beneath later Saxon structures, leading Radford to interpret the site as a 'Celtic' monastery, based on the evidence of similar Irish sites. Also found in this area was an eastern Mediterranean copper censer, from the late sixth or seventh century, suggesting that Glastonbury had Byzantine ecclesiastical contacts.

Philip Rahtz's excavations in the 1960s on Glastonbury Tor yielded further evidence of sub-Roman occupation. Structures were found both on the summit of the Tor and on the terrace platforms, reached by a series of steps cut into the bedrock approaching from the west. Slight remains of wooden buildings were found, associated with hundreds of animal bones (representing prepared joints of ham, beef and mutton seemingly butchered elsewhere and brought to the site), charcoal and burnt stones. A fenced-in eastern hollow yielded Roman tile, a bone needle, an iron lamp-holder and a mysterious stone cairn. The most important area was the south platform, where traces of a large timber

(Below left) Drawing of a bronze escutcheon – in the form of a helmeted head – found during excavations on Glastonbury Tor. (Below) Contour map of Glastonbury, showing excavated features at the Abbey and on the Tor.

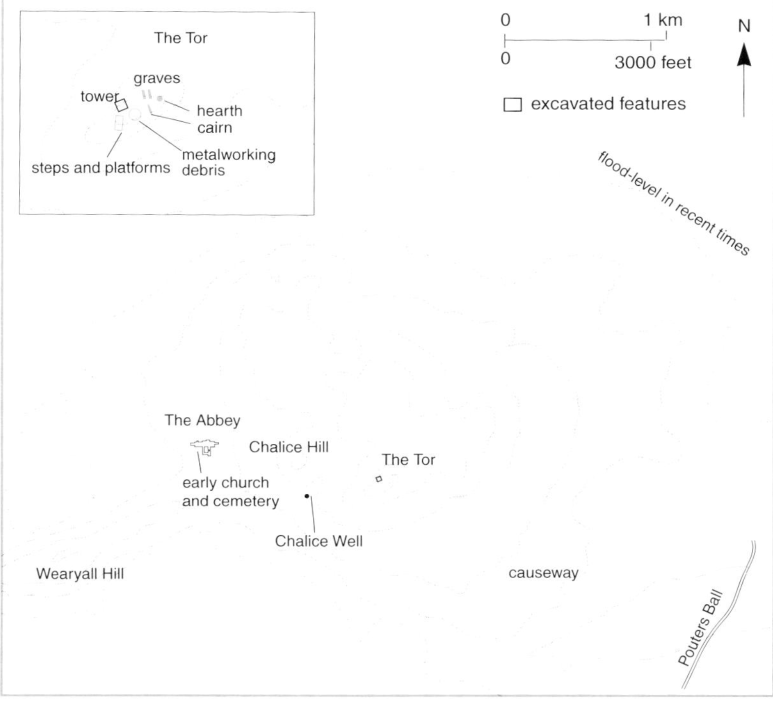

The silhouette of Glastonbury Tor and the tower of St Michael's Church dominate the surrounding Somerset landscape. Here, according to Caradoc of Llancarfan (fl. 1130), was the stronghold to which the King of the Summer Region carried off Guinevere.

building were found along with two hearths, crucibles and other evidence of metalworking, a dozen pieces of imported Mediterranean amphoras and a carved bronze head similar to continental 'Celtic' examples (see previous page).

Though the finds from the Tor are rich, their interpretation is rather difficult. Possibilities for its use include a pagan shrine, a Christian hermitage, the stronghold of a petty chieftain or a defensive signal station used to warn other British settlements of Saxon incursions. Whatever the truth may be, when the new rulers of Wessex began to patronize the Abbey in the seventh century, Glastonbury had probably already earned a reputation as a Christian holy site. By the twelfth century it had become associated with not only Joseph of Arimathea, but also King Arthur, St Patrick and the Holy Grail.

Whithorn and Christian activity

The strongest evidence – literary, epigraphic, and archaeological – for Christian activity in the Brittonic Age comes from Whithorn in south-western Scotland (see plan, below left). Claimed by Bede to be the site of St Ninian's fifth-century monastery, Candida Casa, the area has yielded several Early Christian memorial stones. Peter Hill's excavations in the 1980s revealed at least two phases of Early Christian activity at Whithorn, before it was taken by the Vikings. Fifth- and sixth-century features of the site include small rectangular wattle buildings (one structure had lime-wash residue, giving credence to Bede's 'Shining House' description of Ninian's monastery), a circular 'oratory', a garden, remains of a mouldboard plough, broken 'wine glasses' and yet more imported pottery. Hill sees good reason to believe that the sub-Roman settlement was indeed a monastery, with a surrounding Christian community large enough,

(Below) Plan of excavations at Whithorn, showing the features of the early monastery. (Below right) Excavations at Whithorn, summer 1988. In the background is a reconstructed Viking hut.

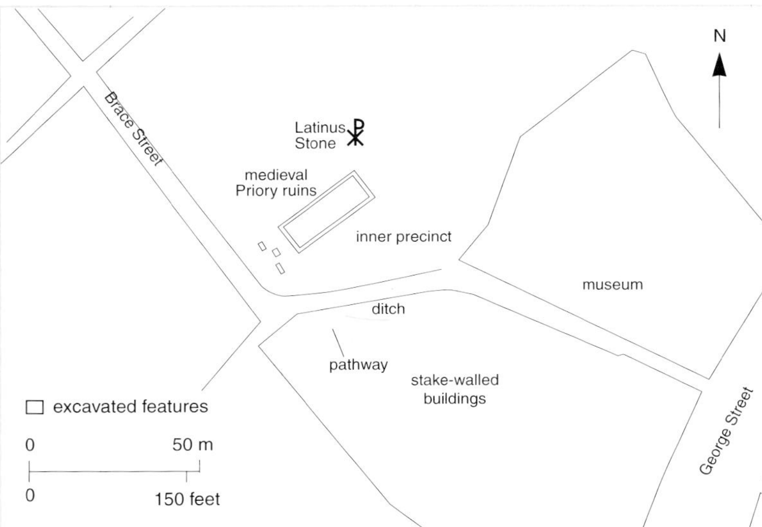

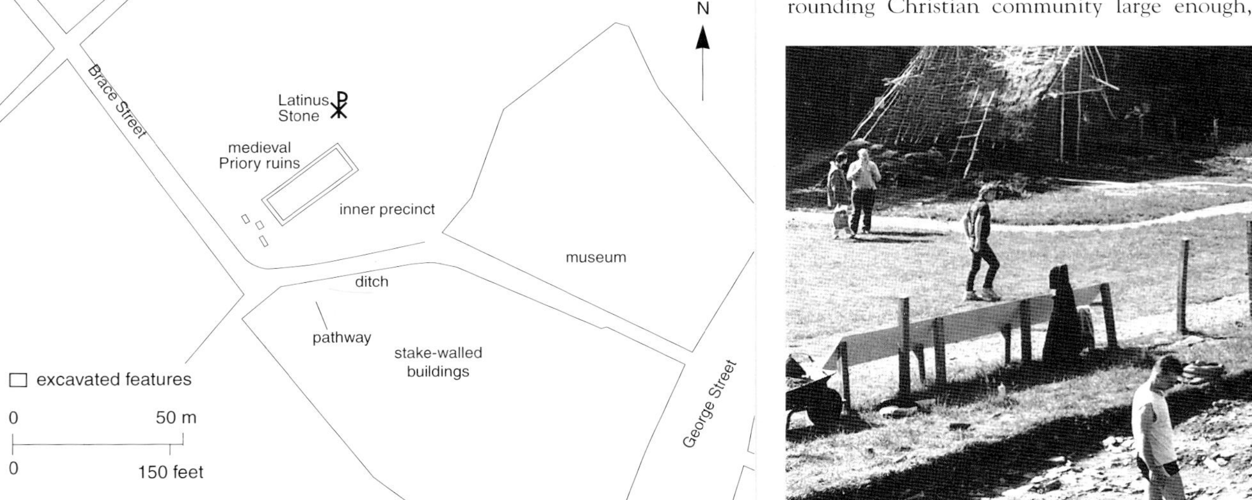

perhaps, to warrant the provision of a bishop such as Ninian, possibly from the nearby Late Roman town of Carlisle.

Wroxeter and urban life

Fourth-century ecclesiastical records do provide us with evidence for British bishops being associated with the towns that were provincial capitals, that is London, Lincoln, York and possibly Cirencester and Carlisle. Most Roman towns in Britain were given major defensive circuits by the late fourth century, making their survival into the fifth century likely. Some historians and archaeologists believe that urban life – if not the towns themselves – was already disintegrating by the early fourth century, and thus sub-Roman Britain must have been completely rural. Other scholars have detected signs of continuity between many Late Roman towns and their medieval successors. Such continuity has been argued for Bath, Canterbury, Chester, Chichester, Cirencester, Exeter, Gloucester, Lincoln, London, Winchester, Worcester and York.

At Verulamium (St Albans), where the medieval town grew up around the Saxon abbey outside the Roman walls, archaeologists found several fifth-century structures and a newly laid water pipe indicating that a nearby Roman aqueduct was still providing water for the town's sub-Roman inhabitants. At Silchester, which did not become a medieval town, excavations have revealed that economic activity at the forum continued into the fifth century (dated by coins and imported pottery and glass), while jewelry and an Ogam-inscribed stone hint at sixth-century contacts with Irish settlers.

But the most dynamic urban activity occurred in the city of Wroxeter. Philip Barker's meticulous excavations of the baths basilica site in the 1970s revealed the constant repair and reconstruction of a Roman masonry structure into the early fifth century. At that point, a large complex of timber buildings was constructed on the site which lasted until the late sixth century when it was carefully dismantled. Described by the excavator as 'the last classically inspired buildings in Britain' until the eighteenth century, this complex included a two-storied winged house – perhaps with towers, a verandah, and a central portico – smaller auxiliary buildings (one of stone) and a strip of covered shops or, possibly, stables. More a villa than a public building, it was perhaps the residence of a 'tyrant' like Vortigern who had the resources to build himself a rural mansion in the middle of the city, with stables and houses for his retainers.

Wroxeter and other archaeological discoveries are helping to dispel the myth of the Dark Ages in Britain. With or without Arthur, fifth- and sixth-century Britain certainly developed a more vibrant character than the label 'sub-Roman' would imply.

(Above, top) Reconstruction drawing of the fifth-century timber building complex at Wroxeter. This complex incorporated the still-standing masonry wall of the baths basilica, now called the Old Work (above right in the photograph).

THE PEOPLES OF POST-ROMAN BRITAIN

(Right) The Venerable Bede, depicted in an initial from a twelfth century copy of his Life of St Cuthbert, *has more than any other author shaped our image of Britain in the early Middle Ages. His* Ecclesiastical History of the English Peoples, *written in the early eighth century, uses a myriad of source materials to describe the multi-ethnic Britain of the fifth and sixth centuries.*

THE ROMANS MADE a clear distinction between citizens and non-citizens in the provinces of the early Empire. In the year 212, by edict of the emperor Caracalla, virtually all free peoples living within the borders of the Empire became citizens, while those beyond the *limes* were barbarians. Post-Roman Britain inherited this distinction, but it became increasingly hard to maintain as some barbarians were intentionally settled within the *limes*, and others seized such land at will.

Inscribed slab from Glamis, Angus (eighth century), showing typically mysterious Pictish symbols accompanying an interlaced cross. Of all the peoples of post-Roman Britain, the Picts remain the most enigmatic.

In 731, a Northumbrian monk and scholar named Baeda – better known to us as the Venerable Bede – completed his *Ecclesiastical History of the English People*. Bede writes that the Britain of his day was inhabited by four peoples, defined by the languages that they spoke. To begin with, he says, the inhabitants were all Britons, who had sailed to Britain from Gaul and spread out across the island from the south. Then came the Picts, who had sailed in a few ships from Scythia (the steppeland to the north of the Black Sea) to Ireland before settling in northernmost Britain. 'In the course of time,' continues Bede, 'Britain received a third tribe . . . namely the Scots,' who won lands among the Picts and founded the kingdom of Dalriada. Lastly, at the invitation of the British king Vortigern, came the English, 'who came from three very powerful Germanic tribes, the Saxons, Angles and Jutes'. The English, Bede's own people, settled in the eastern part of the island, and soon turned against the Britons. Because of the sins of the Britons, he writes, the English became God's instrument of vengeance upon the natives and were destined to inherit control of the island.

Although Bede's foundation account contains much that is legendary and simplistic, it nevertheless provides us with a basic picture of the ethno-linguistic make-up of Britain between the departure of the Romans and the arrival of the Vikings. More closely contemporary writers, like Patrick and Gildas, use the same ethnic distinctions. Still, we must be careful in following their perceptions of ethnicity, given the obvious biases of early medieval authors. Nor is archaeological evidence conclusive, for artifacts do not speak and therefore cannot inform us of the identities of their users. Carefully scrutinized and used in combination, however, textual, linguistic and archaeological clues can help us piece together a fuller picture of life in the multicultural Britain of the fifth and sixth centuries.

IN THE POPULAR comedic film *Monty Python and the Holy Grail*, Arthur introduces himself to a peasant woman as 'King of the Britons'. The perplexed woman replies, 'King of the who? Who are the Britons?' and Arthur informs her that *she* is a Briton. We can sympathize with her dilemma: 'Britons' is a term that has been used to describe the ancient barbarians who fought Julius Caesar, the medieval Welsh who fought the English, and the mostly English-speaking inhabitants of Britain after the Act of Union in 1707. Today, Briton or 'Brit' is used indiscriminately of citizens of the United Kingdom from London to Northern Ireland to the Scottish Highlands, yet in the sixth century no 'British' kingdom could claim these places. Who, then, and where, were the Britons of the Brittonic Age?

Britons (*Britanni*) was a term used to describe all inhabitants of Roman Britain south of Hadrian's Wall for the almost 400 years of Roman occupation. This included the native Celtic-speakers, the Romanized natives and other provincials in the army and the cities of Britain, and the Roman veterans and officials who had settled in the island permanently. Such was the case in the opening decade of the fifth century, when Britain still maintained the administrative apparatus of a diocese of the Roman Empire (see chart on following page).

By the end of the decade, however, the political situation had changed dramatically. In the

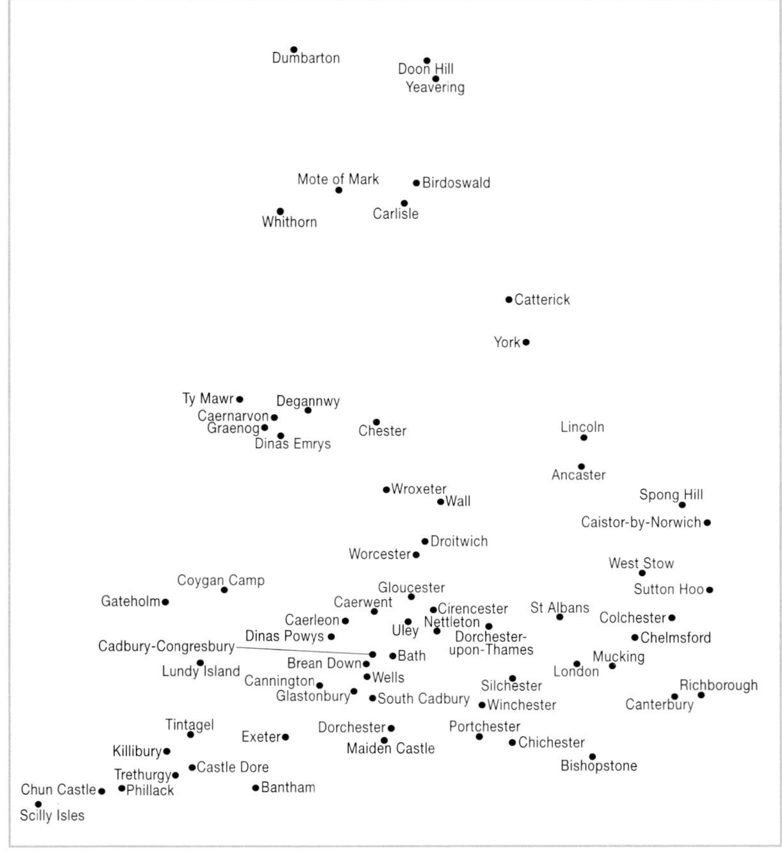

(Above) Important settlements and excavated sites in Britain, c.400–600. Britons, who made up the majority of the population throughout this period, occupied a variety of settlements including Roman towns and fortresses, villas, farmsteads, hillforts and monasteries. New settlements where continental goods are most in evidence (Spong Hill, West Stow, Sutton Hoo, Mucking, Bishopstone, Dorchester-upon-Thames) appeared along the Channel coast and its tributary rivers. Others near the east coast – Yeavering, Caistor, Richborough, Canterbury, Portchester – passed early to Saxon control, while Cornwall, Somerset, Wales and Cumbria remained bastions of British culture.

THE PATCHING HOARD

Some have argued that Britain's money economy collapsed with the withdrawal of Roman troops and the end of Roman administration c.410. The Patching Hoard, discovered in West Sussex in 1997, shows without a doubt that some Britons were receiving both official Roman coin issues and Gallic copies in the mid-fifth century, some fifty years after the end of imperial administration in Britain. Trade with the Roman world, rather than direct imperial payments, is the most likely explanation for this amazing deposit.

Gold solidus *of Valentinian III from the Patching Hoard. This coin is of Visigothic issue, c.440.*

years 406–7, as we have seen, three successive usurpers were raised to the purple in Britain. The last of these, Constantine III, apparently granted the wishes of his troops by taking them to Gaul to secure the western frontier against looting and further barbarian attack. Presumably, he left *his* supporters in command of the civil and military posts in Britain during his absence. Shortly after his departure, however, Britain itself was devastated by northern invaders, most notably Saxons, and the Britons responded by arming themselves to free their cities from the attacking barbarians. This was an illegal act, but it did not seem to matter to the Britons, for Zosimus tells us that they had expelled the 'magistrates' and set up a government of their own choosing, 'no longer submitting to Roman law'.

Aristocratic rule

The character of the government in Britain after the revolt of 409/10 is not an easy matter to discern. Some scholars have taken Zosimus at his (literal) word: the Britons expelled *all* Roman officials from the island, not just the government of Constantine III. Some have even gone so far as to interpret these events as a socio-political revolution, with dispossessed rebels (*bacaudae*) ousting a pro-imperial establishment. While the *bacaudae* were responsible for fifth-century turmoil in Gaul, there is nothing in the written sources to suggest that rural peasants and slaves took control of Britain. On the contrary, there is much to suggest that it was not the dispossessed who took over the reins of government in Britain, but rather the *possessores*.

The *possessores* of sub-Roman Britain undoubtedly came in many shapes and sizes. Decurions, such as Patrick's father, struggled to maintain private country estates, while seeing at the same time to the maintenance of the urban centres that hosted their political assemblies, served as marketplaces for their produce and even as fortifications in times of danger. Archaeological evidence shows us that at Verulamium, for example, they kept the Roman aqueduct working and laid a new water-main, while at Carlisle the town fountain continued to function into the seventh century. They also continued to pave the streets at Winchester, laid new cobble floors for the inner precinct of the temple at Bath, provided for a sluice gate and other flood-prevention work at Cirencester and purchased Mediterranean imports at London and Wroxeter.

Civil and Military Administration

The western portion of the Notitia Dignitatum *gives us a glimpse of the administrative apparatus functioning in Britain in the first quarter of the fifth century, and perhaps even later. The chief civilian official was the governor* (vicarius) *in London. There were also lessor-governors* (consulares *and* praesides) *in each of the five British provinces, while local government was administered through the* civitates *(Gildas numbers them at 28), which were small territorial units, originally tribe-based, focused on major urban centres. Each of these 'cities' was governed by a council of representatives called the* ordo *or* curia; *its members, the* curiales *or* decuriones, *were drafted in from the local aristocracy* (possessores). *Military commands were separated from civilian posts. The* Notitia *lists three major military commands in Britain: the* Comes Britanniarum, *the* Comes litoris Saxonici *and the* Dux Britanniarum (p. 29).

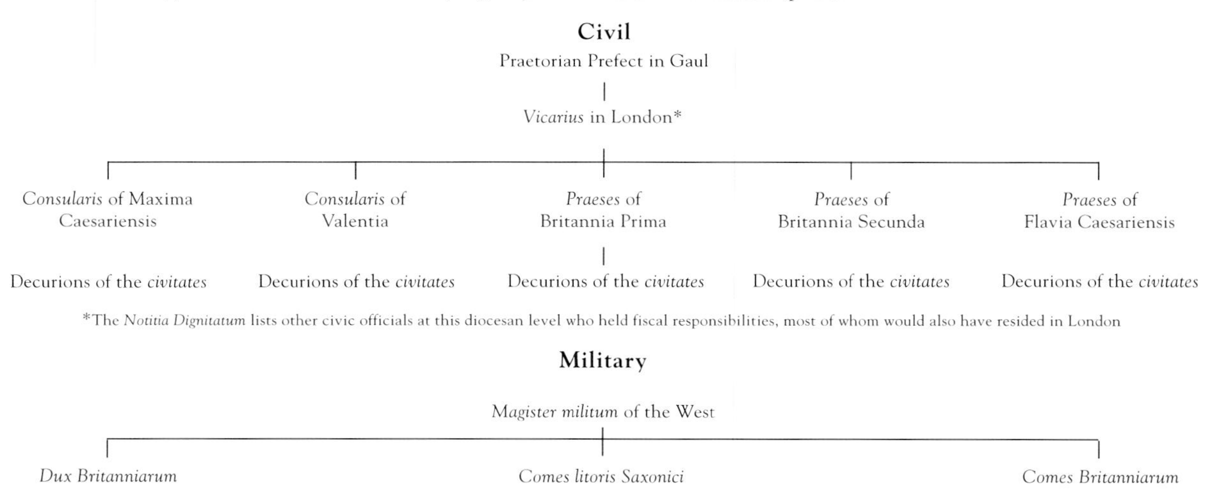

The *possessores* defended their cities using both militias and mercenaries, at least once taking common counsel to tackle a problem affecting more than a single district of Britain. Still, their power and importance were mostly local. Documents and inscriptions show that they gave themselves high-sounding Latin titles like *rector, iudex* and *magistratus*. Their offices had been hereditary under the Empire and these titles might have been passed down as well. But the *possessores* did not appear to be Roman citizens who had simply expanded their powers. They could be seen, and were seen, as 'tyrants'.

Kings and the countryside

Written sources depict a Britain in AD 400 run by an urban-based civilian government, but the Britain of AD 600 was clearly dominated by kings living in rural strongholds. I have argued elsewhere that the 'tyrant' – or *tigernos* – is the key to understanding this transition. Physical evidence of the transition includes signs of the lavish spending on townhouses in the first half of the fifth century, at places such as London and Verulamium, where modest timber, turf and mud-brick structures huddled around the stone mansions of the rich. The complex at Wroxeter (p. 45), which has been described as a country mansion inside a city, had associated smaller structures that could have housed a large personal retinue. Individuals who, taking advantage of such economic disparities, could pull together human resources to defend and maintain the cities would gradually have been viewed as kings.

These landowners could also move their household and retainers to fortified rural settlements, including hilltops, promontories and other easily defended sites, many of which had served as hillforts in the pre-Roman Iron Age. Occupation at British hillforts seems to increase from the fourth century onward and overlaps in many areas with the large *villa* estates. The hillforts had probably remained temporary refuges in the Late Roman period, while after 410 we begin to see the first signs of significant defensive construction at such sites, as well as industrial, agricultural and religious activity. At some Roman forts we see a similar pattern of activity in the fifth and sixth centuries.

Vortigern and the Saxons

Unfortunately, the contemporary written sources do not name the rulers who controlled the sub-Roman cities and hillforts. Gildas speaks of a *tyrannus superbus* – whom Bede calls King Vortigern – who presided over a council that met to discuss the defence of the island against the Picts and the Scots. Their solution was to hire mercenaries from the Continent and settle them in lands in northeastern Britain, presumably to guard the river routes which led to the cities of the south. The date of this settlement is a matter of much debate, though Bede gives it as 449.

These Saxon mercenaries (Gildas, like most Britons, used Saxon as a generic term) were granted supplies and presumably kept the Scots and Picts at bay, for we no longer hear of them as a significant threat. Rather, the threat became the Saxons themselves, for they had increased their numbers and were now plundering the cities that they had sworn to protect. Gildas claims that all the major towns were destroyed by a combination of barbarians, plague and famine. There is little archaeological evidence of such urban destruction. Other signs suggest that most of the towns continued to function through much of the fifth century, but by the sixth the Britons were clearly preferring the protection afforded by the forts and hillforts of the countryside.

The Britons at War

Warfare shaped the lives of the Britons in many ways. Walled cities, Roman forts and amphitheatres, native hillforts and other fortified enclosed places dot the landscape of sub-Roman Britain. But what was warfare like in the Brittonic Age? History and archaeology offer ample answers to this question. Patrick and Gildas both describe British soldiers wielding swords, shields and lances, while their opponents hurled barbed spears which tore the Britons from their city walls. At Tintagel, a graffito etched on slate may depict a sub-Roman warrior equipped with sword, shield, spear, helmet, and what appears to be a whip (right).

Horses had been an important part of warfare for the Britons since Caesar's day, if not earlier, and the early medieval vernacular poetry certainly testifies to the continuing use of cavalry by the British aristocracy. Gildas describes kings who ride chariots, and excavators at Dinas Emrys found three rein-rings from such a vehicle. Archaeologists have also uncovered belt-fittings, spearheads, lead-weighted javelin heads and a shield boss. Compared to the Roman and Anglo-Saxon periods, however, weapon finds are scarce. This may have much to do with it being a newly Christian population of Britons who were giving up the pagan tradition of burial with grave-goods.

(Above) Drawing showing the wood, leather and rivet construction of a typical British round shield.

The British Church

Patrick and Gildas describe a British Church teeming with deacons, elders, priests and bishops. They also describe such pastoral duties as administering baptism, hearing confessions, celebrating the Eucharist, confirming oaths, giving alms, performing sacrifices, serving secular rulers and sometimes pronouncing excommunication. Celibacy was not required, at least not below the level of bishop, and women appear to have played an active role within the church.

The material evidence for British Christianity occurs in four forms: churches, villas, cemeteries and portable objects. Only Silchester, Colchester, Icklingham and Whithorn have produced buildings that have been convincingly identified as churches. None of these structures is architecturally impressive, indicating an urban Christianity of modest means. (A large basilica excavated at Tower Hill in London in the late 1990s, tentatively identified as a cathedral, may force us to alter this opinion for the provincial and diocesan capitals.)

We see a different picture, however, when we look at the Christian evidence from villas. During the fourth century, the villas at Frampton, Hinton St Mary and Lullingstone had extra rooms added, decorated with explicitly Christian artwork. These apsidal rooms, which had associated antechambers, have been identified as private chapels for the use of Christian members of the estate. Many items of domestic use, from silver spoons to gold finger-rings, have also been found bearing Christian symbols like the Chi-Rho, *and* Alpha *and* Omega. *It could be that evidence for urban churches is so rare for Late and sub-Roman Britain because well-to-do Christians preferred to worship in house-churches and other structures less easy to identify archaeologically.*

In rural areas monasticism began to emerge, by the late fifth century, as a strong presence. In Gildas's day there were abbots, monks and nuns following monastic rules, in which they fasted, held vigil, sang psalms and worked in the fields. Whithorn, in southwest Scotland, has yielded the most impressive physical and written evidence for British monasticism (pp. 44–45). Other possible monasteries include Glastonbury, Llandough and Llantwit Major, while hermitages are likely on the islands of Ardwall, Caldey and Lundy.

Reconstruction drawing of the excavated basilica and adjacent cemetery at Colchester.

The British kingdoms

We can now see the formation of political entities that would characterize Brittonic society for much of the early Middle Ages. The *civitas*, a Roman city-state imposed upon a pre-existing tribal territory, seems to have survived in post-Roman Britain, when and if its walled capital could withstand both the post-imperial economy and the increasing barbarian raids. London, Chichester, Silchester, Cirencester, Wroxeter, Chester, York and Carlisle have all been suggested as administrative centres for sub-Roman *civitates*. The larger hillforts such as South Cadbury, Tintagel, Degannwy and Dumbarton may have performed a similar role. Such survival, however, appears strongest in the southwest, the Midlands and the north, and weakest in the southeast where the first Anglo-Saxon political entities emerged (see map on p. 60).

Gildas states that a nobleman named Ambrosius Aurelianus, 'perhaps the last of the Romans', organized and led the Britons' defence against the first Saxon revolts (p. 70). Their success fluctuated until the siege of Badon Hill, a battle whose date is also much debated, but which was probably at the end of the fifth century. After this victory the Britons enjoyed a period of peace with the Saxons (perhaps by treaty) but engaged in bitter civil wars. There was seemingly no Vortigern or Ambrosius to exercise authority over all the Britons, but rather several kings and princes. We know their names, but their dates and territories are less clear (see map on p. 68).

The most prominent kingdom in the south was Dumnonia, which included the modern counties of Devon and Cornwall. It was ruled by a king named Constantinus (Constantine) in Gildas's day, while inscriptions and later sources name Cunomorus (Mark) and Geraint as Dumnonian monarchs. All three make appearances in Arthurian literature. Major centres in Dumnonia included Tintagel and the Roman town of Exeter, and both written and artifactual evidence attests to Dumnonia trading its tin for imported goods from Gaul, Spain and the Mediterranean. Dumnonia, or rather Cornwall as it was called from the eighth century on, held out as an independent British polity until Æthelstan's conquests in the tenth century.

The Britons must also have controlled the territory stretching from Dorset to Oxfordshire, though the names of kingdoms here have not survived. Somerset is dotted with hillforts, like South Cadbury and Cannington which were occupied (and often fortified) in the sub-Roman period, while such towns as Dorchester, Cirencester, Silchester and Bath all show signs of activity in the fifth and early sixth centuries.

Wales eventually became the heartland of the Britons, but not perhaps until the end of the first millennium with the conquests of Æthelstan of Wessex. Border towns like Gloucester, Worcester and Wroxeter continued to operate as political and economic centres through the sixth century, as did forts like Caerleon, Chester and Caernarvon. The first principalities that formed in Wales include Demetia (Dyfed), Brycheiniog, Gwent and Glywysing (Glamorgan), Powys and Gwynedd. Welsh genealogies and charters mention several rulers and their dynasties, but these are often confusing and contradictory and usually reflect political aspirations more than political realities. These Welsh principalities, of course, held out, for the most part, until the plantation of the Norman Marcher Lords following the events of 1066. Here the British language and culture was preserved, not to mention the traditions surrounding the hero Arthur (p. 92).

The northern Britons, whose territory stretched from Liverpool to Edinburgh, developed three large kingdoms: Rheged, Strathclyde and Gododdin. Two smaller kingdoms, Bernicia and Deira, soon passed from British to English control. The northern Britons called themselves *Cumbri*, 'fellow countrymen', while later Welsh sources call them the *Gwyr y Gogledd*, 'Men of the North'. The biography of the British saint, Kentigern, active in Strathcylde *c*.600, suggests that these northern Britons maintained links with their Welsh kin until English expansion permanently separated Wales and Scotland around the ninth century. Though they continued to utilize some Roman towns and fortifications, such as Carlisle and York, the northern Britons increasingly became part of the heroic society most vividly portrayed in the poem *Y Gododdin* (p. 92).

Finally, some Britons fled to lands overseas during the Saxon revolts. Bishops led their congregations to new lands in both Brittany in

Christian or Pagan?

The transition from paganism to Christianity in Britain has long been the most significant religious issue for historians of the period. Scholars still debate, however, the degree of Christianization in Late Roman Britain, as well as the strength of pagan religions in the Brittonic period.

*The written sources, all produced by clerics, are silent on the matter of paganism. Patrick's family had been Christian for three generations, and his only complaint against his fellow-Britons is that there were rebel Christians and apostates among them, not that there were pagans. Similarly, Gildas complains that the Britons had allowed pagan Saxons into their Christian land, and that the British kings had broken their vows to God, but he never mentions British pagans. If paganism were widespread and influential in Britain, Patrick and Gildas would have been all too willing to complain. Nevertheless, it is reasonable to assume that paganism (and probably a mixture of pagan and Christian traditions) was still dominant in the countryside (*paganus*, indeed, meant 'country-dweller').*

Formal pagan worship in Roman Britain had primarily been strong in the Romanized south and east. The number of temples and shrines in these areas, especially in urban centres, decreased in the fourth century (with the exception of the brief reign of Julian the Apostate), and by the end of the century most had gone out of use. Both the discontinuity of worship and the 'desecration' of Romano-Celtic temples c.*400 (at, for example, Chelmsford, Brean Down and West Hill Uley) have been attributed to increasingly influential and zealous Christians. However, there is no direct evidence, literary or physical, that Christians ever engaged in the systematic destruction of paganism in Britain, or even that tensions existed between the two groups. On the contrary, pagan and Christian motifs can often be found together in art from this period, especially in mosaics and on silver-plate.*

Informal worship of pagan gods undoubtedly lingered in the British countryside for several centuries, but would have left few recognizable traces in the archaeological record. Bede and others testify, however, that the traditional sanctity of many pagan sites was recognized by Christians who later established their churches and cemeteries there.

Gold votive plaques dating from the early fourth century. Such plaques were commonly dedicated to pagan gods though these bear unmistakably Christian symbols, the Chi-Rho, *and the* Alpha *and* Omega.

TIMBER FEASTING HALLS

The timber aisled 'hall' is perhaps the most characteristic structure of sub-Roman Britain. Hall-villas and timber barns occur in Late Roman Britain, and perhaps they inspired the hillfort halls of the south and west, such as those at South Cadbury, Tintagel, Dinas Powys and Dinas Emrys. However, the many examples of northern halls – Catterick, Doon Hill, Yeavering, Balbridie – suggest influences other than Roman. To explain these structures, archaeologists often turn to the royal feasting halls prevalent in both the Celtic and Germanic verse of the early medieval period, (in, for instance, the Welsh poem Y Gododdin). *The impressive size of the excavated halls, their internal divisions with private 'apartments' surrounding a central hall, and the presence of large amounts of ceramics and animal bones all argue forcefully for the interpretation that these structures were indeed used for feasting. The occasion may have been a landlord sharing his prosperity with his tenants, a king rewarding his warband, or a noble playing host to an itinerant king, the timing coinciding with a religious holiday or a military victory. The similar design of some Anglo-Saxon feasting halls, like those at Basingstoke and Yeavering, may reflect a significant British component in these communities.*

Conjectural drawings of a typical British timber hall (interior and exterior). In the centre of the hall is a square hearth; towards the back, a wicker dividing screen.

western Gaul, and Galicia in northwest Spain. The settlement of the first Britons in Brittany, though little understood, led to a major linguistic and cultural take-over. Politically, the Bretons were fragmented and dominated by their Frankish neighbours. But their cultural contributions, from Peter Abelard to the Arthurian romances (p. 99), rank significantly in medieval history.

The Loss of sovereignty

By 600, what little political unity the Britons had was shattered by a series of Anglo-Saxon victories. The *Anglo-Saxon Chronicle* describes the Battle of Dyrham in 577, in which the British towns of Gloucester, Cirencester and Bath fell to the West Saxons, effectively driving a wedge between the Britons of Cornwall and Wales. Bede describes the English victory at the Battle of Chester (*c*.616), which cut off Wales from the northern British kingdoms. The latter suffered a serious setback *c*.600 when, as the *Gododdin* narrates, a British warband from Edinburgh fell to the English while trying to retake the fort of Catraeth (Catterick). Although these are both late and difficult sources, the literary evidence, coupled with studies of Anglo-Saxon cemeteries, points to a Germanic culture dominating lowland Britain in the seventh century, with the remaining British settlements in the area scattered and quickly succumbing to the English.

The historical evidence reveals Britons who were proud and who felt these losses to the English deeply. Writers like Patrick and Gildas described themselves and their fellow Britons as *cives* (citizens) of a *patria* (homeland) that was the entire island of Britain, not just the shrinking remnants that would become Wales and Cornwall. Many celebrated their titles or status in stone inscriptions, one Briton proudly proclaiming that he was a constant lover of his *patria* and a preserver of the Faith. Patrick longed to visit this *patria*, and Gildas ached for all its sufferings. The words of both British and English writers reveal fear and hatred dominating relationships between Britons and Saxons. Even those Britons who did not write in Latin saw themselves as 'citizens' – in Welsh *cymry* – and the Saxons as 'foreigners' (*allmyn*). Though divided politically, the Britons shared a common language and a common faith, and for these reasons they saw themselves as superior to and separate from their pagan barbarian neighbors. They saw the struggle as civilization versus barbarism, and cast Arthur as the saviour of the their civilized land.

On What did the Britons Feast?

Sub-Roman Britain was the home of both villa-dining and feasting warlords. Patrick and Gildas tell us that their fellow Britons consumed pig's meat, wild honey, bread, vintage wine, butter, garden vegetables, eggs, 'British cheese' (Britannicus formellus)*, milk, whey, buttermilk and the Celtic beer called cervisa which had been popular among the Roman soldiery. At various British sites excavators have found the remains of wheat, barley, spelt, oats, hazelnuts, limpets, oysters, and the butchered and cooked bones of cattle, pigs, sheep and goats, as well as fragments of cooking utensils, corn-drying kilns, plates, silver spoons, iron knives, pitchers and wine glasses.*

Bronze hanging-bowl, found at St Paul in the Bail, Lincoln (fifth or sixth century).

'Flaunting Their Wealth in Dazzling Robes'

British penannular brooch.

Constantius of Lyon used this phrase to describe the British Pelagians in the fifth century. We know very little about what kinds of clothes the Britons wore, for jewelry, not clothing, survives best in the archaeological record. However, gold and silver finger-rings, bone pins and combs, metal belt-buckles and fittings, silver amulets and both annular and penannular brooches have been found at many sub-Roman sites. Of all the Britons' material remains, the brooches can boast the greatest artistic merit, perhaps inspiring the later 'interlace' masterpieces of Hiberno-Saxon jewelry. Over one hundred enamelled objects from the period 400–700 have also been found in Britain, and from these we can infer that red was the favourite sub-Roman colour, followed by yellow, blue and green; multicoloured millefiori *enamels also appear occasionally. Gildas criticizes many Britons for ostentatiously showing off their wealth, driving their horse-drawn carriages, paying too much attention to entertainments and 'regarding themselves as superior to the rest of men'.*

Kingdoms, peoples and major settlements in post-Roman Scotland. Throughout the early Middle Ages, Scotland was an ethnically diverse land. Britons dominated the lowlands in the early years from their kingdoms of Gododdin, Strathclyde and Rheged. They were soon joined by Angles who took over the kingdom of Bernicia, which was later incorporated into Northumbria. Irish newcomers settled in Argyll and the Hebrides where they were known as the Dalriada Scots. But in most of the isles, the Highlands and the northeast, the Picts maintained control until the Viking Age.

BEDE IS SURPRISINGLY uncritical of the Picts, who were in direct competition with the English over land in northern Britain. For Patrick and Gildas, however, the Picts were an utterly barbarous and dangerous nation. So dangerous were they to their security, that the Britons chose to bring barbarian warriors from the Continent to set against the Picts. The creation of Anglo-Saxon England is, in a sense, the result of the activities of these early inhabitants of Scotland.

Caledonians

The origins of the Picts are obscure and much debated. When the Roman general Agricola pushed into the Scottish Highlands in the late first century AD he met resistance from the Caledonians. Historians now believe that this was a confederation of Highland tribes named, by Tacitus, after the Roman word for Scotland, Caledonia. These peoples of central and southern Scotland eventually developed a sophisticated metalwork tradition comparable to that of the continental Celts. Beyond the Caledonians, in Caithness and in the Orkney and Shetland Isles, were a culturally distinct group who built stone huts and towers called duns and brochs and many-roomed radial huts known as wheelhouses. The ruins of these structures are some of the most spectacular sights to be found in Scotland today.

When the Roman emperor Severus campaigned in central Scotland in the early third century he was opposed by two tribal groupings, the Caledonii and the Maeatae. Archaeological evidence suggests that these tribes were based on hillforts, and thus more closely resembled the British tribes of the south. These peoples of central and southeastern Scotland also inhabited underground houses called souterrains as well as crannogs – artificial islands built on platforms over a lake – a northern British settlement type which made its way to Ireland.

Duns and brochs are characteristic of northwest Scotland in the Roman period. This reconstruction drawing of a cross-section from Dun Telve (above) shows wooden lean-to structures erected against an inner wall of unmortared stone. The broch of Clickhimin, Shetland (right), was of similar construction and included an outer wall and gatehouse for greater defence.

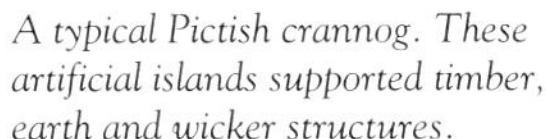

A typical Pictish crannog. These artificial islands supported timber, earth and wicker structures.

North and south

By the end of the third century the tribes of Scotland were once again becoming aggressive. When Constantius and his son Constantine came to northern Britain in 306, they led Roman armies against a people called the *Picti*. The Picts thus make their first appearance in the written record, but they appear as an enigma. Were they simply one of the many Caledonian tribes? Or were they recent invaders of Scotland?

The Roman historian Ammianus Marcellinus described the fourth-century Picts as being composed of two groups, the Dicalydones (surely related to the *Calidones* mentioned in other sources) and the Verturiones. This may represent the north/south distinction we see in the archaeological record as well as in later written sources. It may have been hard for the Romans – as indeed it is for us – to distinguish the Picts from the Britons living north of Hadrian's Wall, such as the Votadini and the Selgovae. It has been suggested that the Romans had established diplomatic relations with these northern tribes so that they could act as a buffer between the Picts and the Roman settlements near the Wall.

As we have seen (p. 30), Pictish raiding of Romano-British settlements increased in the second half of the fourth century. Both Magnus Maximus and Stilicho are credited with victories over them. We do not know whether or not the Picts were involved in the barbarian attacks of 408–10 that led to Britain's break with Rome. We do know, however, that they continued to be a nuisance to the Britons in the fifth century. Gildas implies that the Picts often raided Britain in conjunction with the Scots, and asserts that they came by sea in coracles, small wicker-and-hide boats (still found today throughout the

PICTI

The Picts first appear as such in Latin geographies and panegyrics from the beginning of the fourth century. The Latin word picti *means simply 'the painted ones', probably a reference to the common Celtic practice of warriors painting or tattooing their naked bodies before going into battle.* Priteni, *related to both* Britanni *and* Prydein *(the Welsh word for Britain) and meaning 'people of the forms', is the vernacular equivalent used by Britons to describe the barbarians beyond the Antonine Wall. Thus* Picti *is unlikely to be a tribal name, but rather a term describing yet another confederation of hostile northern tribes.*

On the other hand, Picti *may be related to what these people actually called themselves. The linguist Kenneth Jackson developed a theory that the Pictish language, which survives only in place-names and a few inscriptions, is Celtic and belongs to the P-Celtic or Brittonic branch (p. 23). But Jackson also noticed similarities between Pictish and the language spoken by the ancient Celtic inhabitants of Gaul. This is most noticeable in place-names beginning with* Pit-, *such as Pitcairn. Pictish language and culture developed differently from British, showing elements of indigenous/non-Indo-European survival, while their southern neighbours felt the influence of Rome.*

Foundations of the Late Roman signal station on the clifftop at Scarborough, North Yorkshire.

Celtic fringe). Constantius of Lyon records that, around 429, the Picts were attacking the Britons by land, this time with the help of Saxons.

Apparently the Pictish threat was the more serious, for, according to Gildas, the Britons were willing to hire Saxon mercenaries to protect them from 'the peoples of the north'. Since these first Saxons were settled on the eastern side of the island, it appears that the Picts were raiding the northeast coast of England. Today the remains of Roman signal stations in this area testify to this threat, which may have been the Picts' attempt to circumnavigate the Wall, and the stations undoubtedly supported Romano-British naval operations along the coast. In any case, the Saxons were so successful in stopping Pictish attacks that the Picts seem no longer to have been a threat to the Britons. However, it may be that the Saxons had simply replaced the Picts as *the* enemy in the minds of southern Britons, for the northern Britons would have to contend with the Picts, along with the Saxons and the Scots, for control of lowland Scotland in the sixth and seventh centuries.

THE PICTISH SYMBOLS

We know little about the Picts' now extinct language, but they also communicated through elaborate symbols, usually carved in stone or on jewelry (though if they had used other media – wood, leather, body decoration – the evidence would seldom have survived). One of the reasons the Picts appear so mysterious to us is that scholars have never been able to decipher these symbols. Most widespread are the crescent, the double disc, the bull and the Pictish beast (or 'swimming elephant'). Animals in general appear frequently, always in stylized curvilinear designs. Were these totemic symbols of individuals or clans in Pictland? Were they memorials to the dead? Or, as Charles Thomas has suggested, simply boundary markers or charters used by a non-literate people?

We might be able to understand these symbols better if we had a greater knowledge of the pre-Christian religion of the Picts. The carved bulls, for example, may represent a particular cult associated with that powerful animal. But it is dangerous to make elaborate interpretations of these symbols without the corroboration of written sources. If the word Picti does refer to the practice of tattooing, there may be a link between the tattoo designs and the carved symbols. Archaeologists, however, have yet to uncover such a link. The only contemporary written evidence for Pictish religion comes ofrom Adomnán's seventh-century Life of St Columba, *which depicts the saint battling with the pagan wizards (Druids?) who serve the Pictish king Bridei. This episode, however, may be more folktale than truth. Like their language, Pictish religion eventually disappeared under the pressure of aggressive Christianity and, later, the even more aggressive Vikings.*

Pictish symbols like these (top right) have been found inscribed in stones throughout Scotland. Noteworthy examples include (left to right) the Aberlemno Stone, the Burghead Bull and the Easterton of Roseile stone.

The Scots (originally Irish, but by now Scotch) were at this time inhabiting Ireland, having driven the Irish (the Picts) out of Scotland; while the Picts (originally Scots) were now Irish (living in brackets) and vice versa. It is essential to keep these distinctions clearly in mind (and verce visa).

MANY A STUDENT has sympathized with the whimsical confusion of Sellar and Yeatman in their comic history *1066 and All That*. Is it really true that the Irish were originally called Scots, and that the Scots were originally Irish? Well, yes. But it is really not as confusing as it sounds.

Roman writers called Ireland Hibernia, with *Hibernii* becoming the umbrella term for its inhabitants. Beginning in the fourth century, some Irish began raiding Roman Britain. Latin writers called these people *Scoti* (also *Scotti*), which may derive from an Irish verb meaning 'to raid'. Around AD 500 this raiding led to a permanent settlement, in Argyll, and the kingdom of these settlers became known in Latin as Scotia, or 'Scot-land'. Maybe it *is* as confusing as it sounds. But through archaeology we can see cultural similarities between the Britons and the Irish dating back at least to the Bronze Age. Hillforts and timber roundhouses are just two examples.

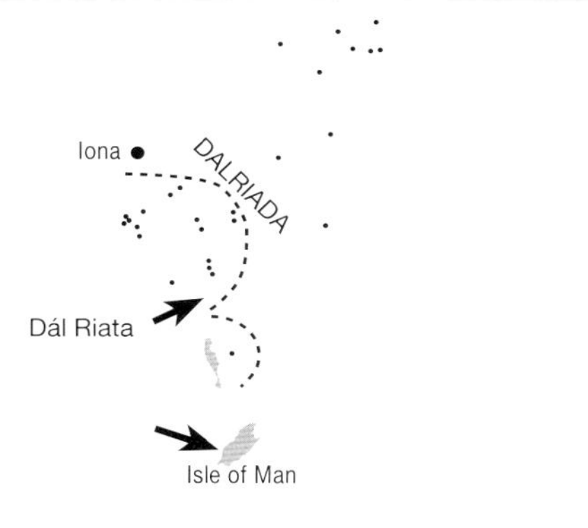

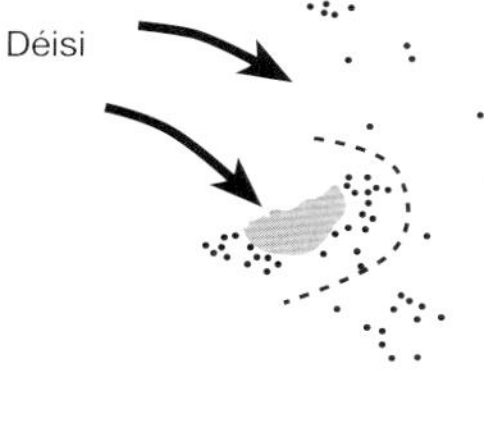

Irish settlement in Britain, AD 400–600. The Irish came to western Britain as both raiders and colonists in the fifth and sixth centuries. They left evidence of their presence in place-names, dynastic names, personal names in inscriptions, and their peculiar script known as Ogam. Dotted lines and shading on the map indicate areas in which such evidence is most highly concentrated. Especially significant were the Dál Riata of Antrim, who settled in Argyll, and the Déisi (literally 'vassals') of Co. Waterford, who established a line of kings in Dyfed.

Invasions

Such similarities raise the question of when, if ever, Ireland became 'Celtic'? The medieval Irish *Lebor Gabála* (Book of Invasions) records a popular tradition that Ireland was populated by sea-demons – the Fomori – who were displaced by several invading peoples: the Partholon and Nemed, from Spain; the *Fír Bolg* (also called *Érainn*), from Greece; the *Tuatha Dé Danann* ('tribes of the goddess Danu'), amiable deities who later retreated to the underground *sídhe* (prehistoric tombs); the Goidels (or Gaels), sons of Mil, who came to be called Milesians; and the Cruithni, from Scotland, who settled in the north. While all of this is entirely legendary, it may reflect, ever-so-slightly, the gradual movement of the Celtic language and La Tène culture to Ireland in the first millennium BC.

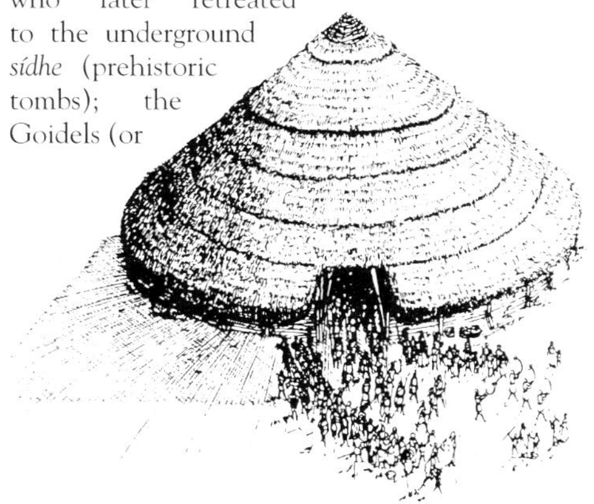

The archaeological record in Ireland, like that in Britain, shows more continuity between Bronze Age and Iron Age cultures than signs of violent change. Both Hallstatt and La Tène metalwork did arrive in Ireland, though later and

A huge circular timber structure excavated at Navan, County Armagh (below, and reconstruction drawing, below left), has revealed a lengthy history for the medieval capital of Ulster, called Emhain Mhacha in the Irish annals. The foundations of such roundhouses have been found throughout Britain as well.

Artist's impression of a coracle bearing Irish settlers to Argyll.

perhaps through trade with Britain and the Continent. Place-names and written records also prove that ancient Ireland was Celtic-speaking, and that the Irish language was related to those spoken in both Britain and Gaul. But, while the Irish and the Britons shared many common terms and concepts, Irish culture developed its distinctive character by remaining on the periphery, rather than becoming part of the Roman Empire.

Though the reasons are unclear, Irish raids on Britain were followed by colonization in the fifth and sixth centuries (see map on previous page). Some have suggested that Roman or Romano-British authorities invited *some* Irish (as *laeti* or *foederati*) to settle in western Britain to guard the coasts from Irish and Pictish raids. It does appear that substantial numbers of Irish settled in Wales and the southwest. A third group of colonists settled in the Cornish peninsula. In these areas we find Irish place-names and inscriptions bearing Irish personal names, some of which are in the Ogam script. The Isle of Man was also colonized by Irish in this period, but though Manx is a Gaelic (Q-Celtic) dialect, both British and Irish were spoken there in the pre-Viking period.

Dalriada

The most significant and lasting settlement of Irish in Britain was of those from the Antrim coast who made the short crossing to Argyll, in southwest Scotland. These Irish belonged to the Dál Riata clan of northeast Ireland, and thus came to found the kingdom of Dál Riata – or Dalriada – in Scotland. The 12-mile crossing would have been made in a *curach*, or coracle, equipped with a sail (above). Upon landing in southwest Scotland, a land then under the control of the Picts, the Irish settled in three regions, each dominated by a kin-group, or *cenél*. They also built impressive fortresses – Dunadd and Donollie, for example – in which they guarded themselves against three aggressive neighbours: the Picts, the English of Northumbria and the Britons of Strathclyde.

We know most about the activities of the Cenél nGabráin, whose king usually held the overlordship of Dalriada. Gabrán was a grandson of Fergus Mór, the legendary founder of Dalriada. He was succeeded c.559 by his nephew, Conall mac Comgaill, who ruled over territory in both Ireland and Scotland from his citadel of Dunadd and who is credited with giving the island of Iona to St Columba. When Conall died, in 574, Dalriada came under the control of Áedán mac Gabráin. Áedán was a very active king who sought to extend the influence of his *cenél* in both Ireland and Scotland. Around 580 he led an expedition against the Picts in Orkney, and a couple of years later he fought the first of many battles for control of the Isle of Man. While fighting in Ireland he lost two of his sons, named Artuir and Eochaid Find. The eldest son bore an Irish name that is the equivalent of Arthur, which has been seen by some scholars as evidence that King Arthur was a northern hero.

IONA

The arrival of the Irish saint and missionary Columba in Scotland in 563 is one of the most significant events in medieval history. Columba's monastery on Iona played host to artists (the Book of Kells *was probably begun there), missionaries (including Aidan, who left Iona to found Lindisfarne, and Columba himself, who was active among the Picts), scholars (such as Adomnán) and political refugees (including several Northumbrian princes). The island was also the resting-place of saints and kings (including, possibly, Macbeth).*

Columba was of royal lineage, a member of the Cenél Conaill of the northern Uí Néill, whose high king ruled at Tara. He was marked at an early age for a career in the Church (his Latin name Columba *means 'dove,' his Irish name* Columb Cille *means 'dove of the Church') and studied under priests and other learned men in northern Ireland (including St Finnian, a correspondent of Gildas). Later he founded monasteries at Derry and Durrow, and eventually a whole network of churches throughout the north became part of the Columban* familia. *Yet Columba could not escape clan politics and, after siding with his family at the Battle of Cúl Drebene in 561, he was excommunicated by clerics of the southern Uí Néill, who had lost the battle.*

Whether as an exile or as a pilgrim, Columba left Ireland in 563 and, according to legend, sailed north until he could no longer see his beloved Erin. Columba and his twelve disciples founded a monastery on Iona that quickly became a cosmopolitan centre. British, English and Pictish monks studied alongside their Irish brethren, welcomed visiting pilgrims and dignitaries, and travelled widely as envoys and missionaries. Columba probably served as the Primate of Dalriada, ordaining Áedán king in what may be the first instance of royal inauguration involving a Christian priest in European history.

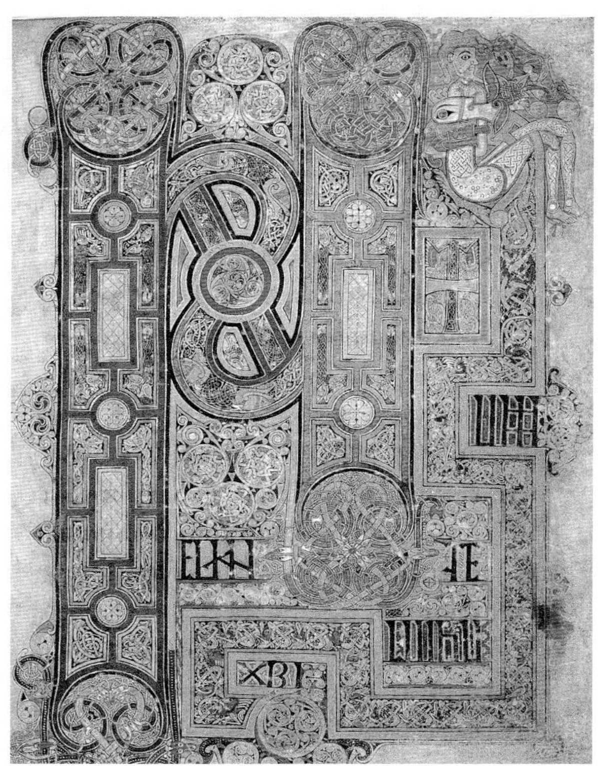

(Right) The beginning of the Gospel of St Mark, from the Book of Kells, *Trinity College, Dublin. (Below) View of the reconstructed medieval abbey from the top of Dùn Ì, the largest hill on Iona.*

THE SAXONS

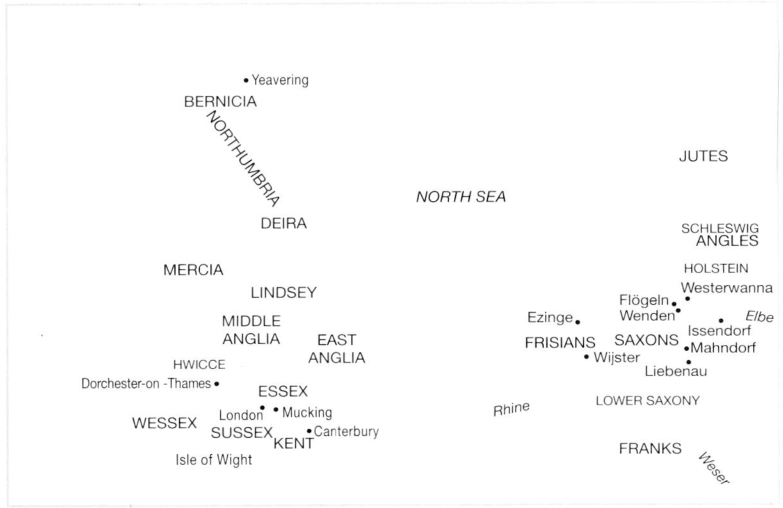

Continental homelands of the Anglo-Saxons and their kingdoms in Britain. Archaeologists are able to identify the continental origins of many Anglo-Saxon settlements in Britain based on important finds in Denmark, northern Germany and the Netherlands that are paralleled in cemeteries across the North Sea. Unlike the Britons, the pagan Saxons continued the practice of burying such goods as pottery and jewelry with their deceased, whether interred or cremated. From Bede and other written sources we know the names and locations of the early Anglo-Saxon kingdoms in Britain. Northumbria, one of the largest and most powerful, came to encompass both Bernicia and Deira.

GILDAS DESCRIBES THE Picts and Scots as crude barbarians, but the Saxons – a 'name not to be spoken!' – he says are 'hated by man and God'. 'Nothing more destructive,' he writes, 'nothing more bitter has ever befallen the *patria* [Britain].' Yet, by his own account, the Britons invited these people to Britain as partners in the war against the northern barbarians. Fortunately for Gildas, he did not live to see his *patria* dominated by these people and given the name of one of their tribes, the *Anglii* or *Englan*.

The Germans

The formation of England was a complex process and is still little understood. The story begins not in Britain but on the Continent, in the north of Germany and in southern Scandinavia, a territory inhabited throughout the Iron Age by various peoples speaking Germanic dialects (see map, above). The Germanic peoples were, in reality, a diverse group of tribes like their Celtic neighbours to the south, and were indeed influenced by the latter. *Germani* was first used to describe these peoples by a Greek historian in the first century BC, though, ironically, it is perhaps a word of Celtic origin. The first Germans to catch the Romans' attention were living on the left bank of the Rhine, and thus were probably Celticized to some extent. In any event, the Germans did not use a single word to refer to themselves until the eighth century AD, when some Germans on the Continent began calling themselves *Deutsche*, 'men of the people'.

While subduing Gaul, Julius Caesar described the movement of some Germanic tribes along the Rhine. When Augustus attempted to conquer the Germans and move the Roman frontier further north, his general, Varus, lost three entire legions in AD 9 when they were massacred by the Germans in the Teutoburg Forest. A disheartened Augustus then made the rivers Rhine and Danube the official boundary between Roman and German territories. But these early contacts resulted in the first ethnographic study of the northern barbarians – Tacitus's *Germania*. His recording of such tribal names as the *Anglii* (Angles, in central Denmark) and the *Frisii* (Frisians, who today still inhabit the Frisian Islands off the coast of The Netherlands) is some of our earliest evidence for people who would later have an impact on British history.

The first and second centuries AD are characterized mainly by stability and interaction along this frontier. Germans were recruited into the Roman army as auxiliaries, trade routes brought Scandinavian amber into the Empire and the Germans adapted, from Mediterranean example, a form of alphabetic writing called *futhark*. Peace and stability resulted in an increased population in central Germany, which put some pressure on the *limes*. Third-century emperors had to campaign against aggressive tribes along the Danube, who were finally brought under control by the time of Diocletian. But it was pressure from the far east – particularly from steppe nomads such as the Huns – which sent the Goths and other Germanic peoples moving south and west and into the Roman Empire in the fourth century.

The Saxon Shore

We have seen that both Britain and Gaul were vulnerable to seaborne attacks, which became quite serious by the later fourth century. According to Ammianus Marcellinus, these North Sea raiders included such peoples as the Franks, then inhabiting the north bank of the Rhine, and the *Saxones*, whom Ptolemy in the mid-second century had placed in the region of modern Holstein. The Saxons may have constituted the most serious threat, for at about this time the coastal fortifications along both sides of the English Channel were reorganized into the system which came to be called *litus Saxonicum*, 'The Saxon Shore' (p. 29).

The Gundestrup cauldron, a large silver vessel of the first century BC *found in a bog in Denmark. Though found in Scandinavia, this remarkable object shows both Celtic and Thracian elements. Originally a diplomatic gift between Danubian tribes, its value was evidently recognized by Germanic neighbours who later came to possess it.*

Gildas describes the Saxons coming to Britain in three ships (he uses their term, 'keels'), later supplemented by additions from their homeland. Bede believed that there were three distinct Germanic peoples who settled in Britain: the Angles, the Saxons and the Jutes. And Procopius, in the sixth century, had recorded that Britain was inhabited by Angles and Frisians. Many have turned to archaeology to clarify the settlement question. Archaeologists working both in Britain and in northern Europe have uncovered cemeteries yielding pottery (holding cremated remains), jewelry and weapons which can help to date and identify the ethnicity of fifth-century Germans. Evidence of parallel finds on both sides of the North Sea at least partially validates Bede's claims, and points to a North-Angle/South-Saxon settlement pattern in Britain by the sixth century. The Jutes, whom Bede places in Kent and on the Isle of Wight, can also be identified from the archaeological record as a distinct group with cultural affinities with southern Scandinavia. Frisians, Alamanni, Swabians and Franks have also left slight traces in the artifacts and place-names of Britain in the fifth and sixth centuries.

The *adventus Saxonum*

Though we now know where they came from, archaeologists have not been able to answer the 'why?' part of the *adventus Saxonum*. The written evidence states unequivocally that the Saxons (to use the generic term) came first in small numbers as mercenaries, as we have learnt, followed by larger and larger contingents who gradually overwhelmed districts in the north and east of Britain. This, according to Gildas and Bede, was a military take-over that led to mass migration (Bede says that the Angles' homeland was in his day deserted) and to centuries of bitter hostility between the Christian Britons and the pagan Saxons. Even after the conversion of some of the Saxons, the rivalry continued on the battlefield and at the church council. Symbolic of this antipathy is the name that the Saxons gave to the Britons: *wealas*, 'foreigner or slave', from which 'Welsh' derives.

Archaeologists have disputed this scenario. Many have suggested that a small number of well-armed Germanic warbands came to Britain and engineered several take-overs of important British political centres. These warrior elites then intermarried with the Britons, who chose to convert to the culture of their conquerors. Thus Anglo-Saxon culture came to dominate large populations of non-Germanic Britons. Mass migration, they would argue, never took place, and there is very little archaeological evidence for violent destruction in the towns of Roman Britain. According to this theory, the Anglo-Saxons were always a minority – though a culturally dominant one – in the Brittonic Age.

Some scholars are now suggesting that we modify this model, in the light of the latest Continental finds which support Bede's story and show that at least some women and families accompanied the Germanic warriors to Britain. The number of cremation cemeteries which have now been recorded show that the pagan Saxon settlements were hardly minuscule; there

Square escutcheon from a hanging bowl found at Sutton Hoo. Note the inlaid enamel and millefiori.

(Above) King Edwin's royal villa at Yeavering, probably a British fortress captured by Northumbrian Angles in the late sixth century. The Great Enclosure in the foreground may have been constructed by northern Britons. (Right) The Alfred jewel, a masterpiece of late Saxon craftsmanship. Its association with the famous Wessex king comes from the inscription Alfred mec heht gewyrcan, *'Alfred had me made'.*

are, moreover, thousands of English place-names which quickly replaced their British predecessors. English did, after all, become the dominant language in most of lowland Britain. Even the Scandinavian dialects of the Vikings and the French of the Normans – both groups who were, primarily, small warrior elites – could not supplant the language of the Anglo-Saxons.

When the first Saxons came to Britain they were, according to Gildas, given lands by treaty. Archaeology has revealed some of these early settlements, such as Mucking in Essex and Dorchester-on-Thames, which were mostly rural communities and farmsteads though often placed in strategic positions guarding important river and land routes. Saxon graves and *Grubenhäuser* (sunken-floored houses) have also been found in Roman forts – Portchester, for example – and in Roman towns such as Canterbury and Colchester. It was once thought that the early English settlers avoided Roman towns, fearing – as in the Old English poem 'The Ruin' – that they were built by giants and inhabited by ghosts. We now know that neither were all of the towns in ruins nor did the Saxons avoid them. Most towns in the fifth century had British populations still in residence, while some may even have had Saxon federates protecting them. By the end of the sixth century, Roman missionaries were organizing new English dioceses around these once-Roman towns.

Bede and the early history of England

It is important to remember that the Saxons themselves produced no contemporary written evidence for their settlement in Britain. It was not until after their conversion to Christianity that they began leaving records, in either Latin or their vernacular. Such early records include laws, charters, poems, letters and, of course, Bede's *History*. Anglo-Saxon history, then, technically begins when the Roman monk Augustine landed in Kent in 597. Bede describes this event, and preserves letters written by Pope Gregory I to Augustine giving encouragement and advice for his new mission in a strange land.

Bede says that Augustine came first to the *metropolis* of Canterbury, where he worshipped along with the wife of the local English king in an old Romano-British church. The Anglo-Saxons by this time had established several kingdoms in the north and the east (see map on p. 60), centred around Roman towns or new royal fortresses such as Yeavering, recently taken from the British.

Some Britons did co-operate with their English neighbours, in war and religion, and many even intermarried. Much later the Welsh Britons interrupted hostilities to support Alfred, King of Wessex, in his attempt to halt Viking expansion in Britain. Alfred the Great is an historical figure that in many ways the legendary Arthur resembles. Both kings came to the throne through unlikely circumstances, both became champions of their people by defeating foreign invaders and both demonstrated enlightened rulership and Christian devotion. It is ironic that, after the Norman conquest, most medieval English writers chose not to celebrate the great deeds of their historic, and English, King Alfred, but rather those of a shadowy – and British (that is, Welsh) – king named Arthur, who was famous for *defeating* the English. The reasons for Arthur's fame among the English are complex, and thus we should now turn to the chronicles of medieval Britain to help us understand this process.

Artist's impression of Saxon warriors rowing a keel. Gildas says that Saxon mercenaries came to Britain 'in three keels, *as they call warships in their language', and were later joined by larger contingents. Excavated ships range from 50 to 75 ft (15–23 m) in length and contain about 20–40 oars, indicating warbands of 100 men or less.*

The Birth of Arthur

And then the two
Dropt to the cove, and watch'd the great sea fall,
Wave after wave, each mightier than the last,
Till last, a ninth one, gathering half the deep
And full of voices, slowly rose and plunged
Roaring, and all the wave was in a flame;
And down the wave and in the flame was borne
A naked babe, and rode to Merlin's feet,
Who stoopt and caught the babe, and cried, 'The King!
Here is an heir for Uther!'

Alfred Tennyson, 'The Coming of Arthur' from *Idylls of the King*

GEOFFREY OF MONMOUTH and later medieval writers related the unusual circumstances of Arthur's conception. These were, that Uther Pendragon, then High King of Britain, became enamoured of Igraine, the beautiful wife of Duke Gorlois of Cornwall. Discovering the king's affection, Gorlois removed his wife from Uther's court and whisked her away to his impregnable Cornish fortress, Tintagel. Uther followed in hot pursuit with his army, ready to make war against Cornwall for the sake of Igraine, and summoned the wizard Merlin to give him advice. Merlin told Uther to draw Gorlois out of Tintagel by ordering the army to attack another of his castles. After Gorlois departed, leaving Igraine behind, Merlin changed Uther into a likeness of the duke so that he could enter Tintagel unharmed. Uther lay with Igraine that night while her real husband was killed by Uther's army. Igraine later gave birth at Tintagel to a boy who was named Arthur. Though Uther and Igraine were now married, Arthur was given to Merlin so that the heir to the throne of Britain would be kept safe from harm. The Norman castle at Tintagel now bears the name 'King Arthur's Castle', while a tunnel beneath is known as 'Merlin's Cave'.

Illustration, by Gustave Doré, of 'Merlin and the Child Arthur' (1868), from Tennyson's Idylls of the King.

[illegible]

[illegible]

ceritaibz · [illegible]

tuum ipenaibz [illegible]

mopem legem

abiciens gen[illegible]

IV
THE CHRONICLES OF THE BRITONS

Britain, the best of islands . . .
is inhabited by five races of people:
the Norman-French, the Britons, the Saxons,
the Picts and the Scots.
Of these the Britons once occupied the land from sea to sea,
before the others came. Then the vengeance of God
overtook them because of their arrogance
and they submitted to the Picts and the Saxons.
Geoffrey of Monmouth, *History of the Kings of Britain*

BEDE AND THE *Anglo-Saxon Chronicle* provide the basic chronological outline for the early history of England. Various Irish annals similarly chronicle the early histories of Ireland and Scotland. While not always reliable, these works tell us much about the political, military and religious activities of the Anglo-Saxons, the Picts and the Scots. But what about the Britons? Did they produce their own chronicles, or must we rely on the testimony of the abovementioned 'outsiders' to tell us about the Britons in the years following Roman withdrawal?

The Britons did indeed compose written accounts of their history in the early Middle Ages. In fact, the only extensive narratives of sub-Roman Britain come from two native sons, Patrick and Gildas. But neither British writer intended his work to be historical, and they are not chronicles in the strict sense of the word. The earliest chronicle material from the Britons was collected in the eighth and ninth centuries and recorded in the so-called *Welsh Annals*. This work is often associated with the *Historia Brittonum*, attributed to the British monk Nennius. Both were used by the Briton Geoffrey of Monmouth in constructing his ambitious *History of the Kings of Britain* in 1136. Neither Patrick nor Gildas mentions Arthur or Merlin, yet all these works have been used by modern writers to reconstruct 'Arthurian' history. Whether or not one believes in an historical Arthur, it is crucial for students of the Brittonic Age to understand exactly what these texts are and how a historian might use them.

The earliest complete manuscript of Gildas's De Excidio Britanniae*; produced in Canterbury in the tenth century and now in the British Library. This page shows the damage done by a fire in the eighteenth century.*

PATRICK AND GILDAS

Known sixth-century British kings and their kingdoms. Many – if not most – of the early medieval kings of the Britons are unknown to us, or, like Arthur himself, are obscured by centuries of legends that grew up around their names. There are, however, a handful of names which have survived in contemporary or near-contemporary chronicles, charters and inscriptions. From the testimony of Gildas we know five of these kings, but their locations are mostly matters of conjecture.

GODODDIN
Mynyddog Mwynfawr
STRATHCLYDE
Rhydderch Hael
TRIBE/KINGDOM
Ruler
RHEGED
Urien
Cadfan
Maglocunus
Cuneglasus
GWYNEDD
Constantine
DEMETAE
Vortipor
Aurelius Caninus
Aergol
Tewdrig and Meurig
Ergyng dynasty
Constantinus
DUMNONIA
Cunomorus

THE FIRST BRITISH historical voice of the period is that of Patrick. Born into the urban aristocracy in the waning years of Roman Britain, Patrick was kidnapped at the age of sixteen and sold into slavery in Ireland. Years later, after escaping and becoming a priest, he returned to Ireland as a missionary bishop. He has left us a spiritual autobiography and a letter written to the British tyrant Coroticus, and while neither work is a history proper each gives us glimpses into the lives of priests and soldiers of the Brittonic Age. The 'providential' approach taken by Patrick also established a trend followed by later British writers such as Gildas and Geoffrey of Monmouth.

Gildas provides a second British voice for historians. But if his writings are more substantial than Patrick's, he tells us less about himself. He says that he was born in the year of the siege of Badon Hill, and that he was writing in the forty-fourth year since that battle. The date of Badon,

Foundations of a Roman granary at Birdoswald, a fort on Hadrian's Wall. Excavators found traces of a timber hall built upon this spot in the fifth century, and some scholars have identified the adjacent village as Patrick's hometown.

Aerial view of Tara, the ancient Fort of Kings. The British saint Patrick allegedly faced down the Irish king's magi at Tara.

however, is a subject of much debate, suggestions ranging from c.430 to c.520. In the Middle Ages he was known as St Gildas Sapiens ('The Wise') and he enjoyed a respectable reputation among historians, including Bede. Two biographies, one Breton and one Welsh, were written in the eleventh and twelfth centuries respectively. Unreliable because of their late dates and thus seldom used by modern historians, these *Vitae* have nevertheless sustained the tradition that Gildas came from northwestern Britain and studied in a monastic school in Wales. It is unclear from his own writings whether he was a monk or a secular cleric, although Welsh hagiographic tradition honoured him as a monastic saint and his Breton cult considered him the founder of the monastery of St Gildas de Rhuys.

Gildas's reputation – then and today – rests mainly on his work *De Excidio Britanniae* (On the Ruin of Britain). The *De Excidio* is an epistle that consists implicitly of three parts: an 'historical' Preface, a 'Complaint' against the British kings and a 'Complaint' against the British clergy. Though it is the Preface that has captured the attention of most historians, it is the Complaint sections that betray the purpose of their author and (presumably) the interests of the original readers. Unfortunately, the 'historical' Preface is not historical at all, but rather a selective recounting of events during the Roman occupation of, and subsequent withdrawal from, Britain whose purpose it is to illustrate the 'wicked' behaviour of the Britons. Recently, several scholars have pointed out Gildas's use of the Old Testament 'jeremiad' to rebuke his fellow-countrymen, following a convention of Christian historiography that explains earthly calamities (such as the barbarian invasions) as God's punishment for the sins of 'His people' (Israelites/Romans/Britons).

The Preface, then, is a narrative of past British 'sins' and 'calamities' which foreshadow the even greater sins of Gildas's own day. The worst of the calamities is the invasion of the Picts and the Scots, which caused the Britons to appeal 'to Agitius, thrice consul' (Bede corrects Gildas's spelling to Aëtius) of Rome. When the Romans failed to respond, 'all the members of the [British] council, together with the proud tyrant', decided to hire Saxons 'to beat back the peoples of the north'. Soon, however, the Saxons turned against the Britons, inflicting an even more deadly 'plague': many towns were destroyed, and most of the survivors were either 'butchered in the mountains' or fled to 'lands beyond the sea'. The remnant mounted a resistance, led by Ambrosius Aurelianus, which brought some success against the Saxons:

VORTIGERN

*According to Gildas, the Britons convened a council to decide on a defensive strategy for Britain, and 'all the members of the council, together with the proud tyrant (*superbo tyranno*) decided to hire Saxon mercenaries. The name Vortigern (Latin* Vortigernus*, Welsh* Gwrtheryn*) appears in two early manuscripts of the* De Excidio*, as well as in the* First Life of St Gildas*, in place of 'the proud tyrant'. In Bede's writings he appears as* Vertigernus *and* Vurtigernus*, while in the* Historia Brittonum *he is* Guorthigernus*. By the eighth century at least, he was recognized as a powerful British king. Since Vortigern is almost certainly a British name meaning 'overlord' –* Vor- *'over',* tigernos *'lord' – Gildas may have been making a pun or word-play with* superbo tyranno.

Is this Mount Badon? Liddington Castle, a prominent Iron Age hillfort in Wiltshire that was once known as Badbury Camp, has revealed slight evidence of sub-Roman occupation.

> From then on victory went now to our countrymen, now to their enemies. . . . This lasted right up to the year of the siege of Badon Hill, pretty much the last defeat of the villains, and certainly not the least. That was the year of my birth; as I know, one month of the forty-fourth year since then has already passed.

The period between the victory of Badon Hill and Gildas's writing is a time of respite from the barbarian menace, but it is a peace that breeds corruption. 'Britain has kings,' writes Gildas, 'but they are tyrants; she has judges, but they are wicked.' Gildas's Complaint against the kings is a specific denunciation of five British rulers: 'Constantinus, tyrant whelp of the filthy lioness of Dumnonia'; 'Aurelius Caninus, lion-whelp'; 'Vortipor, tyrant of the Demetae'; 'Cuneglasus, in Latin "red butcher"'; and 'Maglocunus . . . dragon of the island.' Many attempts have been made to identify the locations of these rulers. (Maglocunus is identified from other sources as Maelgwn, king of Gwynedd.) Generally, they appear to have been rulers of Wales and the southwest (see map on p. 68).

Gildas's Complaint against the clergy is not as specific as that aimed at particular rulers, but it is equally colourful. 'Britain has priests,' he writes, 'but they are fools; very many ministers, but they are shameless; clerics, but they are treacherous grabbers.' Though most of the Complaint is biblical sermonizing, beneath the prejudices are rare sociological glimpses. As Leslie Alcock reminds us, Gildas tells us a great deal here about both the politics and church of sub-Roman Britain, a fact often overlooked by historians trying to make sense of Gildas's confused historical narrative.

Ambrosius, 'Last of the Romans'

> *'After a time, when the cruel plunderers had gone home, God gave strength to the survivors. . . . Their leader was Ambrosius Aurelianus, a gentleman who, perhaps alone of the Romans, had survived the shock of this notable storm: certainly his parents, who had worn the purple, were slain in it.'*

Ambrosius Aurelianus is one of the most solidly historical figures of the Brittonic Age, being the only fifth-century Briton to whom Gildas refers by name. Yet we know very little about him. Since Gildas depicts him as Roman, some have suggested that he was from a senatorial family, the Aurelii, and was perhaps named after St Ambrose. Others have said that since his parents had 'worn the purple', his father must have been a British emperor or imperial usurper. Geoffrey of Monmouth picks up on this by making his 'Aurelius Ambrosius' the son of Constantine III, and therefore uncle of Arthur.

GILDAS

FROM THE *FRAGMENTS*

'A wise man recognizes the gleam of truth whoever utters it.'

'When the ship is holed, let the man who can swim swim.'

FROM THE *PENITENTIAL*

'A presbyter or a deacon committing natural fornication or sodomy who has previously taken the monastic vow shall do penance for three years.'

'A monk who has stolen a garment or any other thing shall do penance for two years . . . if he is a junior; if a senior, one entire year.'

'If on account of drunkenness someone is unable to sing the psalms, being benumbed and speechless, he shall be deprived of his supper.'

'He who willingly has been defiled in sleep, if the monastic house is abundantly supplied with beer and flesh, shall make a standing vigil for three hours of the night if his health is strong.'

'For good rulers we ought to offer sacrifice, for bad ones on no account.'

'One who has broken a hoe which was not broken before, shall either make amends by an extraordinary work or perform a special fast.'

Also frequently overlooked are Gildas's other writings, the *Fragments* and the *Penitential*. The *Fragments* are pieces of lost letters, reportedly written by Gildas, dealing with various ecclesiastical affairs. We know from the writings of St Columbanus that Gildas did correspond with British (and possibly Irish) clergy and that he was considered an authority on asceticism. The *Fragments* cover such subjects as excommunication, abstinence, overzealous monks and the roles of bishops and abbots. Both regular and secular clergy, in their various ranks, are dealt with in the *Penitential*. This penitential, along with those ascribed to Finnian and Columbanus, are the oldest known to us, and had a profound influence on the famous Irish penitentials which became the norm for the entire Catholic Church in the Middle Ages. The *Penitential* of Gildas is a brief collection of very simple and practical rules for a British church that was becoming increasingly stratified and monastic.

While more work needs to be done on these last two works, the *De Excidio* has certainly not lacked modern historical commentary. But, as with Patrick, we run into difficulty when discussing dates for Gildas, and his location while he wrote the *De Excidio*. Gildas provides no absolute dates in his writings, though he does describe some events – the rebellion of Magnus Maximus (383–88), the Rescript of Honorius (410), the letter to Aëtius (*c*.430–54, when Aëtius was active in Gaul) – which can be dated by outside sources. Other episodes in his narrative – the siege of Badon Hill, the reigns of the British rulers whom he denounces – are more difficult to date with confidence. There is also debate over whether to place Gildas in the north or in a southern, more Romanized locale. Scholars are far from reaching a consensus on these issues, but recent discussion has focused on a southwestern Gildas (perhaps Dorset or Somerset) who wrote the *De Excidio* sometime in the early sixth century. In his writing, Gildas's geographic perspective was quite broad, encompassing all of the once-Roman territory on the island of Britain, and there is a strong tradition that depicts Gildas as travelling widely.

There is more of a consensus concerning the sources that Gildas used in writing the *De Excidio*. To many readers, Gildas's writing has appeared peculiar and pedantic, a raving sermon issued from a land of barbarians. Recently, however, scholars have demonstrated that, despite his dependence on biblical themes, Gildas's prose style is more akin to that of fifth-century rhetoricians such as Sidonius and Ennodius. It is now evident that Gildas was familiar with most of the books of the Bible (in both the Old Latin version and Jerome's newer Vulgate edition) in addition to works by Virgil (especially the *Aeneid*), Rufinus, Orosius, Sulpicius Severus, Jerome, John Cassian and Prudentius. Such wide reading, accompanied by impeccable grammar and syntax, suggest that Gildas was the recipient of a superior classical education in a British school. Clearly, Gildas came out of a late classical tradition but presented his social and political views in an insular and wholly Christian scheme.

THE WELSH ANNALS

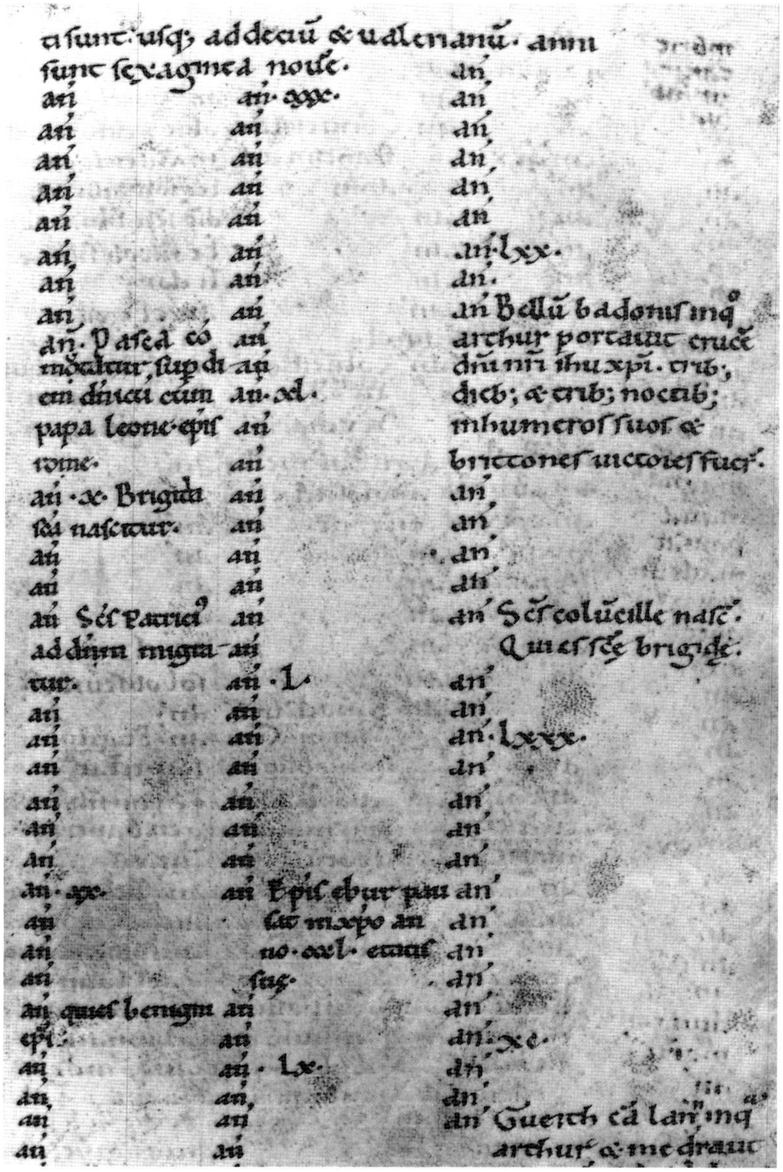

A page from the Harleian manuscript of the Annales Cambriae. *In the far right-hand column are the entries for the battles of Badon and Camlann.*

ANNALS ARE PRIMARILY a way of keeping track of time, secondarily an excuse to record important events associated with those dates. Originally brief documents associated with the reigns of important kings in ancient Mesopotamia and Egypt, annals were adapted by Roman writers such as Tacitus to serve the additional purpose of political commentary. The Christian annalists of the early Middle Ages, however, preferred brief descriptive entries for each year, and the significance of an entry was usually defined by the monastic community that produced the annal. Hence the birth and death days of local saints, the visitation of plague or famine and the sporadic Viking raid were most likely to grab the annalist's attention. Rarely did warrior heroes like Arthur find their way into early medieval annals.

Remarkably, Arthur's first appearance in a written document (p. 94) is indeed in an annal, specifically in two entries belonging to a collection called the *Annales Cambriae* (The Welsh Annals):

> [AD 518] *Bellum Badonis in quo Arthur portavit crucem domini nostri Iesu Christi, tribus diebus et tribus noctibus, in humeros suos, et Brittones victores fuerunt.* (The Battle of Badon, in which Arthur carried the cross of our lord Jesus Christ for three days and three nights on his shoulders, and the Britons were the victors.)

> [AD 539] *Gueith Camlann in qua Arthur et Medraut corruerunt; et mortalitas in Britannia et in Hibernia fuit.* (The conflict at Camlann, in which Arthur and Medraut perished; and there was a pestilence in Britain and Ireland.)

Though the dates have been debated (the *Annals* do not use the *anno domini* dating system), most have accepted these as authentic entries. Questions remain, however, concerning the compilation of these entries. The *Annals* survive in an English manuscript, now in the British Museum's Harleian collection, which dates to c.1100. They also show the influence of Irish annals, especially in the early entries. The focus of the *Annals*, however, is on Welsh matters, and the last event recorded is the death of the Welsh king Rhodri ap Hywel Dda in 957. From this, it would appear that the *Annals* were written down several centuries after the events of 518 and 539.

Arthurian scholars have tried to push back the date of composition for the early entries, some claiming that they are nearly contemporary with the events they describe and thus important evidence for an historical Arthur (and for his association with Gildas's Battle of Mount Badon). Textual specialists are willing to concede that the *Annals* constitute a record kept by monks at St David's from the late eighth century onwards. Furthermore, the entries in the *Annals* that pertain to northern Britain seem to derive from an earlier set of northern annals which was then used by Irish annalists and which may have had entries going back to the late sixth century. But there is no direct evidence for these northern annals being contemporary records for the fifth and sixth centuries either.

The *Annals* cannot, then, be used as a primary source for an Arthur living in the fifth or sixth centuries. As a primary source for any period they are problematic, due to the possibility that entries were added over a prolonged period of time. The *Annals* can, however, be used as an historical document that shows us the preoccupations of the Britons in the early Middle Ages. Here, amid the records of saints and kings, a British monk decided to record the accomplishments – and passing – of a famous and devout military hero named Arthur. But we are left with questions. Was this Arthur a king? And what was his relationship to the mysterious Medraut?

Arthur and Mordred meet at Camlann, as depicted in a fifteenth-century English manuscript.

MORDRED

Mordred, or Modred, is traditionally the most infamous of the Knights of the Round Table. He makes his first appearance in the Annales Cambriae, *under the Cornish form of the name, Medraut. He is said to have perished in the same battle as Arthur, but the circumstances of his death and his relationship with Arthur are not given (he could have been friend or foe). In Geoffrey of Monmouth's* History, *Mordred is Arthur's nephew, the son of King Lot and brother to Sir Gawain. Mordred turned traitor by seizing the throne from Arthur in collusion with the queen, Guinevere. In late medieval versions of the story, Mordred is made Arthur's son, the product of an unknowingly incestuous union between Arthur and his half-sister, Morgause. When Mordred grew to adulthood he became a Knight of the Round Table like his half-brothers, the sons of Morgause and Lot. In a feud between the sons of Lot and those of King Pellinore, Mordred treacherously killed Pellinore's son Lamorak, who had been the lover of Queen Morgause. Later Mordred became an enemy of Lancelot and was responsible for uncovering his affair with Guinevere, which led to the fall of the Round Table. In some versions Mordred has two sons who survive him.*

Henry Justice Ford, Sir Mordred, and the Last Battle, *from* The Book of Romance, *edited by Andrew Lang (1902).*

Arthur, Leader of Battles

MEDIEVAL AUTHORS did not relate stories of Arthur's childhood, giving later writers, such as Edmund Spenser and T.H. White, the opportunity to add their own contributions to the Arthurian saga. According to Malory's *Le Morte d'Arthur,* King Uther Pendragon sent his only son Arthur away for safekeeping shortly after the child was born. Arthur was raised in obscurity by the kindly Sir Ector, along with Ector's own son Kay. Arthur served as Kay's squire at the latter's first 'tourney', and when Kay forgot his sword Arthur was sent to retrieve it. Arthur found another sword, embedded in a stone and anvil, and he pulled this one out to give to Kay. In so doing the fifteen-year-old proved himself to be the rightful heir to the throne of Britain. However, Arthur still had to fight a series of battles against rebel British kings before he was universally recognized as sovereign monarch. The earliest written account, the ninth-century *Historia Brittonum*, does not specifically say that Arthur was a king, but rather that he fought 'with the kings of Britain, though he was the leader of the battles (*dux bellorum*)'. The battles referred to are those against the Anglo-Saxons, who, as descendants of the rebel mercenaries invited to Britain by King Vortigern, were now enlarging their territories in Britain. Twelve great battles were fought, in which Arthur displayed both his military prowess and his Christian piety. The last was the siege of Mount Badon, a British victory that put a halt to Saxon expansion.

Arthur going into battle in 'How Arthur Drew his Sword Excalibur for the First Time', illustration by Arthur Rackham from The Romance of King Arthur and His Knights of the Round Table, *A.W. Pollard's 1917 abridgement of Malory's* Le Morte d'Arthur.

(Right) This page, from a twelfth-century manuscript containing the Historia Brittonum, *includes the description of Arthur's twelve battles against the Saxons.*

SURVIVING IN THE same manuscript as the *Annales Cambriae* (as well as in some forty other medieval manuscripts) is a longer work entitled *Historia Brittonum* (The History of the Britons). The work begins with a prologue identifying the author and his purpose:

> I, Nennius, pupil of the holy Elvodug, have undertaken to write down some extracts that the stupidity of the British cast out. . . . I have therefore made a heap of all that I have found. . . . I ask every reader to pardon me for daring to write . . . like a chattering bird or an incompetent judge.

Despite the author's assertion of his own ineptitude, this is a real work of narrative history, not merely a collection or annal. Herein we find the story of God's chosen people, the Britons, as they struggle against Roman and Saxon invaders. The latter is a particularly destructive plague visited upon the Britons because of their sins. Thus we have a providential history akin to Gildas's *De Excidio*, with an even stronger strain of nationalism.

Brutus's Voyage to Britain. Illustration from a genealogy produced at the Abbey of St Mary in York c.1300. The Historia Brittonum *begins with the legend of the founding of Britain by the Trojan Brutus.*

The narrative of the *History* builds to a climax as it describes the betrayal of the British king Vortigern by the Saxon mercenary Hengist. It records that, 'In that time the Saxons strengthened in multitude and grew in Britain.' This was the time of the Briton Patrick (whose life had just been described in brief), and of Hengist's son Octha:

> Then Arthur fought against them in those days with the kings of the Britons but he himself was the leader of the battles [*dux bellorum*]. The first battle was at the mouth of the river which is called Glen [*Glein*]. The second and third and fourth and fifth were upon another river which is called Douglas [*Dubglas*] and is in the district of Lindsey [*Linnuis*]. The sixth battle was upon the river which is called Bassas.

> The seventh battle was in the Caledonian wood, that is, Cat Coit Celidon. The eighth battle was in Fort Guinnion in which Arthur carried the image of St Mary, ever virgin, on his shoulders and the pagans were turned to flight on that day and a great slaughter was upon them through the virtue of our Lord Jesus Christ and through the virtue of St Mary the Virgin, his mother. The ninth battle was waged in the City of the Legion. The tenth battle he waged on the shore of the river which is called Tribruit. The eleventh battle took place on the mountain which is called Agned. The twelfth battle was on mount Badon, in which nine hundred and sixty men fell in one day from one charge by Arthur, and no one overthrew them except himself alone. And in all the battles he stood forth as victor.

Here, for the first time in a written document, Arthur is presented as the pre-eminent military hero of the Britons in their struggle with the Saxons. He fights *with* the kings of the Britons, as the leader of the battles (some of them possibly naval battles, given their riverine locations), but is not himself called a king. He is, however, credited with twelve great victories over the Saxons, in which his martial prowess is complemented by his Christian devotion. Though we hear nothing more about Arthur in the *History*, this brief passage established a foundation for his career that would be taken up and expanded by such future writers as Geoffrey of Monmouth, Wace and Layamon.

There are, unfortunately, major problems in using the *History of the Britons* as a source for writing fifth- and sixth-century history. First of all, the authorship of the work has been seriously called into question, because the prologue appears only in the so-called 'Nennian recension' (which was copied into a manuscript between 1164 and 1166) and not in the oldest recension (which dates to 831). Some, following David Dumville, claim that it was a later addition to the main body of the work. Peter Field has argued, to the contrary, that the original author was Nennius, a disciple of the archbishop of Gwynedd, who wrote in the late eighth century. The author, whatever his name, appears to have been a talented compiler of a great variety of sources. The Arthurian material in the *History* is believed to derive from a Welsh (vernacular) poem on the battles of Arthur, a poem which we do not possess but which *may* accurately transmit some details of military campaigns *c.*500. But since many of the sources are not of an overtly historical nature – witness the exaggeration of Arthur's military prowess – this has left the *History* with a chronology that is confusing at best.

Local lore concerning Arthur, like that in 'The Marvels of Britain' attached to the Historia Brittonum, *spread throughout continental Europe in the eleventh and twelfth centuries. This mosaic, from the Norman cathedral in Otranto, Sicily (1165), depicts Arthur* (Rex Arturus) *mounted on a goat doing battle with a monstrous cat.*

Further compromising the integrity of the *History* is an appendix attached to it (at a slightly later date) called 'The Marvels of Britain'. This compilation of local lore includes two items concerning Arthur. The first is a heap of stones at *Buelt* (Builth Wells in south-central Wales) which bears a dog's paw-print, supposedly belonging to Cabal the hound of 'the warrior Arthur', who set his foot on it during a boar-hunt. This stone cannot, it is said, be removed from the heap, for it will always return to the spot. The second Arthurian marvel, in the Welsh district of Ercing, is the tomb of 'Amr, son of Arthur'. Each time one tries to measure the tomb, says the *History*'s author (who has tried it himself), it appears to be a different length!

For the historian, then, the *History of the Britons* comes with a lot of unwanted baggage. It is a compilation of varied source material, some of it containing genuine information about the fifth and sixth centuries, but this is extremely difficult to disentangle from the later traditions and local lore. The most we can say, from this work, with confidence is that Arthur was seen by Britons of the eighth and ninth centuries as a great warrior who was important in the early years of their long struggle with the Saxons. We cannot, however, use the *History* to construct a detailed narrative of the Brittonic Age.

THE KNIGHTS OF THE ROUND TABLE

IN THE EARLIEST written accounts Arthur's companions are not named. But in the early Welsh poems the two most frequently mentioned of his associates are Cei and Bedwyr, who appear in Geoffrey of Monmouth's *History* as Kay the Seneschal and Bedivere the Cupbearer (both positions of high honour at medieval courts). Welsh poems such as *Culhwch and Olwen* depict Arthur as possessing a large band of warriors with colourful names and often magical abilities, while Geoffrey cast these warriors as feudal knights who fought in tournaments in order to win fiefdoms from Arthur. The poet Wace introduced the notion that Arthur and his knights would gather on special occasions around a round table (round to denote the equality of its members), which bore the names of those warriors special enough to be part of Arthur's company. The Order of the Round Table came to represent all that was most noble in medieval chivalry, including protection of the weak and service to one's king and one's lady, and its knights became the subjects of their own tales. The earliest of these involved Sir Gawain, the son of King Lot and nephew of Arthur whose great strength grew mightier with the waxing of the sun. Gawain was especially popular among English writers, while the French seemed to prefer Sir Lancelot du Lac. Lancelot was Arthur's greatest champion until the arrival at court of his son, Sir Galahad, who achieved the Siege Perilous (the special seat at the Table in which any but the most perfect knight would perish). Other notable figures who sat at Arthur's Table include Sir Percival and his brother Sir Lamorak, Sir Gareth (Gawain's youngest brother) and Sir Tristram of Lyonesse, the Cornish knight who was a later addition to Arthur's court.

Sir Galahad arriving at Arthur's court, led by a hermit who seats him at the Siege Perilous. Miniature from an Italian manuscript (c.1370–80) containing the Quest del Saint Graal *and the* Mort Artu.

Geoffrey of Monmouth

(Right) The grandeur of Geoffrey's Arthur is captured in this fifteenth-century illustration of Arthur's army confronting the Saxons, from Jean Wauquelin's Chronicle.

WE HAVE SEEN that the warrior Arthur, real or not, had achieved some fame amongst the Britons of Wales and northern Britain in the early Middle Ages. Still, this is a far cry from being the world-famous Christian king that he would become by the end of the Middle Ages. The key figure in this transformation was a learned Briton of the twelfth century named Geoffrey of Monmouth. Geoffrey's *Historia Regum Britanniae* (History of the Kings of Britain), with a narrative disproportionately devoted to the reign of Arthur, provided an expanded biography for the legendary king that would serve as the basis for the great Arthurian romances in the centuries that followed.

Though some of the biographical details remain sketchy, we know more about Geoffrey than we do our previous Arthurian authors. Gaufridus Monemutensis is a Latinized Norman name, but he describes himself as *pudibundus Brito*, 'a modest Briton'. Not only were there Welsh Britons in twelfth-century Monmouthshire, there were also Bretons, descendants of William the Conqueror's followers. Geoffrey shows sympathies for both the Bretons and the Cornish in his *History*, sentimentally recalling a time when these peoples were connected in the great British empire of Arthur. Geoffrey is especially proud of this name, for in five charters dealing with the Oxford region he adds *Artur* (or a Latin variant) to his own signature, implying that Arthur was either his nickname or his father's name.

Arthur fighting the giant of Mont St Michel. Initial from a twelfth-century copy of Geoffrey's History.

On two of these same charters, which date from between 1129 and 1151, he describes himself as *magister*, implying that he was a teacher at Oxford during these years, before the university was granted its official charter. He must at least have taken minor ecclesiastical orders, for in 1151 he was elected (perhaps due to the fame of his writings) bishop of St Asaph in Flintshire, but it is unlikely that he ever saw his Welsh see, for it was then embroiled in the revolt of Owain Gwynedd. The following year he was ordained priest at Westminster and in 1153 he was one of the bishops who witnessed the important Treaty of Westminster between King Stephen and the empress Matilda. According to the Welsh chronicles, he died two years later.

As an Oxford teacher in the early twelfth century, a time of civil war and intrigue, Geoffrey had occasion to meet some of the most important ecclesiastical and political figures in Britain. Various manuscripts of the *History* are dedicated to King Stephen, and to Robert, Earl of Gloucester (bastard son of Henry I and thus half-brother to Stephen's challenger, Matilda) and Waleran de Beaumont, Count of Meulan. He may even have had an opportunity to tutor Robert's visiting nephew, the future King Henry II, who certainly showed much interest in the Arthurian story (p. 128).

By his own account, Geoffrey's most important patron was Walter, archdeacon of Oxford and provost of St George's College. Geoffrey begins his *History* by saying that, apart from the works of Gildas and Bede, he was unable to discover anything about Arthur and the early kings of Britain, until Walter

> presented me with a very ancient book written in the British language. This book, attractively composed to form a consecutive and orderly narrative, set out all the deeds of these men, from Brutus, the first King of the Britons, down to Cadwallader, the son of Cadwallo. At Walter's request I have taken the trouble to translate the book into Latin.

In this long and fanciful narrative, Geoffrey does indeed trace the reigns of all of the kings of the Britons, from the Trojan refugee Brutus down to the Welsh kings of the seventh century AD. But fully one third of the work is devoted to Arthur and Merlin. Borrowing some details from

the *History of the Britons* (p. 76) Geoffrey explains that Vortigern the traitor was overthrown and replaced by two brothers of the House of Constantine, Aurelius Ambrosius and Uther Pendragon. The latter, with some magical help from Merlin, seduced Ygerna, the wife of one of his counts, and she became pregnant with Arthur. Arthur succeeded Uther as king and continued his father's campaign to rid Britain of the barbarian threat. But Geoffrey's Arthur goes beyond simply defeating Saxons, Scots and Picts: he also slays giants, holds lavish court pageants and chivalric tournaments, and defeats Roman armies in Gaul – twice!

He also marries the beautiful Guinevere, who in the end betrays her husband by supporting the revolt of Mordred, Arthur's traitorous nephew. At the Battle of Camlann (*Camblam*), Mordred perishes and his army is defeated, but:

> Arthur himself, our renowned King, was mortally wounded and was carried off to the Isle of Avalon, so that his wounds might be healed. He handed the crown of Britain over to his cousin Constantine, the son of Cador Duke of Cornwall; this in the year 542 after our Lord's Incarnation.

Geoffrey completed the *History* between about 1136 and 1138, but the earliest extant copies reflect a revised version written in the 1140s. Before his most famous work was published he had written another, the *Prophetiae Merlini* (The Prophecies of Merlin), later incorporated into the *History*. Dedicated to Alexander, bishop of Lincoln, the *Prophecies* are again said by Geoffrey to be his Latin translation of a British source, presumably written by Merlin himself who, by Geoffrey's time, was beginning

EXCALIBUR

Arthur's famous sword makes its first appearance in Geoffrey of Monmouth's History. *Called Caliburnus, it was forged on the Isle of Avalon. Its name comes from the Latin* chalybs *(steel), and thus Excalibur translates as something like '[cut] from steel'. Though Arthur pulls a sword from a stone to become king, Excalibur is apparently a different one, given to him by the Lady of the Lake, along with a magical scabbard that prevents its wearer losing any blood in battle. Morgan le Fay manages to steal both sword and scabbard, but Arthur eventually retrieves Excalibur, though the scabbard is lost. Once, he lends Excalibur to Gawain, but wields it again at his last battle, Camlann, after which he orders Bedivere (or Griflet) to return it to the water, from whence it came. Many view this episode as a reflection of an ancient pagan ritual, in which swords were left in pools or wells as votive deposits. The Welsh called Excalibur Caladvwlch, cognate with the Irish Caladbolg – from* calad *(hard) and* bolg *(lightning) – a sword borne by heroes of Irish legend.*

Excalibur departs, from an early fourteenth-century French manuscript.

Ygerna gives the infant Arthur into the care of Sir Ector de Marys, from a fourteenth-century northern French manuscript.

to achieve some fame as an accurate prophet of British politics (p. 154). Geoffrey places these prophecies, which include Arthur as 'the Boar of Cornwall', in the context of an episode from his *History* when the young 'Ambrosius Merlin' (he was simply Ambrosius in the *History of the Britons*) visits the tormented British king Vortigern. When asked to explain why the foundations of the king's fortress keep sinking, Merlin reveals a hidden pool beneath the foundations, from which two fighting dragons emerge:

> Alas for the Red Dragon, for its end is near. Its cavernous dens shall be occupied by the White Dragon, which stands for the Saxons whom you have invited over. The Red Dragon represents the people of Britain [i.e., the Britons], who will be overrun by the White One: for Britain's mountains and valleys shall be levelled, and the streams in its valleys shall run with blood. The cult of religion shall be destroyed completely and the ruin of the churches shall be clear for all to see. The race that is oppressed shall prevail in the end, for it will resist the savagery of the invaders. The Boar of Cornwall shall bring relief from these invaders, for it will trample their necks beneath its feet.

For the Britons' descendants in Wales, these prophecies – and especially the symbol of the Red Dragon – would remain politically potent throughout the Middle Ages. Nor had Geoffrey finished exploring the legend of Merlin. Around 1150 he composed a long Latin poem called the *Vita Merlini* (Life of Merlin). For his *History*, Geoffrey had taken the figure of the prophetic boy Ambrosius from the *History of the Britons* and combined it with a figure from Welsh literature, the northern bard Myrddin (p. 95), Latinizing the name to Merlinus (Merdinus would have had unpleasant connotations for his French-speaking readers). Afterwards, Geoffrey learned more about this Myrddin, including the bard's participation in the Battle of Arderydd (Arthuret) in 575 and his subsequent life as a mad prophet roaming the forest of Celidon. This story became the basis for Geoffrey's *Life of Merlin*, which served as a kind of sequel to Merlin's adventures in the *History*. Also making appearances in this poem are Taliesin, the famed Welsh bard (p. 94), and the enchantress Morgen, the Morgan le Fay of later Arthurian romance (see p. 85).

It should be apparent by now that the Arthurian material presented by Geoffrey of Monmouth is hardly the stuff of a history chronicle. Like Gildas and the author of the *History of the Britons*, Geoffrey worked with

GUINEVERE

Guinevere (also Guenevere and Guenièvre) first appears in Geoffrey of Monmouth's History *as a beautiful Roman noblewoman whom Arthur marries and makes his queen, but who later betrays him for Mordred. According to Malory, she is the daughter of King Leodegrance of Cameliard, who gives her to his political ally, Arthur, together with the Round Table as a wedding gift. In most versions of the story Guinevere bears Arthur no children, a fact to which modern novelists attribute her infidelity. One tradition makes her the mother of Arthur's son Loholt, while the* Alliterative Morte Arthure *gives her two sons by Mordred. There are also early hints that Guinevere was Arthur's second wife. The Welsh tradition has Arthur married to three women named Gwenhwyfar, which means 'white shadow'. Several tales speak of Guinevere's abduction by a king named Melwas (or Meleagant), and of her rescue by Arthur or Lancelot. Some scholars take the abduction motif as as proof that Guinevere is an archetypal goddess or bride of an Otherworld deity.*

Detail of Guinevere from 'The Story of Tristan and Isolde', a stained glass window designed by William Morris.

a variety of sound historical material. But, even more than the earlier *History of the Britons*, Geoffrey's writings rely on an immense body of vernacular tradition and outright fable which is impossible to date and authenticate. Moreover, many of the stories in his *History of the Kings of Britain* seem to be of Geoffrey's own invention, and he seldom refrains from elaborating or exaggerating on other occasions. Even in his own times, Geoffrey had his critics – most notably William of Newburgh – who believed that Geoffrey was a fabricator of history. Gerald of Wales, who in some instances actually borrows material from Geoffrey, relates the humorous tale of a possessed man who was exorcised by placing a copy of the Bible on his chest. When the Bible was replaced by a copy of Geoffrey's *History*, the demons returned in even greater number!

These critics, however, were far outnumbered by enthusiastic readers throughout Europe. Kings, historians and poets would all turn to Geoffrey's *History* for its thrilling accounts of Arthur and Merlin, not to mention the ancient British kings Leir and Cymbelin (who became Shakespeare's Lear and Cymbeline). Geoffrey's account became *the* account of early British history, and would serve the dynastic ambitions of British kings from the Plantagenets to the Stuarts (pp. 128–36). All of these 'chronicles of the Britons' came to have far greater import than the sober history chronicles written by more capable hands. As historical evidence for an enigmatic period they are troublesome, but as the foundational material for one of the world's greatest literary traditions they remain much-discussed works.

(Right) Arthur slaying a giant, detail from a fifteenth-century English manuscript. From the time of Geoffrey onwards, Arthur is frequently cast in the role of giant killer.

MORGAN LE FAY

Morgan (Morgaine, Morganna) first appears in Geoffrey's long poem, Vita Merlini, *as the ruler of the Isle of Avalon, where Arthur was taken after the Battle of Camlann. Here she is the eldest and most beautiful of nine sisters, is skilled in the arts of healing and can change her shape and fly with wings, thus leading to her medieval reputation as 'Morgan the Fairy'. In most versions she is related to Arthur, Malory making her the daughter of Igraine and Gorlois and thus Arthur's half-sister. As a young girl she was a pupil of Merlin and became one of Guinevere's ladies-in-waiting. She married King Urien of Rheged and bore him a son, Uwaine (Yvain, Owain), who once had physically to stop his mother from killing Urien. Morgan took as a lover the knight Accolon of Gaul and plotted with him to steal Excalibur and kill Arthur. She also had plans to make Lancelot her lover, once holding him captive, though later she tried to expose his affair with Guinevere to Arthur. While seemingly jealous of her half-brother, and attempting to humiliate him on many occasions, Morgan surprisingly appears on the barge that carries Arthur off to be healed at Avalon. These many sides of Morgan are appropriate for a character whose origins are divine, being perhaps related to the ancient Celtic goddess Modron (or Matrona), or to the Irish triune-deity Morrigan.*

Frederick Sandys, Morgan le Fay *(1864).*

V

THE LEGENDS OF THE BRITONS

Within a few years Arthur won all the north,
Scotland, and all that were under their obeissance.
Also Wales, a part of it, held against Arthur,
but he overcame them all . . .
through the noble prowess of himself
and his knights of the Round Table.

Thomas Malory, *Le Morte d'Arthur*

IT IS MISLEADING, to be sure, to portray the 'Arthur question' as being mainly an historical one. Some – but by no means all – scholars are interested in the historicity of Arthur. In fact many consider the greater issue to be the Arthurian legend and its transmission into some of the greatest literature of the European Middle Ages. As with tracing the Arthur of history, this quest too has its twists and turns, its uncertainties and its enigmas. But the literature itself is very real and substantive, we can analyze it and measure its impact, which was widespread and immediate. While no contemporary chroniclers took notice of the *warrior* Arthur, bards and poets lined up to sing the praises of the *king* Arthur in the twelfth and thirteenth centuries. The resultant literature, in vogue at the most powerful courts of medieval Europe, would go on to become one of the most enduring myths in the western world.

Arthur, wounded by Mordred at the Battle of Camlann, is carried away in a wagon. Shield and banner display Arthur's heraldic device, the three crowns. Illustration from a fourteenth-century Flemish manuscript.

Both queen and mistress of England's Henry II are depicted in Evelyn de Morgan's painting, Queen Eleanor and the Fair Rosamund (c.1900). *Eleanor was a patron of Arthurian writers, while Henry set up a retreat for himself and Rosamund at Woodstock, in imitation of Tristan and Isolde.*

WHEN GEOFFREY of Monmouth published his *History of the Kings of Britain* in around 1136, he was not the first chronicler of the Anglo-Norman era to mention Arthur. In his *Gesta Regum Anglorum* (Deeds of the English Kings), completed in 1125, William of Malmesbury stops his narrative to chastise the Britons for their oral traditions concerning Arthur: 'This is that Arthur of whom the trifling of the Britons talks such nonsense even today; a man clearly worthy not to be dreamed of in fallacious fables, but to be proclaimed in veracious histories.' Henry of Huntingdon was a little more sympathetic to the Britons when he composed his *Historia Anglorum* (History of the English) in 1129. Borrowing from both the *Historia Brittonum* and (in later revised editions) Geoffrey's *History*, Henry includes an account of Arthur's twelve victorious battles against the Saxons, who are the real subject of this work.

This Anglo-Norman fascination with the early history of the Britons, and especially with Arthur, continued even after some critics attacked the veracity of Geoffrey's story. The scholars, it would appear, were outvoted by the monarchs, particularly the new Angevin king of England, Henry II (r. 1154–89), who wished to learn more about his newly acquired subjects. The Britons were as alien – and exotic – to the French-speaking king as were the Anglo-Saxons. Unlike the Anglo-Saxon kings, however, the British king Arthur – or at least Geoffrey's version – had conquests which extended to Ireland, Scotland and Gaul, territories which the Angevin monarch, too, sought to control. There were several good reasons to resurrect an ancient

WACE'S *ROMAN DE BRUT*

'After the death of Uther the king, he was carried to Stonehenge and there buried within, by the side of his brother. The bishops sent word to each other, and the barons assembled; they summoned Arthur, Uther's son, and crowned him at Silchester. He was a young man of fifteen, tall and strong for his age. I will tell you what Arthur was like and not lie to you. He was a most mighty knight, admirable and renowned, proud to the haughty, and gentle and compassionate to the humble. He was strong, bold and invincible, a generous giver and spender, and if he could help someone in need, he would not refuse him. He greatly loved renown and glory, he greatly wished his deeds to be remembered. He behaved most nobly and saw to it that he was served with courtesy. For as long as he lived and reigned, he surpassed all other monarchs in courtesy and nobility, generosity and power.'

Arthur faces a giant in this miniature from a fourteenth-century manuscript of Wace's Roman de Brut.

British king (over a more recent English one) as a literary symbol for the multi-ethnic empire Henry II was attempting to build (p. 128).

Wace

Many French writers recognized this Arthurian interest amongst the Plantagenets and capitalized on it. The courtly market was creating a great demand, and extremely rich and powerful patrons were willing to subsidize such literary projects. One of these patrons was Henry II's wife, Eleanor of Aquitaine. In 1155 an Arthurian 'chronicle' called the *Roman de Brut* (Romance of Brutus) was published with a dedication to Eleanor. Its author was a Norman named Wace, born on the island of Jersey in the early twelfth century. At some point around 1150 Wace came into favour with the Plantagenets, and Henry II himself commissioned Wace to write, in 1160, the *Roman de Rou*, a verse history of the dukes of Normandy (a title Henry inherited, through his mother, the empress Matilda, from William the Conqueror).

It is, however, his Arthurian 'chronicle' which earned him the most fame and lasting influence. The *Brut* is one of the earliest works to introduce Celtic myths and themes into French literature. It also introduced two of the most important Arthurian motifs: the Round Table, and the Britons' hope of Arthur's return from Avalon. Wace takes Geoffrey of Monmouth's account of Arthur and expands the story with elements possibly taken from the Breton storytellers whom he mentions as keeping the Arthurian tradition alive (p. 99). Like Geoffrey's *History*, Wace's *Brut* crosses the line from chronicle into fiction – which is a modern distinction, in any case – and moves Arthur closer to the world of courtly romance. As such, it would have a great impact on fellow French literati, such as Marie de France and Chrétien de Troyes, whose poetry delighted courtly society yet made no claims to be history.

Layamon

Wace's successor Layamon, however, would take one step back towards the 'heroic history' of Geoffrey and the *Historia Brittonum*. A priest at Arley Regis in Worcestershire, Layamon translated Wace's *Roman de Brut* in English alliterative verse sometime between 1199 and 1225. Layamon's *Brut* is nearly twice as long as its French model, and substitutes descriptions of Dark Age brutality for the latter's talk of love and chivalry. Layamon was obviously writing for a different audience than Wace, that is for English readers who had some interest in pre-Conquest history and Anglo-Saxon verse. This makes it all the more puzzling that an Anglo-Saxon priest would choose to glorify the deeds of a British king whose fame rested on his struggle *against* the Anglo-Saxon invaders who were the very ancestors of Layamon and his readers!

Layamon, like Wace, also seems to have introduced further Celtic elements into the Arthurian story. Elves bless Arthur at his birth, for example, and Argante (probably a corruption of Morgant) receives Arthur in Avalon to cure his wounds. Some have suggested that Layamon's apparent lack of sympathy for Arthur's Saxon foes is an *apologia* for the Norman Conquest: just as the Britons' sins were punished by a plague of Saxons, so too the Saxons' sins were redressed by the Normans who now ruled the island. Others see Layamon as simply being caught up in the wave of Arthurian enthusiasm that swept Europe beginning in the late twelfth century. For most continental European *and* English writers of the Middle Ages, Arthur was simply a great hero of the past who happened to come from the island of Britain. But for those most closely associated with the legends, the Breton and Welsh descendants of the Britons, Arthur was not just a colourful character who lived in the pages of romances and old chronicles. He was a potent political symbol and a long-cherished part of their cultural heritage.

Original illustration of three elven women blessing the birth of Arthur in Layamon's Brut.

LAYAMON'S *BRUT*

'*Arthur was mortally wounded, grievously badly;*
To him there came a young lad who was from his clan,
He was Cador the earl of Cornwall's son;
The boy was called Constantine; the king loved him very much.
Arthur gazed up at him, as he lay there on the ground,
And uttered these words with a sorrowing heart:
"Welcome, Constantine; you were Cador's son;
Here I bequeath to you all of my kingdom,
And guard well my Britons all the days of your life
And retain for them all the laws which have been extant in my days
And all the good laws which there were in Uther's days.
And I shall voyage to Avalon, to the fairest of all maidens,
To the Queen Argante, a very radiant elf,
And she will make quite sound every one of my wounds,
Will make me completely whole with her health-giving potions,
And then I shall come back to my own kingdom
And dwell among the Britons with surpassing delight."'

The Beguiling of Merlin

THE STORIES OF ARTHUR and of Merlin may originally have been separate traditions, Merlin's deriving from that of a mad prophet of northern Britain named Myrddin. But after Geoffrey of Monmouth brought the prophet/magician into the story of Arthur's conception, subsequent medieval authors felt the connection too compelling to ignore. Modern writers have made Merlin responsible for Arthur's upbringing and for arranging the Sword in the Stone episode. Since he had been something of an advisor to King Uther, Merlin was given the same role in the early years of Arthur's reign, using his magic and foresight to protect the young king and to help build the fellowship of the Round Table. It was Merlin who helped Arthur win the sword Excalibur (from the Lady of the Lake) and it was Merlin who predicted future greatness for the young Lancelot, as well as the betrayals of Guinevere and Mordred. But despite his supernatural powers (in some versions Merlin is said to have been the son of the Devil, who had seduced an unsuspecting nun), Merlin knows his own doom is inescapable. After teaching some of his magical arts to Morgan le Fay, Arthur's vengeful half-sister, Merlin takes in as apprentice a young girl named Nimuë (Niviene or Viviane in other versions) who had been in Morgan's service. Merlin dotes on his young pupil and teaches her his most powerful spells, but Nimuë turns on the wizard and uses his own magic to trap him in a tree, a crystal cave, or, as some versions have it, simply a fortress of air. A repentant Nimuë later becomes the new Lady of the Lake and uses her magic to help Arthur, but Merlin remains in his enchanted sleep until some future day when Arthur and Britain will need his powers most.

Gustave Doré, 'Vivien and Merlin Repose', illustration for Tennyson's Idylls of the King *(1868).*

HISTORY, GENEALOGY and myths were all the domain of the bard in Celtic cultures. From Caesar and other classical sources we know that the Iron Age Britons had bards as well as the more (in)famous Druids. While the sources for Roman Britain do not discuss them, bards begin to reappear in the records of the Brittonic Age. Gildas alludes to them as entertainers and flatterers at the courts of the British kings. Eventually, all courts in Wales and northern Britain had resident bards. The names of the most famous from this period – Aneirin, Taliesin and Myrddin – have survived in later sources. The most important of these later manuscripts are the Black Book of Carmarthen (c.1250), the Book of Aneirin (late thirteenth century), the Book of Taliesin (early fourteenth century), the White Book of Rhydderch (c.1350) and the Red Book of Hergest (c.1400). Scattered through these manuscripts are the wild and wondrous tales that make up the Welsh Arthurian tradition.

Aneirin

Aneirin was a court bard in the northern British kingdom of Manau Guotodin, the kingdom of the Votadini or Gododdin, centred around what is now Edinburgh. Sometime around AD 600, a British warband organized by the Gododdin's chieftain, Mynyddog Mwynfawr (Mynyddog the Wealthy), travelled south to Catraeth (probably the Roman town of Catterick in Yorkshire) to attack an Anglian settlement. Aneirin apparently witnessed the ensuing battle in which the Britons were wiped out, and composed an elegy to the fallen British soldiers. This poem, called *Y Gododdin*, is widely considered to be the oldest recorded poem from Scotland. It also contains what may be the earliest mention of Arthur (see box on p. 94). Whether or not it can be used to prove the existence of an historical Arthur, the *Gododdin* is testimony to the fame of Arthur among Welsh audiences in the early Middle Ages.

Thomas Jones's The Bard *(1774) shows a Merlin-like figure gazing upon a Welsh landscape (complete with megaliths) laid waste by the English king, Edward I. The British bard, here portrayed as one victim of English expansion, acted as a conduit through which the Arthurian legends passed from early medieval oral tales to high medieval courtly romances.*

Arthur Gaskin, Kylwych, the King's Son *(1901)*.

The Earliest Mention of Arthur

The Gododdin *was composed by the British bard Aneirin c.600. While describing the character of one British warrior who fell in battle against the Angles, Aneirin compares him to Britain's most famous warrior:*

'Gochore brein du ar uur
Caer ceni bei ef arthur
[He (Gwawrddur) fed black ravens on the rampart
Of a fortress, though he was no Arthur]'

Aneirin is saying here that Gwawrddur killed many of the enemy, but that he was still no equal to the great British warrior Arthur. This passing reference to Arthur would appear to be proof that he was already, by the time of the poem's composition, a figure well known to Aneirin's audience in northern Britain.

There are problems, however, with using the Gododdin *as an historical source (and as evidence for an historical Arthur). First of all, it is unclear when this poem was first written down. The oldest extant version is in a thirteenth-century manuscript, the Book of Aneirin, but the language of this version cannot be older than the ninth or tenth century. Even if the poem was written down shortly after the events it describes, the particular line mentioning Arthur may have been added later, when his fame was more widespread. It appears in only one of the early manuscripts containing the poem, which originated in Strathclyde c.800. A similar reference to Arthur is made in* Marwnad Cynddylan *(The Lament of* Cynddylan*), an elegy to a seventh-century prince of Powys. Here Cynddylan and his brothers are described as* canawon Artur Fras, dinas dengyn, *'whelps of stout Arthur, a strong fortress'. Once again, however, the manuscript tradition is too late to be considered contemporary evidence for Arthur.*

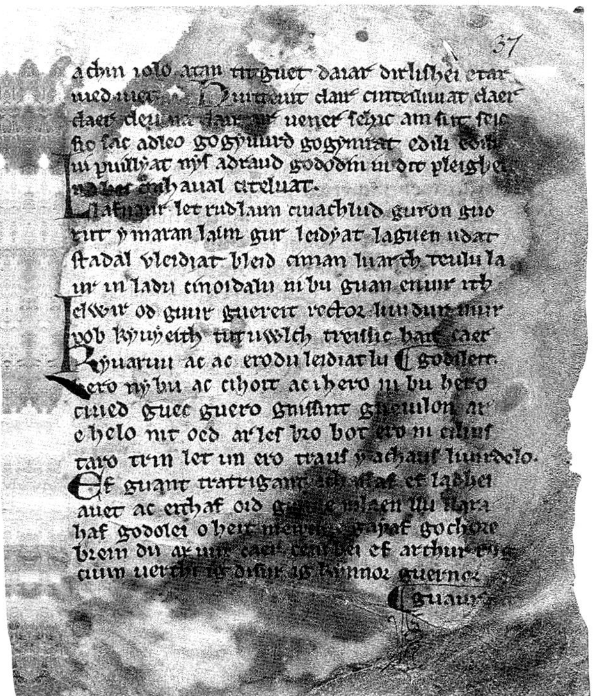

Page from the Book of Aneirin. The stanza shown, from Y Gododdin, *includes the line mentioning Arthur.*

Taliesin

Taliesin was probably the most revered of the early Welsh bards. The historical Taliesin appears to have operated in northern Britain, especially the kingdom of Rheged, in the late sixth century. The contemporary rulers of Rheged (Urien and his son Owain), are praised in poems bearing Taliesin's name. Not all the poems in the Book of Taliesin attributed to the bard are genuine, however, and only five mention Arthur. Most, again, make passing references to him – 'the return of Arthur', 'Arthur the blest', 'the horse of Arthur', 'Arthur's valour' – which attest to Arthur's fame and military prowess. Clearly the bard (or bards) who composed these poems did not feel the need to explain to their audience who Arthur was or why he belonged amongst the prominent figures – both mythical and historical – who are the principal subjects of the poems.

A more substantial role is played by Arthur in *Prieddeu Annwn* (The Spoils of Annwfn). This is an adventure tale describing a raid by Arthur on Annwfn, the Welsh pre-Christian Otherworld (in the poem, 'the fairy fort' and 'the fortress of glass'). Arthur's warriors sail to Annwfn to seize its treasures, the most important of which is a magical cauldron. There are other Welsh tales analogous to this adventure, including a similar episode in *Culhwch and Olwen* (p. 96), where the cauldron rests in Ireland. These stories may all derive from a common Celtic theme of 'raid on the Otherworld'; they certainly contributed to the development of the Grail tradition and its association with Glastonbury, the 'Fort of Glass'. In the poem Taliesin boasts of his own role in Arthur's voyage to Annwfn, implying that the two were contemporaries. But, although the narrator of the poem assumes the persona of Taliesin, the work itself dates to the period c.850–1150.

Myrddin

The third of these venerated British bards is Myrddin, better known by his Latinized name Merlin. While he may have been their contemporary, Myrddin may be less 'historical' than either Aneirin or Taliesin (both of whom are mentioned in the *History of the Britons*). Like the latter, nevertheless, his name was attached to works of many different periods and some have even suggested that Taliesin and Myrddin were names given interchangeably to accomplished Welsh bards, serving as an archetype for 'the poet'.

The earliest poems attributed to Myrddin seem to place him in the northern Britain of the late sixth century, thus making him a contemporary and neighbour of Taliesin. But these early poems exist only in later manuscripts such as the Black Book of Carmarthen. The oldest of them may be 'Yr Afallennau' (The Apple-trees), an ode to a magical apple tree 'hidden in the forest of Celyddon'. In the poem, the narrator Myrddin tells his audience that he has been living in hardship for the past fifty years in the Caledonian woods, hiding from Rhydderch Hael (Roderick the Generous), an historical king of Strathclyde. Before coming to Celyddon, Merlin had served the Cumbrian prince Gwenddolau and the two had fought together (Myrddin had worn a torc of gold, in the style of the ancient Celtic warriors) at the Battle of Arderydd, recorded in the *Welsh Annals* under the year 573. Gwenddolau fell in the battle and, in witnessing the carnage, Myrddin lost his wits, running wild into the forest uttering prophecies and keeping fellowship with animals.

Other Welsh poems also trace these strange adventures, describing a deeply grieving Myrddin who has somehow acquired the gift of prophecy. Scholars have pointed to a similar 'wild man in the forest' tradition in Scottish literature, where the tragic figure is named Lailoken (p. 154). In both traditions the wild man is blest, ironically, with the ability to prophesy, and this has made him an attractive figure to politically minded writers from Geoffrey of Monmouth to the present. Geoffrey, as we have seen, took the figure of Myrddin and combined him with the character of the prophetic boy, Ambrosius, culled from the *History of the Britons*. He thus created the composite figure of Merlin (Merlinus) who came from the town of Carmarthen (Kaermerdin). Geoffrey was also the first to link the figures of Arthur and Merlin, though admittedly there is only a slight relationship in his *History* that was elaborated by later writers of romance.

The Beguiling of Merlin, *photograph by Julia Margaret Cameron for the 1875 edition of Tennyson's* Idylls of the King. *In the Welsh tradition, as in later French and English versions of his story, Merlin is frequently associated with an enchanted forest.*

The Triads

Most early Welsh poetry remains anonymous, collected and added to over the years by countless unremembered bards. This is the case with a large collection of Welsh verses called *Trioedd Ynys Prydein* (The Triads of the Island of Britain), commonly referred to as the Welsh Triads. These poems were grouped in threes – a sacred number but also a mnemonic device – according to a common theme (that is, 'The Three _______ of the Island of Britain'). There are over two dozen Arthurian references in the Triads, and Arthur is sometimes added to a triad, notes Brynley Roberts, 'as a fourth and exceptional example of a particular feature'. The Triads survive in several manuscripts, the oldest dating to the thirteenth and fourteenth centuries, which are based on a collection put together in the eleventh or twelfth centuries. Though relatively late in date, the Triads include tales that must derive from an earlier, oral tradition, for they appear (in altered form) in such early works as *Culhwch and Olwen*.

The Triads constitute a heterogeneous collection, with the growing popularity of Arthur reflected mostly in late additions where Arthur has sometimes ousted other ancient heroes. In the

Original illustration of Ysbaddaden, Chief Giant, father of Olwen and nemesis of Arthur's cousin Culhwch. His eyelids were so heavy, went the tale, that servants had to lift them with pitchforks.

Triads, Arthur is Chief Prince (*Pen Teyrnedd*) of the Island, ruling over Wales, Cornwall and northern Britain from his court of Celliwig, in Cornwall. Praised as a great warrior and hunter, he is served by such men as Cei and Bedwyr and is the rival of King March (Mark of Cornwall). Five of the Triads also refer to Camlann, Arthur's last and fatal battle.

The *Lives* of the saints

One interesting aspect of the Triads is their varied portrayal of Arthur. While he is usually depicted as a powerful king and praised as the defender of the island, some Triads depict him as a proud, destructive monarch who will resort to deceit or force to get what he desires. This negative attitude towards Arthur can also be found in some of the *Vitae* (Lives) of the Welsh saints. In these ecclesiastical hero-tales – the *Lives* of Cadoc, Gildas and Illtud – Arthur is often portrayed as a powerful tyrant, a *rex rebelis*.

Arthur also appears in several of the poems collected in the Black Book of Carmarthen. In *Englynion y Beddau* (The Stanzas of the Graves), a poem about the burial places of Welsh heroes, it is claimed that Arthur's grave is a great wonder because no one knows where it is located. In the praise-poem *Geraint filius Erbin* (Geraint son of Erbin), the poet laments the valiant deaths of the vassals of Geraint and 'Arthur . . . the Emperor (*ameraudur*), the leader in the toil' of the Battle of Llongborth. In other poems Arthur is named as the father of Llachau, while 'the shout of the host of Arthur's warband' is used for a poetic comparison. Arthur makes a more-than-casual appearance in only one untitled poem which begins with the line 'Pa gur yv y porthaur?' ('What man is the gatekeeper?'). This is a dialogue between Arthur and the gatekeeper Glelwyd Gafaelfawr, Arthur's own porter in *Culhwch and Olwen* but here defending a fortress from Arthur and his men. There are references in this poem to Cei and Bedwyr, Arthur's traditional companions, as well as to Uther Pendragon, the monstrous Cath Palug (Palug's cat) and several figures taken straight from Celtic mythology.

The Mabinogion

There are many similarities between the poem 'Pa gur' and the greatest of the Welsh Arthurian prose tales, *Culhwch ac Olwen*. Surviving in both the White Book of Rhydderch and the Red Book of Hergest, *Culhwch* was collected and translated along with ten related prose tales by Lady Charlotte Guest in the early nineteenth century. She named this collection *The Mabinogion*, and it was assumed that all the tales were linked by the theme of youth (*mab* meaning boy or son). *Mabinigion*, however, is actually a scribal error for *mabinogi*, the term now preferred by most scholars.

The *Mabinogi* proper includes only the first four tales or 'branches'. These are purely mythological and not Arthurian. Modern editors, however, see these tales as related to other early compositions and often include the latter in their editions and translations. *Culhwch and Olwen* is the earliest of these related Arthurian tales. It is the story of Arthur's cousin Culhwch ('pig pen'), who is fated to love only one woman, Olwen ('white track'), daughter of the giant Ysbaddaden. Arriving at Celliwig to seek the king's advice, Culhwch is given seven of Arthur's men to help him win Olwen. Her father, however, imposes a series of seemingly impossible tasks on Culhwch before he will consent to the marriage. With the help of Arthur and his warriors, Culhwch eventually completes the tasks, Ysbaddaden is killed and the young lovers are united.

Despite the plot and title, this tale is not so much about Culhwch and Olwen as about the spectacular adventures accomplished by Arthur's company, including Cei and Bedwyr. Arthur himself joins the adventure, sailing away on his ship Prydwen, and appearing to be more the hero from a 'wonder-tale' than the great feudal lord of the French romances. This, along with the spelling and other linguistic features of *Culhwch*, has convinced scholars that the work was composed much earlier than the earliest surviving manuscript copy, perhaps just prior to the eleventh century, making it the oldest full Arthurian story in the Welsh canon.

The Red and White Books contain another three related Arthurian tales which were

OLWEN

‘She came in wearing a flaming-red silk robe with reddish-gold torc studded with precious stones and red gems about her neck. Her hair was yellower than the flowers of the broom; her skin whiter than the foam of a wave, her palms and fingers whiter than the blooms of the marsh trefoil amidst the sands of a gushing spring. Neither the eye of a mewed hawk nor the eye of a thrice-mewed falcon was brighter than her own. Her breasts were whiter than a swan's; her cheeks redder than foxglove: whoever saw her was filled with love of her. Four white clovers would spring up in her track wherever she went. Because of this she was called Olwen, "White-track".’

From Culhwch and Olwen

Olwen, *shown here in a watercolour by Alan Lee (1981).*

THE EARLIEST MENTION OF MERLIN

Merlin is Geoffrey of Monmouth's creation, based in part on a sixth-century figure named Myrddin *(p. 95). As with* Arthur*, the earliest mention of* Myrddin *is in the* Gododdin*: 'Morien defended the fair song of* Myrddin *(*gwenwawd Myrddin*) and laid the head of a chief in the earth.' This line appears only in a late text of the poem, and it has been suggested that the line was interpolated after the original northern poem arrived in Wales and encountered the thriving* Myrddin *tradition. This tradition is evident in another early Welsh peom,* Armes Prydein Vawr *(The Great Prophecy of Britain), written by a cleric in Dyfed c.930: 'Myrdin [sic] foretells that they will meet in Aber Peryddon, the stewards of the Great King.' While this is a clear testimony to* Myrddin*'s reputation in the early tenth century as a great British prophet, the prophecy survives only in later manuscripts, the oldest dating to the fourteenth century.*

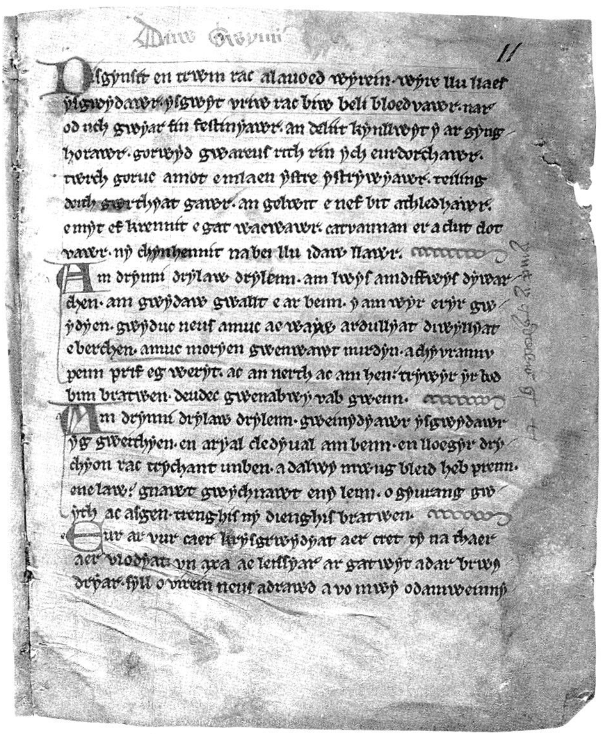

Page from the Book of Aneirin. The stanza shown, from Y Gododdin*, includes the line mentioning* Myrddin*.*

included in Guest's *Mabinogion*: *Geraint ab Erbin* (Geraint son of Erbin), *Owain: Chwedl Iarlles Y Ffynnon* (Owain: Or the Tale of the Lady of the Fountain) and *Ystoria Peredur ab Efrawg* (The History of Peredur, son of Efrawg). Written in the thirteenth century and labelled by scholars the 'three Welsh romances', these prose tales are analogues of three French romances by Chrétien de Troyes: *Erec and Enide*, *Yvain* and *Perceval* (p. 101).

Another Arthurian tale often associated with the *Mabinogi* is *Breuddwyd Rhonabwy* (The Dream of Rhonabwy). It opens with the fictional character Rhonabwy setting off to seek the brother of Madog ap Maredudd, the historical ruler of Powys c.1130–60. Lodging for the night on this journey, Rhonabwy is granted a *drych* (vision) which transports him back to the days of Arthur. In this dream he comes upon Arthur and his men encamped and awaiting the Battle of Badon. Arthur himself is occupied playing a board-game with Owain ab Urien, from which he can not tear himself away, despite messages that his own men are being slain by Owain's ravens! A truce is finally called – without the actual battle happening – and Arthur leaves to gather his forces in Cornwall. With that, Rhonabwy awakens (having slept for three days and three nights) and the story ends with no explanation being given for the strange dream.

As one modern commentator has pointed out, *The Dream of Rhonabwy* shows us an Arthurian world turned upside down. The Battle of Camlan precedes that of Badon, Arthur is abused by minor characters, and the great king is so distracted by a competition against one of his own supporters that he allows his men to die and neglects to face his real enemy at Badon. Its parodying of many Arthurian courtly conventions, and its borrowings from *Culhwch* and Geoffrey's *History*, are good evidence that *The Dream of Rhonabwy* is one of the last original specimens of this thriving medieval vernacular tradition.

THE BRITONS WHO migrated to Brittany in the fifth and sixth centuries (p. 51) brought with them their language, history and myths. Through the centuries they kept alive various traditions about Arthur. Several later authors, including Henry of Huntingdon, mention the common Breton belief that Arthur will one day return. Wace claimed that he had heard of Arthur's Round Table from the Bretons, and he located the enchanted Forest of Brocéliande in Brittany. In the anonymous Breton *Life of St Efflam* (of uncertain date), the saint succeeds in slaying a dragon after Arthur has failed. In the *Legend of St Goeznovius* (a hagiographic tale of the Breton saint Goueznou, allegedly written in 1019), the prologue tells how, in the fifth century, the Saxons were largely cleared from the island of Britain by 'the great Arthur, king of the Britons'.

Medieval Brittany with Arthurian associations. As it was the Breton bards who helped to shape and spread the Matter of Britain, it should not be surprising that they added details of their landscape to Arthur's story. The magical Forest of Brocéliande, identified with the modern forest of Paimpont, is the most noteworthy example. It was said to possess a storm-making spring, which Arthur's knights encounter, and in some French tales it serves as the enchanted prison that holds Merlin captive. Other Breton sites with Arthurian associations include Mont St Michel, where Arthur kills a giant, and Perros, whose Romanesque church bears a sculpture relating the adventures of Arthur and St Efflam. The monastery of St Gildas de Rhuys was allegedly founded by Gildas and was, for a while, the home of Peter Abelard. Dotted lines on the map indicate the borders of the modern départements.

The Breton lays

Arthur's alleged immortality, his pre-ordained return and his association with monsters are clearly all folk traditions kept alive in the oral culture of the Bretons, which manifested itself in the twelfth century in the Breton lays. The word 'lay' derives from the common Celtic term *lai* (modern scholars writing in English often use the original spelling), which was a short, emotional song, played on a harp or other stringed instrument and sung in the Breton language. The song was usually prefaced by an explanatory narrative, probably in verse, in the language of the local audience (these poems eventually became independent of the songs and came also to be called lays). Many Breton bards or minstrels learned to compose their narratives in French, for travelling throughout the vast French-speaking world (of France and England) they could perform at markets, fairs and, if they were lucky, at the courts of the great nobles.

In addition to wandering bards, these courts often had resident poets called *trouvères* who were learned men – and women – composing works of literature to suit the tastes of their aristocratic patrons. For secular compositions they had three traditions from which they could draw: Greco-Roman history and myth, stories about Charlemagne and his paladins (the so-called *chansons de geste*) and what would come to be called the *matière de Bretagne* (the Matter of Britain), derived mainly at first from the Breton lays.

(Left) Tristan playing the harp for Isolde, from a fourteenth-century French manuscript of the Roman de Tristan.

Marie de France

The Matter of Britain – that is of both Britains, Greater and Lesser, meaning Britain and Brittany – was dominated by the stories of Arthur and his knights. Unlike the more historical tales set in the days of Alexander the Great or Charlemagne, the Arthurian legends involved more than just military exploits and kings. They told of love, magic and manners, making them the perfect entertainment for the affluent twelfth-century courts which were often dominated by powerful women. It should not surprise us then that the most famous 'composer' of Breton lays was a woman known as Marie de France. Surprisingly, given her *nom de plume*, she seems to have been a resident of England, composing poems at the Anglo-Norman courts of the Angevin Plantagenets.

Two of Marie's lays were overtly Arthurian: *Chevrefueil* (Honeysuckle) and *Lanval*. The first poem recounts a brief but passionate encounter between Tristan and Isolde in the forest. Their mutual but doomed love is likened, in the poem, to the intertwining of the honeysuckle and the hazel, where one cannot live without the other. *Lanval* is more of a narrative, the tale of a young knight whose fairy lover requires him to keep their love a secret. At Arthur's court Guinevere tries unsuccessfully to seduce the young Lanval, but in repelling her advances Lanval reveals his secret. He is not believed, however, and is accused of insulting the queen by lying to her. Nevertheless, despite breaking his oath, Lanval is saved at the last minute when his otherworldly lady arrives and reveals the truth. This plot is very similar to that of *Graelent*, a non-Arthurian Breton lay.

The Gothic abbey at Mont St Michel, where, according to Geoffrey of Monmouth, Arthur killed a giant who had carried off the daughter of Arthur's vassal, the Duke of Brittany.

THE FRENCH ROMANCES that appeared in the second half of the twelfth century bear many similarities to the Breton lays. Both are verse compositions written primarily to entertain nobles at court, both are concerned chiefly with love and knightly adventure, and both draw heavily upon Arthurian tradition. The romances, however, are longer and more elaborate treatments of these themes. The romance poets increasingly saw themselves as more than just entertainers, and their creations as self-conscious, artistic compositions with permanence. Little did they know that they would not only help make Arthur world famous, but also present Europe with a new and powerful vision of romantic love.

EREC ET ENIDE

'The matter was kept from him until one morning when they lay in bed, where they had been taking great pleasure. They were lying mouth to mouth in close embrace like true lovers, he sleeping and she awake. She began thinking of the things that many people throughout the country were saying about her husband; and when she came to recall them, she could not help weeping. She was so sad and grief-stricken that she unfortunately chanced to utter words for which she afterwards felt much remorse, though she intended no harm. She began to look her husband up and down, gazing at his shapely body and clear features. Then she weeps so abundantly that her tears fall on her husband's breast; and she says: "Alas, what a misfortune that I ever left my country! What did I come here to find? The earth ought to swallow me up when the very best knight, the boldest, most resolute, noblest and most courtly ever to be numbered among counts and kings has on my account utterly given up his whole practice of chivalry. So I've truly brought shame upon him, which I would not have wished at any price." Then she said to him: "How disastrous for you!" With that she fell silent and said no more.'

Walter Crane, *'Sir Geraint and Lady Enid in the Deserted Roman Town'*, *illustration for* King Arthur's Knights *(1911)*.

Lancelot and Guinevere

THE FAMOUS, INFAMOUS and utterly romantic affair between Lancelot and Guinevere appears to have been an invention of Marie, Countess of Champagne, in the late twelfth century. She provided the plot for the *Knight of the Cart*, written by her court poet Chrétien de Troyes, in which the queen is kidnapped and eventually rescued by a young knight who is revealed to be her lover. The knight is Lancelot, the queen's champion, who accomplishes many adventures in her name and defends her from the accusations of her enemies. The irony is that accusations about the queen's adultery were true, forcing Lancelot into the dilemma of whether to defend love or truth. Lancelot's sin prevents him from achieving the Grail Quest, and is eventually exposed by Agravaine and Mordred (in Geoffrey's version it is Mordred who seduces Guinevere into joining him in a plot against Arthur, while modern novelists have made Bedwyr the queen's lover). The exposing of the affair puts Arthur in a dilemma, for to uphold justice means executing his beloved queen for treason and losing his best knight. Guinevere is brought to the stake and Lancelot rides once again to her rescue, but in the ensuing battle many innocent knights are killed and the Round Table is effectively split into factions. Lancelot places Guinevere back on the throne, but Gawain convinces Arthur to wage war on Lancelot at his castle Joyous Gard in France. While the king is away Mordred rebels and holds Guinevere captive, forcing Arthur to return – without Lancelot – to face the most serious threat to his reign. After the Battle of Camlann, in which both Arthur and Mordred fall, Lancelot returns to Britain and tries to convince Guinevere to return with him to his castle. Now a nun, a guilt-ridden Guinevere shuns his advances and advises Lancelot to repent of their love, which had cost so many lives. Lancelot retires to a hermitage and finds consolation only in death.

Lancelot and Guinevere, still separated by Arthur (here in effigy), in Dante Gabriel Rossetti's watercolour King Arthur's Tomb *(1854–55).*

Chrétien de Troyes

The first, and perhaps most important, figure of this genre is Chrétien de Troyes. We know little of his biographical details. Presumably he was from the city of Troyes, in Champagne, or spent enough time there to become associated with it. Chrétien was for a time associated with the court of Marie, Countess of Champagne, and later he claimed as patron Philip of Alsace, Count of Flanders. His literary ouptut included five Arthurian romances written, in octosyllabic lines of rhymed verse, between *c.*1170 and 1191.

The first of these to be written was *Erec et Enide*, analogous to the Welsh romance *Geraint and Enid*. Chrétien uses this story to illustrate the potential conflict between romantic love and chivalry (p. 101). Erec (significantly, perhaps, a Breton name), son of Lac, is in the company of Guinevere when he is struck by a malicious dwarf. Vowing to avenge himself on the dwarf and on the knight who is his master, Erec sets off on a journey which takes him to the house of an aged gentleman and his beautiful daughter, Enide. Erec vows to be Enide's champion in a contest for a sparrow-hawk, which he wins for her by defeating in battle the very knight whom he had been seeking.

Erec returns to Arthur's court to wed Enide, and after elaborate nuptials the two settle down in wedded bliss. In such a state, however, Erec begins to neglect his knightly duties and his subjects begin to murmur and even mock him. Seeing that Enide is distressed, Erec forces her to reveal the content of the rumours about him, which so unsettle him that he orders his new wife to leave with him on an arduous journey. Treating her roughly and keeping his thoughts from her, Erec forces Enide to prove her love and devotion in a series of bizarre encounters with brigands. In the end the two are reconciled, Erec having been convinced of Enide's devotion and Enide having seen proof of Erec's prowess.

CAMELOT

In the oldest Arthurian tales, Arthur is variously depicted as a roving warrior who fights battles across the island, or as an itinerant chieftain with no permanent court. By the twelfth century, however, he becomes associated with particular sites – Celliwig in the Welsh Triads, *Caerleon in* Geoffrey's History *– though he may still have moved his court celebrations according to the Christian calendar. Thus Chrétien de Troyes, in his Arthurian romances, has the king celebrating holy days at various locations in both Britain and Brittany. But in his* Lancelot, *Chrétien tells how, one Ascension Day, Arthur left Caerleon 'and held a most magnificent court at Camelot with all the splendour appropriate to the day'. Camelot gradually became the most prominent of all Arthurian locales, and later romances made it Arthur's permanent seat of government (which mirrors the historical phenomenon of centralized monarchies emerging in the early modern period). The problem is that Chrétien did not precisely locate Camelot, and many have wondered whether or not the fabled castle was simply his invention. Malory identified Camelot with the city of Winchester, Alfred the Great's royal city that became prominent again under the Tudors. In 1542, the English antiquary John Leland wrote, 'At the very south end of the church of South Cadbyri standeth Camallate, sometime a famous town or castle. . . . The people can tell nothing but that they have heard say Arthur much resorted to Camalat.' In the late 1960s, excavation of an Iron Age hillfort beside the village of South Cadbury was launched with the expectations of finding this Cadbury 'Camelot' (p. 42). Others, noting the* Camel- *element of the name, have searched for a suitable spot along the River Camel, or else have scoured similar Roman place-names. Yet still Camelot eludes us.*

'May in Camelot', illustration by Aubrey Beardsley for Thomas Malory, The Birth Life and Acts of King Arthur *(1927).*

SIR LANCELOT DU LAC

'His honour rooted in dishonour stood,
And faith unfaithful kept him falsely true.'
Tennyson, 'Lancelot and Elaine', from Idylls of the King

Lancelot (Launcelot, Lanzelet) is, like Camelot, almost entirely a creation of the French poets. He has no clear counterpart in the Welsh tradition (though some have equated him with Llwch Lleminawc of The Spoils of Annwfn *or the Irish warrior, Llenlleawc, from* Culhwch and Olwen*). Lancelot first appears in Chrétien's* Erec*, and is later the central figure of Chrétien's* Knight of the Cart*. He became – among French writers at least – the most popular of Arthur's knights, with subsequent romances detailing his origins and his other adventures. In most of the romances he is Sir Lancelot du Lac, eldest son of King Ban of Benwick, in France, raised in an underwater kingdom by a fairy (the Lady of the Lake) before coming to Britain to join Arthur's fellowship of knights. In some versions Lancelot is knighted by Guinevere and becomes the queen's own champion, thereby establishing his divided loyalty between Arthur and Guinevere which would lead to great tragedy. Devoted to Guinevere, Lancelot is nevertheless desired by many women, who see him as the 'flower of chivalry'. One of them, Elaine of Corbenic, constructs a ruse to sleep with Lancelot (who thinks it is Guinevere) and conceives a son, Galahad. Knighted by his father, Galahad is destined to surpass Lancelot in prowess and virtue. He achieves the Grail, an achievement which Lancelot's sin prevents him from sharing. In many ways a flawed and tragic figure (Malory calls him* le chevalier mal fait*, 'the ill-made knight'), Lancelot must watch as Arthur and his fellows of the Round Table perish due to a rift that he in part created.*

'Lancelot slays a dragon', illustration by Arthur Rackham for A.W. Pollard's abridgment of Malory, The Romance of King Arthur *(1917).*

Chrétien's next romance, *Cligés*, begins outside the Arthurian world, in Constantinople. There resides a Greek prince named Alexandre, the father of Cligés, who was so brave and proud that he would not be knighted in his own country, but only in the land of the renowned King Arthur. By recounting the adventures of the father before those of the son, Chrétien may consciously have been drawing a parallel with the Tristan story (p. 116). Cligés, like Tristan, is in love with his uncle's wife, Fénice. In fact, Fénice tells Cligés that she will not make the same mistakes Isolde made, and so devises a ruse to escape her marriage. Like Shakespeare's Juliet, she will drink a potion that will make her appear to be dead. When the charade works, a resurrected Fénice is free to be with her true love, Cligés.

Love, rather than honour or fidelity, has become the most powerful motivating force in this second romance. Alexandre launches into long interior monologues on the subject of his simple but intense love for Soredamors, Gawain's sister. Cligés is also concerned chiefly with love, but his affair with Fénice is more worldly and sophisticated. Here the poem's rhetoric changes and we move closer to Chrétien's own world of courtly love and intrigue, where adultery – real or pretended – is celebrated as an aristocratic pastime. The most fashionable courts of twelfth-century France were those dominated by powerful women, such as Eleanor of Aquitaine and the Countess de Champagne, who in turn dominated the lesser male nobility that served them, and who cajoled their own court poets into turning their court games into thinly veiled fiction.

This, at least, is the way Chrétien describes the making of his third and best-known romance, *Le Chevalier de la Charrete* (The Knight of the Cart), also known simply as *Lancelot*. This poem introduces two of the most important elements of the Arthurian tradition: the adulterous affair between Lancelot and Guinevere, and Arthur's fabled court of Camelot. As for the former, Chrétien says that the *matière et san* of this romance (that is, the source material and the

LANCELOT

'When Lancelot joined in the tourney, he alone was worth twenty of the best. And he begins to do so well that no one can take his eyes off him, wherever he is. . . . They all ask frantically: "Who is this man who is fighting so well?" The queen drew to one side a prudent, sensible girl and said: "Maiden, you must take a message [to Lancelot] . . . tell him privately that I bid him do 'his worst'." . . . "Sir, the instructions I bring you from my lady the queen are to do 'your worst'." Hearing this, he replies: "Very willingly!" in the manner of someone who is entirely hers.'

YVAIN

'The knight very knowingly dashed through the proper way, whilst my lord Yvain imprudently rushed after him at a great pace and came so close to catching him that he held him by the back saddle-bow. He was very lucky to be leaning forward, otherwise he would have been sliced right through; for the horse stepped on the wood that supported the iron gate. Down comes the gate like a devil out of Hell, catching the saddle and the horse behind it, slicing it clean through the saddle.'

treatment of it), were supplied by the Countess. With this device, whether truthful or a deceit, he removes himself from responsibility for what is to follow: a celebration – some would say a burlesque – of adulterous love.

The backdrop to this aristocratic affair is a royal abduction. Entrusted to Sir Kay (Cei), Guinevere is abducted by the knight Meleagant after he has defeated the seneschal. Arthur and Gauvain (*sic*) race off to rescue the queen and encounter another knightly rescuer, whose name is withheld by Chrétien for dramatic effect. The unnamed knight rides his horse to its death in his urgency, and is forced to climb into a criminal's cart to reach the castle where the queen is held hostage. Once there, he engages Meleagant in combat, in which his successes and failures are entirely dictated by Guinevere's whim. The queen needs to teach her lover a lesson, for his hesitation over climbing into the criminal's cart was a sign to Guinevere that the knight would place his honour before her rescue. Once the lesson is learned, Lancelot (as he is now revealed to be) is readmitted to Guinevere's bed.

Chrétien's explorations of courtly love and chivalry reach a climax in *Yvain*, or *Le Chevalier au Lion* (The Knight with the Lion), which many scholars believe is his greatest artistic achievement. The knight Yvain wins the love of the lady Laudine after killing her husband. But after they marry, Yvain is coerced by Gauvain into accompanying him on knightly adventure. Laudine gives her new husband permission to be gone for one year, but Yvain forgets to return on the agreed date and loses her love. This leads to more adventures for the tormented Yvain, who looks for a way to expiate his sin. On one adventure he saves the life of a lion, who becomes his constant companion thereafter. The lion is clearly symbolic – Divine Grace or the ideal of devotion are both possibilities – and serves as the device to lead Yvain back to Laudine's love.

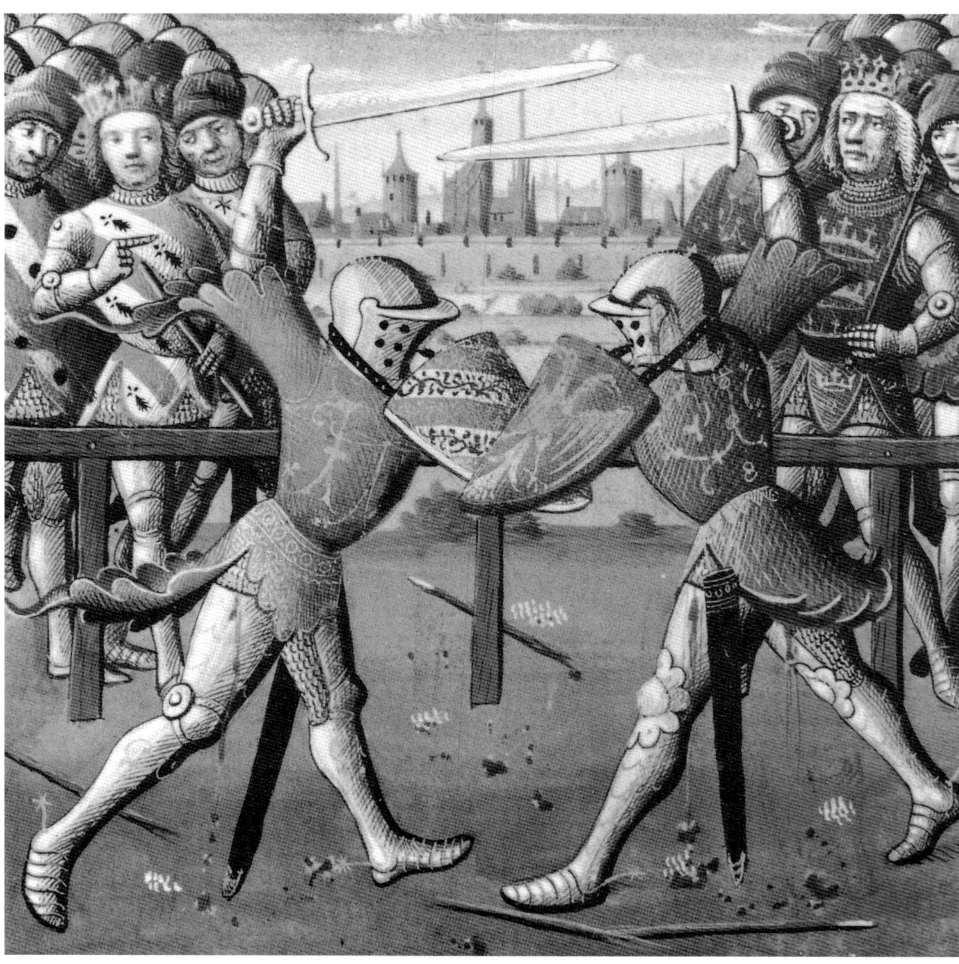

Combat between Lancelot and Gawain, illustration from a fifteenth-century French manuscript of the Cycle de Lancelot.

Chrétien's final romance was *Perceval*, or *Le Conte del Graal* (The Story of the Grail). It is an unfinished work, possibly due to the death of the poet. This is only one aspect of its enigmatic allure. *Perceval* is a unique blend of two separate adventures – those of Perceval and of Gauvain – and three genres: romance, comedy, and religious drama. It begins with the story of Perceval, a naïve youth who, raised in isolation, does not know what knights are. As soon as he encounters them, however, he vows to become a knight and sets off on a series of, mostly comical, adventures. On these adventures he wins armour and the love of the beautiful Blancheflor, displaying impressive physical abilities but for the most part still behaving like a child.

An early lack of education in courtly matters leads to his greatest mistake. After entering the Grail castle and witnessing its mystical procession (see box, below), Perceval fails to ask the question which would have healed the Fisher King (the lord of the castle) and restored his withering land. Perceval also loses Blancheflor, and hears that his mother has died awaiting his return. In this moment of crisis and tragedy, the poet shifts the narrative to Gauvain's adventures. When the reader comes upon Perceval again it is Good Friday and the knight learns the reasons for his failures from a saintly hermit. We hear no more of Perceval, for the story shifts back to the chivalrous Gauvain, who finds himself in a strange land that does not know chivalry.

Lancelot rescues Guinevere, miniature from a medieval French manuscript. Like much medieval manuscript illumination, this illustration represents several episodes in the narrative, read left to right.

This unfinished romance lacks the cohesiveness of Chrétien's other poems, but it did provide the basic framework for centuries of Grail stories that would follow it. In describing the qualities of the ideal knight and the ideal lover, Chrétien made an important contribution to the formalization of European chivalry. The overall impact of Chrétien's works, on the Arthurian tradition and on the medieval world in general, is incalculable.

PERCEVAL

'While they were talking of this and that, out of a room came a youth holding a white lance . . . and from the tip of the lance-head oozed a drop of blood. . . . A damsel, who came with the youths and was fair and attractive and beautifully adorned, held in both hands a grail. Once she had entered with this grail that she held, so great a radiance appeared that the candles lost their brilliance just as the stars do at the rising of the sun or moon. . . . The young man [Perceval] saw them pass, but did not dare ask who was served from the grail.'

Perceval meets a group of knights, French ivory casket (c.1325).

The Vulgate Cycle

Several French romances appeared in the first few decades after Chrétien's poems had set the standard. Many were continuations of his Grail romance, in which German writers also joined (p. 110). But the most ambitious and complete project of the thirteenth century was the Vulgate Cycle, also known as the Prose *Lancelot*. This consisted of five long romances, all in Old French prose: *L'Estoire del Saint Graal* (The History of the Holy Grail), *Merlin*, *Lancelot*, *La Queste del Saint Graal* (The Quest of the Holy Grail) and *La Mort Artu* (The Death of Arthur). They were written over a brief span of time, c.1215–35, possibly by one unknown author, but more likely by at least two. The most ambitious of all Arthurian projects to date, the Vulgate has grand schemes, ranging from the death of Christ to the death of Arthur, and presents an interestingly interwoven discussion of both courtly love and military piety. Translated into several languages, the Vulgate is perhaps best remembered as the source for the climactic medieval Arthurian work, Malory's *Le Morte d'Arthur*.

THE QUEST FOR THE HOLY GRAIL

THERE ARE MANY versions of the Grail story, both medieval and modern, but the most common is that which portrays Arthur's knights in a quest for a sacred Christian object. This Grail was the vessel used by Jesus at the Last Supper and subsequently by Joseph of Arimathea, the secret disciple who entombed Christ's body. Joseph is said to have caught Christ's blood from the Cross in the Grail, which later miraculously nourished him in a Judean prison. Joseph and his son, Josephus, took the Grail on a journey west through the Roman Empire, holding Mass at a round table. The fellowship they initiated eventually arrived in Britain, where for generations the guardian of the Grail was known as the Rich Fisher or the Fisher King. One of these guardians was the Maimed King, so named from a weapon wound that would not heal and which brought a curse on his dominions – the Wasteland. Several generations after its arrival in Britain the Grail appeared briefly at Arthur's court, filling all with joy and amazement. After it vanished from his hall, Arthur's knights each stood and vowed to go in quest, for a year and a day, until they had found the Grail. Each knight had a unique experience on the quest, though ultimately all but three – Galahad, Perceval and Bors – failed utterly, either dying on the quest or returning to Camelot dejected. Perceval's sister, a nun who had received a vision of the Grail, led the three Grail knights to Castle Corbenic where Galahad was able to heal the Maimed King with the aid of the Grail and bring life to his Wasteland. Ultimately the three knights accompanied the Grail to the Holy Land, where Galahad learned its mysteries and was assumed, along with the sacred object, into heaven. Perceval remained in the East as a hermit, while Bors returned to a Camelot that no longer shone so brightly.

Frederick J. Waugh, The Knight of the Holy Grail *(c.1912).*

The Perceval–Grail Tradition

Parzifal

'The knight then dashed
forward o'er the sod.
The lad [Parzifal] thought:
surely here's a god . . .
The rider said, "No God am I,
But His commands I don't deny.
Four knights before thee thou
mayest see,
If right thine eyesight seems
to be."
The lad continued then to say,
"Thou namest knights.
What's that, I pray?
If thou'st not godly fortitude,
Then tell me, who gives
knightlihood?"
"By royal Arthur that is done.
Young sir, when his house
thou'st won,
Then he will give the knightly
name,
The which will never cause
thee shame."'

FRENCH WRITERS dominated the secular literature of the twelfth and thirteenth centuries, in part due to the numerous Arthurian romances that they produced. But the thirteenth century also witnessed two classics of German medieval literature – Wolfram von Eschenbach's *Parzifal* and Gottfried von Strassburg's *Tristan* (p. 116) – and the beginning of an Arthurian tradition in Italian and Hispanic literature.

The *Perceval* Continuators

The most alluring subject for these writers was Perceval and the Grail. The unfinished state of Chrétien's poem was an open invitation for other creative talents to contribute to what was a growing tradition-within-a-tradition. Four verse continuations appeared in the years *c.*1200–30. Some take up the adventures of Perceval, others with adventures of Gawain and minor knights, such as Caradoc and Sagremor. Perhaps the most important contribution of these works is the motif of the broken sword, which Perceval – due to his imperfections – at first fails to mend.

The Didot-*Perceval*

Other writers chose to rework as well as to finish the Perceval story. In doing so they tended to follow one of two paths: either relating the mostly secular adventures of Perceval and other Arthurian knights, or presenting the Grail Quest as part of a long Christian saga. The so-called Didot-*Perceval* falls in the first category. Written *c.*1200–30, it is an anonymous French prose romance drawing from such sources as Geoffrey of Monmouth, Chrétien de Troyes and Robert de Boron. When the young hero in this version first comes to Arthur's court, he sits in the forbidden thirteenth chair (later called the Siege Perilous) of the Round Table, bringing an enchanted darkness over Britain that will only end with the accomplishment of the Grail Quest. This time Perceval asks the right questions at the Grail Castle and brings the quest to a happy conclusion.

Perceval arriving at the Grail Castle. Miniature from an early fourteenth-century French manuscript of Chrétien's Le Conte du Graal.

Parzifal

This first category of Perceval stories draws heavily from the pre-Christian traditions of Europe and integrates these magical (and originally pagan) adventure tales with medieval chivalry and Christianity. The greatest achievement in this group of stories is Wolfram von Eschenbach's *Parzifal*, written *c.*1210. We know very little about Wolfram, other than that he was an unschooled soldier from Eschenbach, near Ansbach in Bavaria, who went on to become perhaps the greatest German epic poet of the Middle Ages. *Parzifal* is written in Middle High German rhymed couplets. It begins with the adventures of Parzifal's father Gahmuret and his marriage to Herzeloyde, and concludes with Parzifal assuming the kingship of the Grail. It is a cohesive and magnificent epic quite unlike anything else in the Arthurian tradition.

The first part of Parzifal's story is a familiar one. Gahmuret dies tragically on a knightly adventure, leading Herzeloyde to raise Parzifal in seclusion, in the hope that he would never enter courtly life. This plan fails after Parzifal encounters his first knights in shining armour – he takes them to be angels – and sets off to be knighted by Arthur. Along the way he rescues and marries the beautiful Condwiramurs, then leaves her in order to become a knight of the Round Table. Failing in his first encounter at Munsalvaesche, the Grail Castle, Parzifal nevertheless is accepted by Arthur, wins the friendship of Gawan (Gawain) and the companionship of his half-brother Feirefiz. Ultimately, he returns to the Grail Castle and heals the Grail King.

What sets *Parzifal* apart from the other Perceval tales is Wolfram's conception of the Grail and his sensitive handling of Perceval's moral development. Whereas Chrétien's Grail had been a mysterious bowl or dish, Wolfram uniquely depicts the Grail as a magical stone – which he calls *lapsit exillis* – sent from heaven during God's war with Lucifer. The stone possessed magical feeding and healing qualities, and came to be guarded by a family of virgin knights

The Grail Knight on his lonely and frightful quest is encouraged by angelic beings. Arthur Hughes, Sir Galahad *(1870).*

(Wolfram calls them 'templars') and maidens, who serve until discharged in the castle of the Grail King. The current king, Anfortas, is maimed and cursed, and it is Parzifal who is destined to ask the question 'What ails you?' which will allow the Grail to heal the king. But first the naïve hero must overcome his ignorance and his anger towards God before he can assume his rightful place at a court higher than Arthur's.

Peredur

Wolfram's epic clearly contains many motifs – a magical stone, a wise hag, a maimed king – which pre-date chivalric romance and which ultimately derive from Europe's ancient pagan past. This borrowing from antiquity is even more explicit in the Welsh contribution to the Perceval tradition, *Peredur*, which assumed written form sometime in the thirteenth century. The young hero of the tale was raised in isolation by his mother but, after seeing knights for the first time, leaves to seek Arthur's court. Insulted by Cei, Peredur leaves the court for a series of adventures during which he is educated by two uncles and the witches of Caerloyw. Inexplicably, he is sidetracked by the Empress of Constantinople, with whom he rules for fourteen years! Back in Britain he learns the true meaning of the marvels he has seen (including a bleeding lance and a severed head on a platter) and is told that he must avenge his maimed uncle. There are many similarities here with Chrétien's *Perceval*, yet no Holy Grail appears and, overall, the tale lacks the clear structure and purpose of the French romance. *Peredur* is a rambling narrative of strange and wonderful adventures without a higher purpose.

Perlesvaus

Peredur bears little resemblance to the tales in the second Grail tradition, which focuses on the Grail as a Christian relic and links Camelot to the Early Christian world. An early example is the enigmatic *Perlesvaus*, or *Li Hauz Livres du Graal* (The High History of the Grail), an Old French prose romance written in the first decade

VULGATE *QUEST OF THE HOLY GRAIL*

'When [the knights] were all seated and the noise was hushed, there came a clap of thunder so loud and terrible that they thought the palace must fall. Suddenly the hall was lit by a sunbeam which shed a radiance through the palace seven times brighter than had been before. In this moment they were all illumined as it might be by the Holy Ghost, and they began to look at one another, uncertain and perplexed. But not one of those present could utter a word, for all had been struck dumb, without respect of person. When they had sat a long while thus, unable to speak and gazing at one another like dumb animals, the Holy Grail appeared, covered with a cloth of white samite; and yet no mortal hand was seen to bear it . . . and at once the palace was filled with fragrance as though all the spices of the earth had been spilled abroad. It circled the hall along the great tables and each place was furnished in its wake with the food its occupants desired. When all were served, the Holy Grail vanished, they knew not how or whither. And those that had been mute regained the power of speech, and many gave thanks to Our Lord for the honour He had done them in filling them with the grace of the Holy Vessel. But greater than all was King Arthur's joy that Our Lord should have accorded him a favour never granted to any king before him.'

of the thirteenth century. Long and complex, *Perlesvaus* attempts to relate the fate of Perlesvaus (Perceval) and the Grail quest to the entire saga of Camelot. It relates the adventures of Gauvain and Lancelot – both of whom fail to achieve the Grail – as well as those of Perlesvaus, who ultimately avenges his mother, frees the Grail Castle from 'the King of Castle Mortal', and returns peace and prosperity to Arthur's entire realm.

Galahad and Perceval rest for a moment, and discuss their love for the quest. From a fourteenth-century French manuscript.

Robert de Boron

The key figure in this trend of depicting the Grail not as a magical object with pagan roots but as a relic with ties to Jesus, is the Burgundian poet Robert de Boron. Robert, probably a cleric, wrote three Arthurian romances *c.*1200: *Joseph d'Arimathie*, or *Le Roman de l'Estoire dou Graal* (The Chronicle of the History of the Grail), *Merlin* (of which only a small part is extant) and *Perceval* (now lost but probably the basis for the Didot-*Perceval*). Written in Old French octosyllabic verse, they present a new Christian saga of the Grail that was to inspire the Vulgate Cycle, Malory and many writers up to the present day.

Robert's Grail saga traces the journey of the sacred vessel, from the Crucifixion to the arrival of Joseph of Arimathea in the West with both the Grail and the bleeding lance (here identified as the Spear of Longinus which pierced Christ's side on the Cross). On these travels a Mass is held at a round table and Joseph's brother-in-law Hebron (or Bron) is appointed the Rich Fisher (he brought fish to the table) to be guardian of the Grail. Bron and his sons continue to preach as they travel to the Vales of Avalon, where they will await a descendant – the 'third man' – who is destined to be the ultimate keeper of the Grail. This man will come from the company of a third table, Arthur's Round Table.

The Vulgate *Quest of the Holy Grail*

With its obvious Trinitarian symbolism, Robert's Grail is a most sacred relic linking the tables of Christ and Arthur. This link proved too attractive to ignore, and French prose versions of his Grail poems soon appeared, strengthening that connection. They depict Perceval as the 'third man', the one to achieve the Grail. But in the Vulgate Cycle, which drew both from Robert's poems and the prose versions, a new hero becomes the perfect Grail knight: he is Sir Galahad.

Galahad makes his first appearance in the Vulgate *Quest of the Holy Grail*. He is, however, the culmination of an elaborate genealogical scheme (later written down in the Vulgate *History of the Holy Grail*), which joins the House of David and the Grail family through the contrived union of Lancelot and Elaine of Corbenic: the first Fisher King, Alain, had brought the Grail (here the dish from which Christ ate the Passover lamb) from Sarras to Corbenic Castle, founding a family of royal Grail guardians culminating in Elaine's father, Pelles. In order to heal his brother, the Maimed King, and restore prosperity to the land, Pelles contrives a liaison between Elaine and Lancelot, a blood-descendant of Jesus himself. Galahad is the product of this union.

Joseph, his son Josephe, Merlin, Arthur and Pelles all prepare the way for the coming of the Good Knight. The *Quest* focuses on a trinity of stainless champions – Galahad, Perceval and Bors – aided by Perceval's sister, a nun. These heroes ultimately meet, after separate adventures, to celebrate a Grail mass (performed by Josephe himself) at Corbenic Castle before accompanying the Grail back to Sarras. There its mysteries are revealed to Galahad, whose spirit ascends into heaven with the Grail and the Spear. Perceval dies later in Sarras, while only Bors returns to Arthur and Camelot.

This depiction of the Grail as a Christian relic, not as a magical pagan object, came to dominate literature from Malory to Tennyson and beyond, and the Grail itself would become arguably the most famous Christian relic in the world.

Galahad achieves the Grail. Illustration from a fifteenth-century French manuscript of Gaultier Moap, La Quête du Saint Graal et la mort d'Arthur.

GALAHAD

'My good blade carves the casques of men,
My tough lance thrusteth sure,
My strength is as the strength of ten,
Because my heart is pure.'

Tennyson, *'Sir Galahad'*

Sir Galahad (or Galaad) is probably a late addition to the Arthurian saga. His name may have been created (from the Palestinian region of 'Gilead', mentioned in the Old Testament) by the author of the Vulgate Quest of the Holy Grail, *though some have suggested it came from the figure of Gwalhafed in* Culhwch and Olwen. *His story is certainly a product of the thirteenth-century Christianization of the Grail adventure. Galahad is the son of Lancelot and Elaine of Corbenic, a contrived union (Elaine's father and nurse help trick Lancelot into sleeping with Elaine) necessary to produce an heir descended from both the House of David and the Grail kings. Lancelot knights Galahad just before his son comes to Camelot and takes his seat – the Siege Perilous – at the Round Table. His short life represents a quickened fulfillment of sacred destiny, hastended along, as in Tennyson's poem, by his ever-present and powerful vision of the Grail.*

This vision is shared with Perceval's sister, who arms Galahad for the quest with the Sword of David (he already carries a white shield, bearing a red cross painted with blood from the Grail). She is his spiritual partner, and his companions are the two purified knights, Perceval and Bors. After many adventures (including Galahad's healing of the Maimed King) the trio find the Grail at Corbenic and set sail with it to Sarras, the mythical land of the Saracens in the East. There Galahad is eventually crowned king, but his only ambition is to uncover the mysteries of the Trinity which the Grail possesses. Drinking from the vessel and peering deep within, his spirit shudders with pure Truth and his soul breaks free of his body to accompany the Grail to heaven. In Idylls of the King, *Tennyson describes Galahad galloping on his horse across a bridge ascending to heaven, its tiers bursting into flames behind him.*

George Frederick Watts, Sir Galahad *(1862).*

TRISTAN AND ISOLDE

SIR TRISTAN (Tristran, Tristram) of Lyonesse was a young knight in the service of his uncle Mark, King of Cornwall. His name, which the poets took to mean 'sad birth', commemorates the loss of his mother, who died giving birth to him. When Anguish, the king of Ireland, demands tribute from Cornwall, Tristan volunteers to fight the Irish champion on behalf of his uncle. He defeats and kills the Irish giant Morholt (or Marhaus), who is also brother-in-law to the Irish king. But, in the course of doing so he is severely wounded by Morholt's poisoned weapon and travels incognito from Cornwall to Ireland to be cured. There he is healed by Anguish's beautiful daughter, Isolde (Iseut, Iseult), whom he teaches to play the harp. Anguish offers his daughter's hand in marriage to any knight who succeeds in slaying a dragon that has been terrorizing his kingdom. Tristan slays the dragon and asks for Isolde's hand, not for himself but for his uncle King Mark. Having thus revealed himself as the Cornish champion who defeated Morholt, Tristan incurs Isolde's hatred, but Anguish must nevertheless fulfil his pledge and turn his daughter over to the knight. On the fateful voyage back to Cornwall, Tristan and Isolde both unwittingly drink a love potion intended for the wedding couple, and are bound by an inescapable and eternal love. Although Isolde weds Mark, she commands her maid, Brangwen, to take her place in the nuptial bed. Tristan and Isolde continue their affair and deception of Mark for years, though Tristan's enemies try several times to expose them. Once, the couple is forced to flee to a wooded retreat, but eventually duty and honour force Isolde back to Mark, and Tristan into exile in Brittany. Overseas he meets and marries another Isolde, known as Isolde of the White Hands, though his love for the Irish Isolde prevents him from ever consummating this marriage. In some versions of the story Tristan is murdered while playing the harp for his true love by a jealous Mark. In other versions, Tristan suffers a fatal wound and calls for Isolde to come from Cornwall to heal him. His wife becomes jealous, however, and tells him that the ship arriving from Cornwall bears a black sail, rather than the white sail which would signal Isolde's arrival. When Isolde of Ireland does land she finds Tristan dead of despair, and she herself dies on the spot of a broken heart. The two lovers are buried side by side, where two vines growing from their graves meet and intertwine.

Tristan and Isolde drink the fatal love potion while crossing from Ireland to Cornwall, from a medieval French manuscript.

The Tristan Tradition

Unlike Arthur, the historicity of Tristan is supported by a surviving piece of material evidence, the so-called 'Tristan Stone' found near Castle Dore in Cornwall. The inscription reads DRUSTANUS HIC IACIT CUNOMORI FILIUS, 'Here lies Drustan, son of Cunomorus'.

Gottfried

'Now when the maid and the man, Isolde and Tristan, had drunk the draught, in an instant the arch-disturber of tranquillity was there, Love, waylayer of all hearts, and she had stolen in! Before they were aware of it she had planted her victorious standard in their two hearts and bowed them beneath her yoke. They who were two and divided now became one and united. No longer were they at variance: Isolde's hatred was gone. Love, the reconciler, had purged their hearts of enmity, and joined them in affection that . . . they shared a single heart. Her anguish was his pain; his pain her anguish.'

SO POWERFUL IS the Arthurian saga that it can attract other, independent tales and characters and attach them to the story of Camelot in such a way that few remember them as having ever been separate entities. This is partly true of the Grail stories, which have origins in such disparate sources as Christian apocrypha and Celtic myths. But nowhere is this phenomenon more remarkable than in the Tristan tradition. A great literary tradition in its own right, this saga of a Cornish knight and his doomed love for an Irish princess is an ancient tale that will forever be linked, albeit peripherally, with the Arthurian legends.

Tristan is a popular figure in early medieval Welsh literature, appearing several times in the Triads. In this early Welsh tradition he is known as Drystan son of Tallwch, a name that probably represents an historical Pictish prince, Drust son of Tallorc. Was the Tristan story originally a northern one, ask some scholars, transmitted by the Welsh and relocated in Cornwall? Aside from the origin of the names, the story's basic components can also be found in early Irish literature, for example in *The Wooing of Emer* and *The Pursuit after Diarmaid and Gráinne*. It may be significant that Tristan's lover, Isolde, is almost always represented as an Irish princess.

Eilhart von Oberge

Wherever it originated, the tale was without doubt widely circulated by the Britons, first in Wales, Cornwall and Brittany, and subsequently to Anglo-Norman, French and German audiences. The literary scholar Joseph Bédier first proposed, in the early twentieth century, the idea of an archetypal Tristan tale, which passed from Brittany to France c.1150. Thus Tristan began to make appearances in the works of Marie de France, Chrétien de Troyes and other French poets of the mid-twelfth century.

Soon afterwards there developed two separate Tristan traditions. The earliest representative of the first of these – sometimes called the 'primitive' version – is the *Tristrant* of Eilhart von Oberge. Written in Middle High German verse, perhaps as early as 1170 and certainly no later than 1190, this is the oldest complete Tristan romance. It differs markedly from more famous versions of the Tristan story, introducing several motifs from German and Scandinavian myths. But the most significant variance is that here Tristrant and Isalde drink a love potion so powerful that to start with they cannot stand to be apart for even a day, though after four years the potion fades and the lovers voluntarily separate, Tristrant taking another wife and Isalde returning to Mark. They later resume their affair through the use of disguises and other comical devices, and when they both die Mark repents of his interference and has them buried in a single grave.

Béroul

The presence of farce and non-courtly elements, not to mention Tristrant as a member of King Arthur's hunting party, indicates that Eilhart was already diverging from the archetypal Tristan story, but in a different direction from most contemporary French versions. An exception is the Anglo-Norman poem *Tristran* written by Béroul c.1175-80. This fragment includes several comic episodes showing Tristran and Iseut fooling, and eluding, a jealous Mark, thus resembling more a medieval *fabliau* than medieval romance. In this aspect, and in its depiction of the love potion as having only temporary effect, Béroul's narrative is very close to Eilhart's. It, too, features an appearance by Arthur and his knights, though Tristran is not yet shown as a member of the Round Table.

Thomas

Also fragmentary is the *Tristan* ascribed to one 'Thomas of Britain' (which could mean either Britain or Brittany). It is an Old French romance, in octosyllabic couplets, written c.1175 probably at the Angevin court of Henry II and Eleanor of Aquitaine. Under such influences, Thomas reworked his source material (the 'archetype' Tristan?) to present a more mature and sophisticated courtly love story. In Thomas's version the love potion has no fixed duration, nor does it completely control the lovers; it is, rather, the symbol of two people for whom love is the sole law guiding their behaviour. Here Tristan and Iseut take full responsibility for their love, and Tristan marries the second Iseut solely in an attempt to forget his true love.

Gottfried von Strassburg

Thomas's *Tristan* is the earliest example of the second Tristan tradition – the 'courtly' version – which is, in many ways, similar to the courtly love tradition of Lancelot and Guinevere. Its lasting impact can be seen in the *Tristan* of

Gottfried von Strassburg, widely considered to be the classic form of the Tristan romance. This unfinished poem was written in Middle High German rhymed couplets in around 1210. It is debatable whether this is technically an Arthurian poem, for Arthur's court is never mentioned. Gottfried tells us that the 'authentic version' of the Tristan story was told by Thomas, a 'master-romancer' who had 'read the lives of all those princes in the books of the Britons'.

Like Thomas, Gottfried offers a sophisticated exploration of courtly love and tragedy, employing long introspective monologues and classical allusions. This is in evidence right from the start, when Gottfried narrates the tragic deaths of Tristan's parents, foreshadowing those of Tristan and Isolde. Tristan is conceived on the deathbed of his father, while his grieving mother dies in childbirth. The child is kidnapped, but eventually finds his way to Cornwall where he becomes a favourite of King Mark. Tristan goes to Ireland to win Mark a bride, but on the return voyage he and Isolde drink the love potion intended to be drunk by Isolde and Mark. As with Thomas, Gottfried's love potion is merely symbolic of the powerful love that will rule the lives of Tristan and Isolde and lead ultimately to their destruction.

This destruction is delayed, however, by various tricks which deflect Mark's suspicion. When the two lovers can stand it no longer they run away to live in a forest cave, where they eat no food but are nourished merely by gazing at one another. This idyll comes to an end when they return to court and are discovered in bed together by Mark, who banishes Tristan. The poem breaks off as Tristan, wandering through Europe in grief for Isolde, meets another woman bearing her name and contemplates marrying her.

The Prose *Tristan*

Like Chrétien's *Perceval*, these unfinished and fragmentary Tristan poems proved to be an invitation for later writers to rework and complete the story. The most ambitious completion is the so-called Prose *Tristan*, a lengthy French romance that survives in two versions, dating respectively to the second and third quarters of the thirteenth century. Here we learn more about Tristan's lineage and early life, his tutor Governal, his rival Palamedes (who is desparately in love with Iseut himself) and a companion named Dinadan, who is constantly questioning and challenging the precepts of courtly love and chivalry. Here also Tristan becomes a knight of the Round Table, assuming the seat of Morholt (whom he had killed in combat for Mark). Mark himself becomes more explicitly a villain, in one version killing Tristan as he is singing to Iseut.

The Prose *Tristan* was enormously popular and much imitated in other European literature, probably because it brought the two compelling stories of Tristan and Arthur together in a cohesive and convincing manner. It was also to have a great influence on the English writer Thomas Malory, who would bring it and the Vulgate stories together with Arthur's saga in the late medieval masterpiece *Le Morte d'Arthur*.

John Duncan, Tristan and Isolde *(1912).*

Tristan and Isolde in bed, detail from an ivory casket (c.1200).

Tristan fighting in a tournament, as depicted in a French manuscript illustration of 1463. Such tournaments, held by European princes and potentates, were called 'round tables' in the later Middle Ages in imitation of Arthur's gatherings.

What place is there within the bounds of the empire of Christendom to which the winged praise of Arthur the Briton has not extended? Who is there, I ask, who does not speak of Arthur the Briton, since he is but little less known to the peoples of Asia than to the Bretons? . . . The Eastern peoples speak of him as do the Western, though separated by the breadth of the whole earth. Egypt speaks of him, and the Bosphorus is not silent. Rome, queen of cities, sings his deeds, and his wars are not unknown to her formal rival Carthage. Antioch, Armenia, and Palestine celebrate his feats.

Alanus de Insulis

THE ARTHURIAN TRADITION in the Middle Ages was truly international. Alanus de Insulis, writing with only slight exaggeration, bore witness to this fact as early as the 1170s. Though originally a product of the 'Celtic fringe', and occasionally glimpsed in Latin chronicles and saints' lives, Arthur quickly captured the attention of French-speaking audiences in England and France. From 1200 to 1600, Arthurian stories were also composed in, or translated into, English, Scots, German, Spanish and Portuguese, Provençal, Italian, Dutch, Old Norse and Icelandic, Swedish, Danish, Greek, Czech, Russian, Hebrew and Yiddish! Arthurian tournaments and pageants were also held across Europe, and Arthurian knights and ladies appeared in art and architecture from the Romanesque to the Renaissance.

There follows a brief survey of some of the most significant examples of the Arthurian legend's impact on the medieval world.

Ireland

The *Lorgaireacht an tSoidhigh Naomhtha* is an Irish translation of the Vulgate *Quest of the Holy Grail* (or of an English version) produced in the fourteenth or fifteenth century. Several Irish tales of the fifteenth and sixteenth centuries use Arthurian characters and settings, and an Arthurian 'riding' was held in Dublin in 1498.

Scotland

Scotland is the setting of the French romance *Fergus*, written by Guillaume le Clerc in the early thirteenth century for Alan of Galloway. But of the indigenous material, only two Scottish Arthurian romances have survived: *Lancelot of the Laik* and *Golagros and Gawain*, both Middle Scots adaptations of French romances written in the late fifteenth century, along with the Middle Scots poem *Sir Gawan and Sir Galeron of Galoway*. In addition to these romances, however, Arthur, along with Gawain and Mordred, appears frequently in the medieval Scottish chronicles.

(Right) Arthur's Seat, Salisbury Crags, Edinburgh. This 'Seat' may have once been a hillfort.

Burgundy and the Low Countries

The early popularity of the Arthurian legends in the Low Countries is evidenced by the frequent appearance of names such as Iwain and Walewanus (Gawain) in Flemish charters of the twelfth century. Chrétien de Troyes dedicated his *Perceval* to his patron Philip of Flanders, while prose versions of both *Cligés* and *Erec et Enide* were produced for Burgundian audiences. *Perchevael*, a Middle Dutch translation of Chrétien's *Perceval*, was produced in the early thirteenth century. The most productive Dutch Arthurian writer was Jacob van Maerlant (c.1230–90), who produced several translations and adaptations of the French romances. The manuscript known as the *Lancelot-Compilatie* contained no fewer than ten Arthurian romances, most of them Dutch translations of French works. One exception is *Walewein end Keye*, which is an indigenous thirteenth-century romance describing the adventures of Gawain after he had been accused by Kay of bragging.

Scandinavia and Iceland

Testament to the widespread dissemination of the Arthur legend in this part of the world is a manuscript known as the *Hauksbok* which includes two Old Norse translations of Geoffrey of Monmouth's works: the *Merlínusspá* (c.1200) and the *Breta So gur* (early thirteenth century). At the same time, writers at the court of the Norwegian king Hákon IV (who reigned 1217–63) were responsible for several Old Norse prose translations of Arthurian tales, including *Parcevals saga*, *Tristrams saga ok Ísöndar* and *Ívens saga*. The *Tristrams saga* (which itself derives from Thomas of Britain's *Tristan*) was particularly popular in Iceland, giving rise to several folktales and a fifteenth-century ballad called 'Tristrams Kvæði' (a Danish version was called 'Tristram og Jomfru Isolt'). In 1303 *Ivan Lejonriddaren*, a Swedish translation of Chrétien's *Yvain*, was made in rhymed couplets.

(Left) An illuminated initial from the Flateyjarbok, *a manuscript containing the saga of Arthurian enthusiast Hákon IV (wearing the crown). This Norwegian king commissioned several translations of French Arthurian romances.*

Germany

In 1281 German merchants gathered at Magdeburg for an Arthurian competition sponsored by the city's burghers. The poet Hartmann von Aue had introduced Arthurian literature to the German-speaking world in c.1200 with his two romances *Erec* and *Iwein*. The Swiss author Ulrich von Zatzikhoven composed, shortly after this, the romance *Lanzelet*. Wirnt von Grafenberg's *Wigalois* (c.1200–15) narrates the adventures of Gawein's son, while Gawein himself is the focus of Heinrich von dem Türlin's *Die Crône* (c.1230). Wolfram von Eschenbach's *Parzifal* was followed by *Der Nüwe Parzefal*, by an unknown author, a century later and, in the fifteenth century, Parzifal's adventures were included in Ulrich Fuetrer's *Das Buch der Abenteuer*. Building on the works by Eilhart von Oberge and Gott-fried von Strassburg, the Tristan tradition came to be particularly appealing to German audiences. Both Ulrich von Türheim (1235) and Heinrich von Freiberg (1290) attempted to complete Gottfried's *Tristan*, and Tristan was to appear repeatedly in late medieval German chapbooks.

The Cathedral in Magdeburg, Germany, the city in which an Arthurian pageant was held in 1281. Arthur so dominated German medieval literature that German courtly epic is called Artusepik, *'Arthurian epic'.*

The Byzantine and Slavic World

A Greek poem called *Ho Presbys Hippotes*, written c.1300, concerns an old knight whom neither Gawain, Lancelot, nor Tristan is able to defeat. This is significant in being one of the earliest examples of Arthurian literature from this

(Below) Prince Charles Bridge, Prague, built c.1357. The fourteenth-century Czech king John of Luxemburg built a wooden hall to house Round Table festivities.

(Right) Mount Etna, Sicily, with Graeco-Roman theatre in the foreground. Local legend, first recorded in the early thirteenth century, claims that Arthur lies sleeping inside the mountain.

vast and varied territory. But in these lands there is discernible – as in much of continental Europe – a particular fascination with the Tristan story. One of the earliest complete versions of the Tristan story is *Tristram a Izalda*, a Czech work of the late fourteenth century. Earlier that century, in 1319, an Arthurian tournament was held in Prague, where *minnesinger* were accustomed to compare their kings to Arthur. Then there was the *Povest' o Tryshchane*, a Slavic version of the Prose *Tristan*, produced in the sixteenth century and often called the *Byelorussian Tristan*.

The Middle East

The first Arthurian tournament on record anywhere is that held on the island of Cyprus in 1223. Then, almost two hundred years after the First Crusade, in 1286, when Henry II of Cyprus was crowned King of Jerusalem at Acre, a lavish pageant including fighting and imitation 'round tables' was held. These tournaments remind us of the integral role played by crusader knights in spreading the Arthurian legends.

The Round Table of the Last Supper, from a twelfth-century Syrian manuscript.

Italy

The Arthurian legends arrived in Italy at an early date, as witnessed by the Arthurian scenes depicted at the Italian cathedrals of Modena, Bari and Otranto. One early legend claimed that Arthur was not dead, but sleeping inside Mount Etna! Both Dante (1265–1321) and Boccaccio (1313–75) make allusions to Arthurian figures and themes, most famously in Dante's *Inferno* where Francesca blames the description of Lancelot and Guinevere's first kiss as having been responsible for her and Paolo's damnation. Examples of Italian Tristan stories include the *Tristano Riccardiano* (1280), the *Tristano Panciaticchiano* (fourteenth century) and *La Tavola Ritonda* (1340). Arthur and his knights make frequent appearances in the Italian *cantari* of the thirteenth and fourteenth centuries, especially in the compositions of Antonio Pucci (*c.*1310– 88). Other Italian singers began fusing the stories of Arthur with those of Charlemagne (r. 768– 814), making them contemporaries, as in Ariosto's masterpiece *Orlando Furioso* (1516).

Spain and Portugal

The Christian kings of Aragon were particularly fond of Arthurian celebrations. These are on record for Valencia in 1269, Saragossa in 1286, Barcelona in 1290 and Calatayud in 1291. The *Queste del Saint Graal* was translated into both Spanish (*Demanda del Sancto Grial*) and Portuguese (*Demanda do Santo Graal*) in the fifteenth century, which also saw translations of the Tristan story, such as the Aragonese *El Cuento de Tristán de Leonís*. An anonymous Catalan poet gave us the Provençal romance *Jaufré* (1220), while the Spanish poet Garci Rodríguez de Montalvo reworked earlier anonymous verse to create *Amadís de Gaula* (1508). The *Amadís* is known to readers of Cervantes, for it is this romance which so obsessed Don Quixote that he set out on a tragi-comic quest to outdo the deeds of Arthur's knights.

(Right) The Aragonese coat of arms on the façade of the Lonja de la Seda in Valencia. Alfonso the Magnanimous of Aragon is said to have preferred the arms of Tristan on his shield at tournaments.

The Late Medieval English Tradition

THOUGH FRENCH LITERATURE dominated at the courts of medieval England, it should surprise no one that as soon as an English vernacular tradition developed it would include stories about King Arthur and his knights. Arthur appears as a character in no fewer than twenty Middle English romances written between the latter half of the thirteenth century and the beginning of the sixteenth. He and his knights also appear in numerous songs, poems and works of art in this same period, and ultimately in one of the most ambitious and acclaimed works in all of medieval literature, Malory's *Le Morte d'Arthur*.

The Wife of Bath, illustration from William Caxton's 1484 edition of Chaucer's The Canterbury Tales.

The Middle English lays

Arthur made his first appearances in English literature through the chronicles and pseudo-chronicles. Many of these, such as Layamon's *Brut*, were written in verse and were inspired by Geoffrey of Monmouth's *History*. The majority of English authors, however, drew their inspiration from the French songs and romances popular at Anglo-Norman courts. One such example is a group of Middle English lays, based on Breton oral compositions, which were written in the fourteenth and fifteenth centuries. Included in this group are several versions of Marie de France's *Lanval*, the most notable being *Sir Launfal* by Thomas Chestre (in the late fourteenth century). Chestre is also the likely author of *Libeaus Desconus*, a poem featuring Gawain's son Gyngalyn as the 'Fair Unknown'.

Chaucer

The most famous English author to make use of such lays and romances is Geoffrey Chaucer, as he admits in *The Canterbury Tales*, in the Prologue to 'The Franklin's Tale':

> Thise olde gentil Britouns in her dayes
> Of diverse aventures maden layes,
> Rymeyed in hir firste Briton tonge,
> Which layes with hir instrumentz they songe.

Of course, Chaucer's versions of these lays and romances in *The Canterbury Tales* (*c*.1400) are not straightforward celebrations of chivalric ideals, but usually laced with irony and satire. It is ironic, to begin with, that Chaucer's Wife of Bath should choose for her tale an Arthurian romance, given her earthy and non-courtly demeanour. But 'The Wife of Bath's Tale' is a clever reworking of the Gawain and the Loathly Lady theme found in other, less famous English romances. Here, an unnamed young knight has raped a maiden and stands in judgment before Arthur and Guinevere. The queen spares the knight's life if he will seek and find the answer to the question, 'What do women most desire?' An old hag promises to give the knight his answer if he, in return, will promise to marry her. The desperate knight fulfils his promise, but rejects the woman on their wedding night, saying that she repels him because of her age, ugliness and low birth. After chiding her husband for his lack of gentility, the woman asks him whether he would have her old, ugly and faithful, or young, beautiful and possibly unfaithful. The knight answers by giving her the choice – granting her the sovereignty that is what she says all women most desire – and she rewards him by becoming perpetually fair and constant.

Geoffrey Chaucer, from a late-sixteenth-century English manuscript.

The English Gawain tradition

Though unnamed in 'The Wife of Bath's Tale', in other versions of this romance the knight is Gawain. Gawain had, early on in the French Arthurian tradition, attained a reputation for being a model of chivalry and courtly manners (though he is rarely featured as the subject of his own romance). This reputation, however, led many poets to use Gawain to make gentle criticisms of such medieval aristocratic values, to the extent that later French portraits of Gawain were sometimes unflattering. In the Middle English literary tradition, however, Gawain is restored to the position of paragon of prowess and courtesy, and he is featured in several romances as the chief protagonist.

GAWAIN

Sir Gawain (Gauvain, Gawein) has long and close associations with King Arthur. As Gwalchmei he appears in the early Welsh tradition, and as Walwanus in the histories of William of Malmesbury and Geoffrey of Monmouth. In the later French and English romances he is the eldest son of King Lot of Lothian and Orkney. His mother, Morgause (or Anna), was Arthur's sister, or half-sister, and thus as Arthur's nephew he achieved a position of prominence at Camelot at an early age. He is usually depicted as being courteous and well-mannered, making him attractive to the ladies – a mixed blessing and cause of many of his adventures (and misadventures). His great strength was, curiously, said to increase until noonday and decrease with the setting of the sun, while his hot temper led him into frequent feuds. His sometimes violent nature prevented him from achieving the Holy Grail, though he was the first to vow to make the quest. In some romances he marries a woman named Ragnell, and his sons appear occasionally as Round Table knights. Gawain is always depicted as having strong affection for family members and, usually, for Lancelot as well. This friendship turned to revenge when, after the rescue of Guinevere at the stake, Gawain held Lancelot responsible for the deaths of his brothers Gareth and Gaheris. After challenging the reluctant Lancelot to a duel, Gawain suffered injuries from which he died soon after. Before his death, however, he forgave Lancelot and asked him to come to Arthur's aid against Mordred.

Detail from William Dyce's Sir Gawain Swearing to be Merciful and Never be Against Ladies *(1854), fresco from the Royal Robing Room, Westminster.*

The most famous of these stories is *Sir Gawain and the Green Knight*, written by an anonymous northwest Midlands poet *c*.1400. Written in alliterative stanzas, it is one of the true masterpieces of medieval verse romance. The poem begins with the appearance of the wondrous Green Knight at Arthur's New Year's Day feast at Camelot. The visitor unleashes ridicule and contempt upon Arthur's court, until the valiant Gawain volunteers to replace Arthur in accepting the knight's challenge to deliver one uncontested blow with his axe, and to receive the same a year later. With one mighty swing Gawain beheads the stranger, only to see the body retrieve its gruesome head, from which issues a reminder to Gawain of his promise. The Green Knight then gallops away.

Almost a year later Gawain leaves Camelot to find the Green Chapel and receive his blow. On the way he is received at a castle whose lord and lady entertain him lavishly during the last three days before his scheduled meeting with the Green Knight. Before going off to hunt, the lord suggests a game, whose content he does not make clear, but in which it is agreed that he and Gawain shall – that evening – exchange that day's 'winnings'. In the absence of the lord, his lady tries to seduce Gawain, but the knight only permits a few kisses and embraces. On his return from hunting, the lord demands of Gawain whatever he had 'won' that day and Gawain is obliged to exchange the same number of kisses with the lord. He does not reveal the source of these, however, nor does he admit to the green girdle which the lady has given him as a good-luck token. When New Year's Day arrives, Gawain journeys to the chapel and meets the Green Knight, who, after first feigning two swings (intended to unnerve Gawain), delivers the promised blow. But it only grazes Gawain's neck. This is meant as a punishment for Gawain, it turns out: had he not concealed the girdle the Green Knight would have missed altogether, for he reveals himself to be Sir Bertilak, the lord who played host to Gawain at his castle. He explains that the entire game, including the seductions, was arranged by Morgan le Fay to discredit Arthur and his knights. Gawain henceforth wears the girdle as a reminder of his failure, but the other knights of the Round Table adopt similar badges in honour of Gawain's courage.

The Alliterative *Morte Arthure* and the Stanzaic *Le Morte Arthur*

Sir Gawain and the Alliterative *Morte Arthure* (late fourteenth century) are part of a general revival of alliteration in English poetry. *Morte Arthure* furthers this homage to Old English verse by using archaic terms and epic themes. The poem begins with a great military adventure: Arthur defies the Roman emperor and sets off to conquer the Empire, leaving Mordrede behind as regent. Though he slays giants and defeats Roman armies on the Continent, Arthur loses his companions Kayous and Bedwere in the fighting. Even more disturbing is the news he receives that Mordrede has seized both his crown and his queen. Returning to England he is able to defeat Mordrede's allies at sea, but loses Gawain in a land campaign. A grieving and vengeful Arthur defeats Mordrede's forces in Cornwall and slays the usurper, but himself receives a mortal blow and is buried at Glastonbury after turning over the reins of government to Constantyne.

SIR GAWAIN AND THE GREEN KNIGHT

'For barely had . . . the first course in the court
been courteously served,
When there heaved in at the hall door an awesome fellow
Who in height outstripped all earthly men.
From throat to thigh he was so thickset and square,
His loins and limbs were so long and so great,
That he was half a giant on earth, I believe. . . .
Men gaped at the hue of him
Ingrained in garb and mien,
A fellow fiercely grim,
And all a glittering green.'

Illustration from a medieval English manuscript of Sir Gawain and the Green Knight.

(Right) King Edward IV, who reigned 1461–83, led the House of York against the House of Lancaster in the Wars of the Roses, the strife which so influenced Malory in his depiction of the Arthurian saga. Mid-sixteenth century portrait, by an unknown artist.

The Alliterative *Morte Arthure* drew upon the pseudo-chroniclers – Geoffrey of Monmouth, Wace and Layamon – whereas the Stanzaic *Le Morte Arthur* deals with essentially the same episode in Arthur's reign but it derives from the French romance *Mort Artu*. Not surprisingly, given his place in the French tradition, Lancelot plays a more prominent role, though his love for Gaynor (Guinevere) is revealed to be as much responsible for the fall of Camelot as is Mordred's usurpation. From its French source the Stanzaic *Morte* includes such episodes as Lancelot and the Maid of Astolat (p. 140), Guinevere and the poisoned apple, and Gawayn's vengeance upon Lancelot for the deaths of his brothers. Furthermore, the anonymous poet of the *Morte* introduces original scenes such as the adder whose appearance sparks the final battle (here located on Salisbury Plain) and the poignant farewell scene between Lancelot and Guinevere.

Malory

All these scenes made their way into the masterpiece which marks the culmination of English chivalric romance, the *magnum opus* of medieval Arthurian literature, Sir Thomas Malory's *Morte d'Arthur*. So, too, did the diverse traditions discussed throughout this chapter – the chronicles, the French romances, the stories of Tristan and those of the Grail Quest – which come together in one great prose epic that would be responsible for the way all succeeding centuries viewed the story of Arthur. But, like Arthur himself, this work is shrouded in mystery.

In 1485, England's first printer, William Caxton, published a book called *Le Morte d'Arthur* attributed to one 'Sir Thomas Maleoré, knyght'. An earlier text, known as the Winchester manuscript, bears the same attribution. The author concludes his work by stating that it was finished in the ninth year of the reign of King Edward IV (that is, 1469/70), and asks the reader to pray for his deliverance: he is, he confirms elsewhere, a knight prisoner.

Who is this Thomas Malory, the knight who composed a chivalric epic in jail? It turns out that there are records for nine men bearing this name in the years 1469–70, which has lead to a great deal of speculation and controversy surrounding the authorship of the *Morte d'Arthur*. The strongest candidate is Sir Thomas Malory of Newbold Revel in Warwickshire. This man was indeed a knight and a prisoner, having been accused of rape, theft, church-robbery, cattle-rustling, extortion and attempted murder! The 1460s witnessed the height of the Wars of the Roses, and this Thomas Malory was caught in the middle of Yorkist and Lancastrian feuds which may have led to politically motivated charges against him. He was apparently freed by the Lancastrians in 1470 and when he died, a year later, was afforded a very expensive burial at Greyfriars, Newgate.

A life-long Arthurian enthusiast, Malory was amazingly adept at collecting a wide variety of sources and reworking them – and in many cases improving them – to fit his vision of Camelot (all the more so since he neither owned the books nor had easy access to the libraries that contained them). The most important of these sources are the Vulgate Cycle, the Prose *Tristan*, the Alliterative *Morte Arthure* and the Stanzaic *Le Morte Arthur*. He chose some episodes and discarded others, creating a narrative chain that extends from the conception of Arthur to the death of Lancelot. The achievements of Arthur (aided by Merlin) are recounted early on, then the emphasis is shifted to the adventures of his greatest knights: Balin the Savage, King Pellinore and his son Tor, the cousins Gawaine and Uwaine, Launcelot, Gareth, Tristram, Palomides, Lamorak, and the Grail knights Galahad, Perceval and Bors. Tristram's story is the most extensive of these tales, though the least satisfactory in terms of unity and purpose, while the Grail Quest is a strong adaptation of the Vulgate *Quest*, with the emphasis placed on Galahad.

As in the French romances, Arthur tends to fade into the background during the recounting of his knights' adventures. After Malory describes Arthur's foreign and domestic wars, the

WILLIAM CAXTON

Until 1934, the earliest edition of Malory's Le Morte d'Arthur *known to us was the Westminster edition published (in 1485) by William Caxton. But in that year an older, slightly damaged manuscript (now in the British Library) was discovered at Winchester College. In 1947 Eugene Vinaver published an edition of the Winchester Malory, which he showed differs and is independent from Caxton's. Vinaver also challenged Caxton's vision of the* Morte d'Arthur *as a whole and complete work, saying that Caxton had imposed unity on what Malory had intended to be eight separate books.*

William Caxton's trademark and initials.

The Death of Lancelot

'Then went Sir Bors unto Sir Ector, and told him how there lay his brother, Sir Launcelot, dead; and then Sir Ector threw his shield, sword, and helm from him. And when he beheld Sir Launcelot's visage, he fell down in a swoon. And when he waked it were hard any tongue to tell the doleful complaints that he made for his brother. "Ah Launcelot," he said, "thou were head of all Christian knights, and now I dare say," said Sir Ector, "thou Sir Launcelot, there thou liest, that thou were never matched of earthly knight's hand. And thou were the courteoust knight that ever bare shield. And thou were the truest friend to thy lover that ever bestrad horse. And thou were the truest lover of a sinful man that ever loved woman. And thou were the kindest man that ever struck with sword. And thou were the goodliest person that ever came among press of knights. And thou was the meekest man and the gentlest that ever ate in hall among ladies. And thou were the sternest knight to thy mortal foe that ever put spear to rest." Then there was weeping and dolour out of measure.'

From Malory's Le Morte d'Arthur

Illustration by Wynkyn de Worde for the 1498 edition of Malory's Le Morte d'Arthur.

focus begins to move away from the greatest of kings to the greatest of knights, Launcelot. Malory follows Launcelot closely through his ups and downs. When an unhappy Launcelot takes to calling himself *le Chevalier mal Fait*, 'the Ill-Made Knight', we wonder (as T.H. White did) if the imprisoned author is commiserating with his hero. Indeed, though the book builds up to the dramatic climax of Arthur's passing, it ends with Lancelot's death and a powerful eulogy delivered by his brother Ector (see box, above).

Thomas Malory's death prevented him from witnessing the tremendous impact his book would have – and not just on the Arthurian tradition. Caxton's publication of Malory's *Morte d'Arthur* ushered in an Indian summer of English chivalry, actively promoted at the courts of the new Tudor monarchs. At the very time that Italian Renaissance artists were promoting classical virtues and heroes, the quintessential medieval king was made relevant for a new age. His deeds, as told in splendorous detail by the rogue knight from Newbold Revel, were welcomed as the proud family inheritance of a bold and ambitious breed of English monarchs.

VI

Monarchy, Chivalry and the Return of Arthur

Then loudly cried the bold Sir Bedivere:
'Ah! my Lord Arthur, whither shall I go?
Where shall I hide my forehead and my eyes?
For now I see the true old times are dead,
When every morning brought a noble chance,
And every chance brought out a noble knight.'

Alfred Tennyson, *Idylls of the King*

THE LEGENDS OF the Britons provided great entertainment for aristocratic audiences throughout medieval Europe. With the exception of some ballads and *fabliaux*, Arthurian works relied on the patronage and tastes of the nobility until well after the invention of the printing press. Fortunately, British royalty has shown an enthusiasm for Arthur from the middle of the twelfth century onwards. This royal interest has not been limited to entertainment, however, for several British monarchs have tried to emulate Arthur, evening claiming him as an ancestor. As Britain went on to create a world empire, Arthur and Camelot have grown from medieval literary subjects to universal symbols, transcending any particular culture and becoming applicable to any age. In the nineteenth century, artists as diverse as Alfred Tennyson, Mark Twain and Richard Wagner understood this symbolic dimension of Arthuriana, making their own significant contributions to the tradition and ensuring its appeal to modern audiences in the next century and beyond.

Chivalry in Victorian England: Knight at the Eglinton Tournament *(c.1839), painting by Edward Henry Corbould of Lord Eglinton dressed for his infamous tournament, held in 1839 as part of a conscious attempt by the British nobility to revive chivalry and Arthurian ideals.*

(Right) 'The Rescue of Guinevere', sculpted c.1120–40 on the archivolt above the Porta della Pescheria of the cathedral at Modena, Italy.

THE INTERNATIONALIZATION OF the Arthurian legends began very early on. As early as 1120, a sculptor in northern Italy was carving 'The Rescue of Guinevere' in the archivolt above the north portal of Modena Cathedral (right). Two of the queen's rescuers are named, as Artus of Bretania and Galvagin, and indeed Arthur and Gawain (in their various forms) became popular names on the Continent in the twelfth century. This age is full of accounts of travellers encountering local Arthurian stories and storytellers, as well as geographic features in Britain, Brittany and even in more distant lands.

The first impetus for this widespread interest in Arthuriana was, perhaps, the First Crusade (1096–99), during which French and Breton knights must have carried Arthurian stories first to Italy and thence to the Middle East. But its longevity ultimately depended on the patronage of the Plantagenet dynasty in England. Robert, Earl of Gloucester and supporter of the empress Matilda during the civil war of the mid-twelfth century, was a patron of William of Malmesbury, Henry of Huntingdon and Geoffrey of Monmouth. Robert was also for a time the guardian of Matilda's young son, Henry Plantagenet, who, we can presume, must have come into contact with these writers or their works at an early age.

(Above) Henry II, first Plantagenet king of England, here depicted in a miniature from a medieval manuscript.

Henry II and Richard I

As king of England after Stephen's death in 1154, Henry displayed an active interest in the Arthurian legend for both its entertainment and its political value. He was so impressed with Wace's *Roman de Brut*, a copy of which Layamon says was presented to Queen Eleanor, that he commissioned the clerk to write a history of the dukes of Normandy. Marie de France, thought by some historians to be the half-sister of Henry, dedicated her Tristan lay *Chevrefueil* to the 'noble king', while the Anglo-Norman poet Thomas gave the hero in his *Tristan* the gold lion shield device often used by Henry. Besides entertainment, the Matter of Britain gave Henry a royal predecessor in Arthur whose antiquity was

The Crusader assault on Jerusalem in 1099, as depicted in a fourteenth-century French manuscript. The Crusades played an important part in spreading the Arthurian legends throughout Europe and to the Middle East.

ARTHUR'S GRAVE

Arthur's end has always been something of an enigma. The Welsh tradition made no mention of its location, and the Bretons denied that Arthur ever died. But Henry II announced that, from information provided by a Breton singer, he had located Arthur's grave at Glastonbury Abbey. An excavation was conducted by Glastonbury monks in 1190 or 1191, which revealed a coffin containing the bones of a large man together with smaller bones and a lock of golden hair. An inscribed cross was also found which indeed identified this as Arthur's grave, though it was subsequently lost. The Latin inscription (below, right) from William Camden's drawing of the cross translates 'Here lies the famous King Arthur in the Isle of Avalon'. (Gerald of Wales recorded that it also mentioned Guinevere, presumably on the reverse side.)

(Above) Drawing of the Glastonbury Cross from William Camden's Britannia *(1607 edition). (Left) The exhumation of Arthur and Guinevere at Glastonbury Abbey. Modern illustration by Judith Dobie.*

ARTHURIAN HERALDRY

Medieval heraldry, originating in the twelfth century, consisted of shield devices and helmet crests used to identify a knight in battle, at a tournament or on his seal. They were hereditary and carried legal status. The authors of the Arthurian romances assigned such devices to Arthur and his knights. Among the most frequently seen are (from left to right) Arthur's, the three gold crowns on a red (English) or blue (French) background; Gawain's, a gold pentangle on a red background; Lancelot's, three red stripes on a silver or white background; Galahad's, a red cross on a white background; Perceval's, a red heart on a white background; and Tristan's, a gold harp on a green background. The symbols often refer to specific episodes in the romances, though Arthurian heraldry has also evolved over time.

greater than that of Charlemagne, whose legacy was claimed by Henry's Capetian rivals. Indeed, if we are to believe Geoffrey of Monmouth, Arthur's deeds were even greater than Charlemagne's and included the conquests of Ireland, Scotland, Wales and Gaul – a veritable master plan for Henry's own territorial ambitions.

It was said that a British bard disclosed to Henry the secret location of Arthur's grave shortly before the monarch's death in 1189. Henry encouraged the Glastonbury monks to look for the grave, and the excavation (see box, p. 129) was carried out with the support of Henry's successor, Richard I (r. 1189–99). Many have presumed that the excavation was a hoax perpetuated by the Abbey in order to increase donations from pilgrims and royals. Archaeologists, however, have proved that the excavation did take place and that the site was inhabited in the fifth or sixth century. As for the cross, the style of the inscription (of which there remains a drawing by William Camden) suggests it is much older than twelfth century, but probably not as old as sixth century. But since both the bones and the cross have been missing since the sixteenth century, the mystery of Arthur's grave continues.

Finding Arthur and venerating his remains at a new Glastonbury shrine would provide a Plantagenet counter to the Capetian cult of Charlemagne. It might also quiet the so-called 'Breton hope': in 1187 the son born to Geoffrey Plantagenet (Richard's brother) and Constance of Brittany was named Arthur, 'the hope of his people' according to one chronicler. Was the christening of Henry II's grandson with the name Arthur done in honour of the Plantagenets' adopted forebear, or in the hope of Breton independence?

Richard must have felt some loyalty to this Arthur, for he declared his young nephew heir to the English throne. Henry's youngest son John, however, had no wish to see a reigning King Arthur II. John and his mother, Eleanor of Aquitaine, loathed both Constance and Arthur, and then Arthur made the fatal mistake of allying with the Capetian Philip Augustus. While Arthur was besieging Eleanor's castle in 1203, John captured his nephew and had him executed – by some accounts, strangling the sixteen-year old with his own hands!

Edward III

The official dynastic worship of Arthur continued unabated, however. In 1191, during the Third Crusade, Richard gave a sword that he claimed was Excalibur to his friend Tancred of Sicily. Even his brother, King John (r. 1199–1216), possessed Arthurian relics in his royal regalia. Edward I (r. 1272–1307) returned to Glastonbury Abbey for a state visit at Easter 1278, and he and his queen put Arthur's remains on display before having the bones reinterred in a great tomb at the high altar. Of the Plantagenets, Edward III (r. 1327–77) was a particularly avid Arthurian, visiting Glastonbury, collecting Arthurian texts and wearing clothes embroidered with symbols from the Tristan romances. In 1344 the king proposed a revival of the Order of the Round Table. Though he went on to found the Order of the Garter instead, Edward encouraged the aristocratic pageants called 'round tables' that had been popular since the thirteenth century, and he may have been responsible for the construction of the Winchester Round Table (p. 134).

ARTHURIAN PAGEANTS

Geoffrey of Monmouth, in 1136, was the first to describe Arthur and his knights engaging in chivalric entertainments. The twelfth century saw the rise of the tournament movement in western Europe, and by the thirteenth century these aristocratic games could be found from Ireland to Outremer. Not surprisingly, European knights sought to mimic their Arthurian heroes in these tournaments, while noble ladies joined them in their imitations in the less violent pageants.

Both the church and monarchs such as Henry III of England tried to halt the spread of these dangerous entertainments in the thirteenth century. But the most effective deterrent was expense. By the fourteenth century only the richest nobles could afford to participate in the tournaments, and membership became even more restricted through the advent of secular orders, including the Order of the Golden Fleece in Burgundy, and the Order of the Garter in England (Edward III formed the Order of the Garter after an abortive attempt at an Order of the Round Table). Chivalric pageantry reached its climax at the Burgundian court of Duke Philip the Bold in the late fifteenth century. Thereafter, English imitations in the Tudor period became purely ceremonial, but no less devoted to Arthurian themes.

Arthur presiding over a tournament, from a fifteenth-century Flemish manuscript.

TRY AS THEY might, the Plantagenets could not claim sole possession of Arthur. When Geoffrey of Monmouth vividly depicted the pageantry of Arthur's plenary court, he made Arthur an international symbol of the aristocratic culture of chivalry. Medieval nobles across Europe and in the Crusader States sought to emulate their Arthurian heroes, and Arthur took his place alongside historical figures such as Charlemagne and the crusader Godefroy de Bouillon among the so-called Nine Worthies.

One English knight who tried to emulate the chivalry of the Arthurian romances was Sir Thomas Malory (p. 124). Writing at the height of the Wars of the Roses in the mid-fifteenth century, Malory captured all the violence and pageantry of his age, yet gave us an Arthur and his Round Table knights who stood for a higher purpose than the petty feuds of the kingdom outside the walls of Camelot. This was a powerful and promising myth, and the first to be ensnared by it was the printer William Caxton. In the preface to Malory's *Le Morte d'Arthur*, Caxton wrote:

> I have . . . emprised to imprint a book of the noble histories of the said King Arthur, and of certain of his knights, after a copy unto me delivered, which copy Sir Thomas Malorye did take out of certain books of French, and reduced it into English. And I, according to my copy, have set in imprint, to the intent that noble men may see and learn the noble acts of chivalry, the gentle and virtuous deeds that some knights used in those days. . . . For herein may be seen noble chivalry, courtesy, humanity, friendliness, hardiness, love, friendship, cowardice, murder, hate, virtue and sin. Do after the good and leave the evil, and it shall bring you to good fame and renown.

ARTHUR AND THE NINE WORTHIES

Arthur had truly 'arrived' in medieval culture when he was included in les neuf preux, *the 'Nine Worthies' celebrated in European arts from the early fourteenth century. The group consisted of three pagans (Hector of Troy, Alexander the Great, Julius Caesar), three Jews (Joshua, King David, Judas Maccabeus) and three Christians (Arthur, Charlemagne, Godefroy de Bouillon) who achieved great military success. Mentioned in some late medieval literary works, the Nine Worthies are more often found in the visual arts. Tapestries, sculptures, manuscript miniatures, murals and stained glass windows are just some of the media which bore their likenesses. Jean, Duc de Berry, and the Habsburg emperor Maximillian I are two of the more notable collectors of this art.*

The Nine Worthies appear together in a castle hall in this medieval French manuscript illustration. Arthur, third from the right, flies his heraldic standard: three golden crowns.

Henry VII

Caxton published his version of *Morte d'Arthur* in 1485. That very year, an English baron who bore the Welsh family name Tudor returned from exile in Brittany to march against the king of England at Bosworth Field. Fighting under the banner of the Red Dragon, Henry Tudor defeated Richard III and established a new dynasty which would not only view Arthur as a symbol of their vigorous monarchy, but indeed as a beloved ancestor. For Henry VII (r. 1485–1509) laid claim to the English throne by uniting, through marriage, the warring houses of York and Lancaster, as well as by being a descendant of Cadwallader (the last king of the Britons according to Geoffrey of Monmouth) and ultimately of Arthur himself.

When Henry's new wife Elizabeth became pregnant, the king transported his queen to the city of Winchester to await the royal birth. A son was delivered in the city that Malory had identified as Camelot, and in the shadow of the great Round Table the boy was christened Arthur, 'that there might once more be a king of that name in Britain'. Of course, Henry's plan that his eldest son should reign as Arthur II, with Catherine of Aragon at his side, came crashing down with Arthur's premature death in 1502. All hope was transferred to Arthur's brother, Henry, who married Catherine and became if not Arthur reborn (*Arturius Redivivus*) – then 'Arthur magnified'.

Henry VIII

Henry (r. 1509–47) was a chivalric youth, an athlete who enjoyed jousting and the pageants that had fallen out of fashion in England since the days of Edward III. In 1511, he spent over £4000 on a tournament at Winchester (in which he himself participated) celebrating the birth of his son, yet another Prince Arthur (this Arthur lived only 52 days). In 1520, at the Field of the Cloth of Gold, Henry defiantly faced the French king Francis I with pennants and trappings depicting Arthur as a world conqueror. Two years later another rival, the emperor Charles V, paid a state visit during which Henry escorted the young Habsburg monarch to Winchester and showed off its great Round Table, newly repainted in Tudor green and gold and now bearing the image of an enthroned Arthur with Henry's visage.

Not all writers of the Tudor period accepted the Arthurian myth. As early as 1485 Caxton noted that some men 'holde oppynyon that there was no suche Arthur, and that all suche bookes as been maad of hym ben but fayned and fables'. Early Tudor chroniclers, such as Fabyan and Rastell, showed some learned scepticism over Arthur's exploits as told by Geoffrey of Monmouth and his imitators. But the real attack came from the Italian humanist Polydore Virgil, brought to court by Henry VII. In his *Historia*, of 1534, Polydore dismisses Geoffrey and the medieval chroniclers, and asks why, if Arthur had lived, his exploits are not to be found in the early histories of Gildas and Bede? Such doubts were seen by some to contradict Tudor ancestral claims and, coming from a foreigner, to be anti-English. An emotional backlash, coming mainly from emerging Protestant nationalists, resulted in a flurry of mid-sixteenth-century chronicles of early British history that exalted the deeds of Arthur and became enormously popular.

Many of these Tudor chronicles, including that of Raphael Holinshed, explicitly retold Arthur's conquests to bolster contemporary Tudor claims over Scotland and Ireland (both Henry and his daughter Elizabeth passed legislation that cited Arthurian chronicles as justification for the Tudors' use of the term 'Imperial Crown'). The most vigorous defence of Arthur's historicity came from John Leland (c.1503–52), who attacked Polydore's negative logic with both archaeological and documentary evidence of Arthur's existence. Separating the more fantastical elements, like the Brutus legend, from that of Arthur, Leland admits to the inclusion of fictitious material but declares that this is insufficient for denying Arthur altogether.

Prince Arthur Tudor, son and heir of Henry VII, in a contemporary portrait.

(Left) Henry VII, founder of the Tudor dynasty (here in a bust by Pietro Torrigiano). Born at Pembroke Castle, exiled in Brittany, the young prince was, according to contemporary Welsh bards, another Arthur, who would rise to rescue the Welsh from Saxon tyranny.

The Winchester Round Table, which hangs in the great hall of Winchester Castle. This massive (18 ft, or 5.5m, in diameter) oak table top, constructed no earlier than the thirteenth century, was believed by Caxton and many others to be the authentic table of Arthur. It was painted early in the reign of Henry VIII, perhaps for a state visit by the emperor Charles V in 1522.

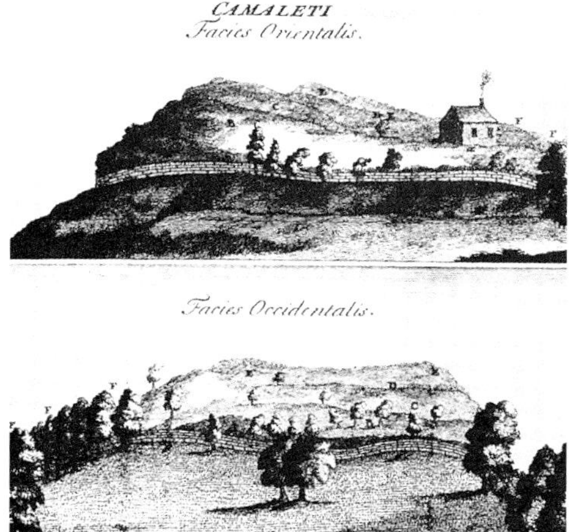

Sketches of the cncient hillfort at South Cadbury, from Musgrave's Antiquitates Britanno-Belgicae *(1719). Beginning in the sixteenth century there are records of this site being identified by locals as Arthur's Camelot.*

The Elizabethans

These pro-Arthur chronicles remained popular and influential during the reign of Elizabeth I (1558–1603), as those who have delved into the source material for Shakespeare's history plays can easily attest. Elizabeth, like her father in his youth, had a penchant for court pageant and ceremony that recalled with nostalgia the heyday of English chivalry. Among her summer 'progresses' through the countryside was a stay at Kenilworth, in 1575, where Robert Dudley, the earl of Leicester entertained the queen with actors playing Arthur and the Lady of the Lake. In 1581 English tournaments were officially revived to celebrate, annually, Elizabeth's accession, with Burgundian-style tilting matches that were to remain popular into the early Stuart years. But

(Above) Sir John Gilbert, The Field of the Cloth of Gold *(nineteenth century). The young Henry VIII held spectacular Arthurian-style tournaments at his banqueting house in Calais, most notably in the summer of 1520 when he was joined by the French king, Francis I, for two weeks of revelry.*

the most remarkable of these neo-chivalric institutions was the Elizabethan Society of Archers, also know as 'Prince Arthur's Round Table'. In Shakespeare's *Henry IV, Part II*, Shallow boasts 'I was then Sir Dagonet in Arthur's show' (a hollow boast, for Dagonet was Arthur's fool).

There are many interesting links between Elizabethan literary figures and the Society of Archers. One of the Elizabethan chroniclers, Richard Robinson, dedicated his translation of Leland's Arthurian essay to Lord Grey of Wilton, Sir Henry Sidney and 'the Worshipfull Societie of Archers, in London yearly celebrating the renoumed memorie of the Magnificent Prince Arthure and his Knightly Order of the Round Table'. Sir Henry was the father of the courtier and poet Sir Philip Sidney, who in turn was the friend of Lord Grey's secretary, Edmund Spenser. Philip Sidney had toyed with the idea of converting his masterpiece, *The Arcadia*, into a series of Arthurian stories. In his *Defence of Poetry*, he maintains that 'honest King Arthur will never displease a soldier'. Like Shakespeare, however, Sidney never produced a work devoted specifically to Arthur, though he would himself often assume the role of an Arthurian knight in Elizabeth's court pageants.

Elizabethan pageantry. This sixteenth-century miniature by Nicholas Hilliard depicts George Clifford, Earl of Cumberland and Queen's Champion, at a tournament in 1590 in which he styled himself 'Knight of Pendragon Castle'.

(Right) Gloriana, 'greatest Glorious Queene of Faerie londe'. The so-called 'Rainbow Portrait' of Elizabeth I, attributed to Marcus Gheeraerts.

Woodcut of 'The Red Cross Knight Slaying a Dragon' from an early edition of Spenser's The Faerie Queene *(1590).*

Edmund Spenser is the one Elizabethan literary giant who managed to tackle the Arthurian legend and bring something new to it. Spenser's connections with Tudor Arthurian enthusiasts are impressive. In addition to those mentioned above, his first teacher, Richard Mulcaster, was a member of the Society of Archers, and his Cambridge classmate Richard Harvey published a defence of Geoffrey of Monmouth's *History*. In his prefatory letter to Sir Walter Raleigh, Spenser states his reason for including Arthur in *The Faerie Queene* (1590): 'I labour to portraict in Arthure, before he was king, the image of a brave knight, perfected in the twelve private morall vertues, as Aristotle hath devised.' Uther, Merlin and Tristram all make appearances in *The Faerie Queene*, and the Red Cross Knight owes much to Malory's Sir Galahad. Spenser even amends his chronicle sources to bring Arthur more directly into the Tudor blood lines.

In this great allegorical epic, Prince Arthur represents the virtue of Magnificence. He enters the story at critical points in its action, like divine grace visiting the questing knights, before leaving again for his personal quest. His ultimate goal is union with Glory – that is, with Gloriana, or Elizabeth – which is the reward of all virtuous action. In dedicating an Arthurian epic poem to Elizabeth, Spenser follows Virgil 'by raising the popular material of legend to the dignity of classical form'. Despite its limited use of traditional Arthurian themes, Spenser's *Faerie Queene* has been credited with keeping the Arthurian story alive among writers from 1634 to 1816, a period when Malory's work was unprinted and little known even among English readers.

THE FAERIE QUEENE

'Faire virgin (said the Prince) ye me require
A thing without the compass of my wit:
For both the lignage and the certain Sire,
From which I sprong, from me are hidden yit.

Thither the great Magicien Merlin came,
as was his use, ofttimes to visit me:
For he had charge my discipline to frame,
And Tutours nouriture to ouersee.
Him oft and oft I askt in priuitie,
Of what loines and what lignage I did spring:
Whose aunswere bad me still assured bee,
That I was sonne and heire vnto a king,
As time in her iust terme the truth to light
should bring.

Well worthy impe, said then the Lady gent,
And Pupill fit for such a Tutours hand.
But what aduenture, or what high intent
Hath brought you hither into Faery land,
Aread Prince Arthur, crowne of Martiall band?'

Edmund Spenser, *The Faerie Queene, Book I, Canto IX, Verses 3–6*

THE FAERIE
QVEENE.
Disposed into twelue books,
Fashioning
XII. Morall vertues.

LONDON
Printed for William Ponsonbie.
1590.

The title page of Spenser's The Faerie Queene, *1590.*

The Stuarts

The death of Elizabeth in 1603 announced the end of the flowering of English chivalry and Arthurian romance. Jousts and pageants continued through the reign of her cousin and successor, James I, but Arthur was not a necessary ingredient in the Scottish king's absolutism. His eldest son, Prince Henry, did take Arthur as his personal symbol, and commissioned Ben Jonson and Inigo Jones to produce the Arthurian masque *Prince Henry's Barriers* in 1610. But this prince, who some predicted would be another Arthur, died young, and his brother Charles I (r. 1625–49) preferred classical to Arthurian themes. A more substantial work was John Dryden's 'dramatick opera' *King Arthur: or, The British Worthy*, first produced for James II in 1685, which, like *The Faerie Queene*, celebrates the monarchy through association with Arthur. But this first Arthurian opera is primarily remembered for the music of Henry Purcell (1659–95), perhaps the greatest English composer of the baroque period, and the story is Arthurian in name only.

THE PLANTAGENETS AND Tudors firmly established Arthur's association with the English monarchy. The Stuarts had inherited this, the association with Arthur remaining sufficiently strong for enemies of the Stuarts to become, by extension, enemies of the Arthurian romances. Many seventeenth-century Parliamentarians and Protestants were offended by the aristocratic and chivalric elements of these 'fables', as they saw them, and preferred to look back to Saxon law for the foundations of modern England, rather than to the Trojan Brutus (Geoffrey of Monmouth's eponymous founder of Britain). This led some of the leading literary figures of the day, such as Ben Jonson and John Milton, to abandon projected Arthurian works. In the rational eighteenth century, writers remained suspicious of medieval themes, and it is perhaps unsurprising that Arthur appears in burlesques such as Henry Fielding's *Tom Thumb* (1731). Not until the early nineteenth century would English writers return to Arthur for use in serious and ambitious projects.

Victoria and Albert

It would be somewhat misleading to state that the nineteenth-century revival of Arthur was inspired by another long-reigning British queen. Yet the Hanoverian Victoria (r. 1837–1901) was, even more than Elizabeth I, an imperial monarch in need of connection with Britain's illustrious past, and she willingly allowed the Arthurian mythology of her day to add to her mystique. In Spenser's *Faerie Queene*, Prince Arthur had been portrayed as Elizabeth's consort; in Tennyson's *Idylls of the King*, Victoria's consort Prince Albert was portrayed as Arthur, while Prime Minister Disraeli referred to his queen as 'the Faery'. Victoria commissioned painters to portray Albert as a chivalric figure, and Albert commissioned artists to decorate the queen's chambers at Westminster with scenes from Arthurian legend (p. 139). Their third son was christened Arthur.

Behind all this, however, is the general Gothic Revival that launched a fashion for medievalism in art and architecture, as well as in literature, throughout Europe. Britain fully embraced a return to its glorious – or fabulous – medieval past, launching a Victorian Cult of Chivalry. Modern Britons collected armour and discussed neo-feudalism in Parliament (see box, below). British writers dug up the medieval knight and reinvented him as a modern gentleman. Sir Walter Scott, whose novel *Ivanhoe* boosted the Gothic Revival in both Britain and America, vowed to edit a new version of Malory's *Le Morte*

Jessie M. King, 'King Arthur's Tomb', illustration for William Morris's The Defence of Guenevere and Other Poems *(1904).*

EGLINTON AND THE YOUNG ENGLAND PARTY

The first decade of Queen Victoria's reign saw a chivalric revival – in politics and at play – led by the peers of the realm. On 28 August 1839, the wealthy young aristocrat Archibald Montgomery, thirteenth Earl of Eglinton, hosted an earnestly medieval pageant complete with jousting. Unfortunately, it rained violently and the Victorian knights stumbled around in the mud while their ladies and other onlookers ran for the umbrellas! Though they were ridiculed in the poetry and newspapers of the day (this cartoon appeared with the caption 'Aristocratic Sense; Or, the Eglinton Tomfooleryment'), this did little to stop the Cult of Chivalry in Britain. In 1842 a faction of the Tory party in Parliament, led by Benjamin Disraeli and Lord John Manners, initiated what came to be known as the Young England movement. Mostly young aristocrats, they promoted a sort of neo-feudalism, calling for loyalty to the monarchy and to High Church ideals. But these conservatives also embraced social activism, calling for a return of noblesse oblige, *under which the rich and well-born were sworn protectors of the poor. Though the Tory party later split over repeal of the Corn Laws in 1846, Disraeli, like Tennyson, continued to search for new ways to make chivalric ideals relevant for modern society.*

Edwin Landseer, Queen Victoria and Prince Albert at the Bal Costumé of 12 May 1842.

Photo-portrait of Alfred Tennyson as 'The Dirty Monk', by Julia Margaret Cameron, to illustrate Idylls of the King and other poems *(1875).*

d'Arthur. That never materialized, but by 1816 several new and inexpensive editions began to appear. One, in 1817, was a deluxe edition by Robert Southey, then poet laureate of England, and many others – often lavishly illustrated – followed.

Tennyson

It was a later poet laureate, inspired by Malory, who would make the most ambitious and compelling contribution to the Arthurian repertoire of the Victorian age. Alfred Tennyson was a student at Cambridge in the 1830s when he first conceived his grand scheme: to rewrite the Arthurian legend for the modern world, in a new national epic. Intended to take twenty years, the project spanned Tennyson's lifetime, with his first Arthurian poems being published in scattered collections. Of these early works, 'Sir Galahad' and 'The Lady of Shalott' stand out as both critical and popular successes, and constitute an important part of the early corpus of his work that earned Tennyson laureate status in 1850.

THE QUEEN'S ROBING ROOM

Queen Victoria's 'Robing Room' at Westminster Palace is adorned, floor to ceiling, with homages to Britain's medieval past. In 1847 Prince Albert chose the artist William Dyce to lead the ambitious project. The Prince followed Dyce's recommendation that the stories of King Arthur, particularly those of the English writer Thomas Malory, should be the chief subject of the Westminster decorations. From 1848 to 1864 Dyce worked on a series of allegorical Arthurian frescoes, but both Albert and Dyce died before the fresco project was completed. In 1870, however, the artist Henry Hugh Armstead did complete a series of eighteen bas-relief panels in the oak frieze which depict events in the lives of Arthur and Galahad. Foliated stained-glass windows and heraldic stencils on the ceiling complete the effect – reviving Arthurian chivalry in celebration of a modern British Empire.

(Top) The Knights of the Round Table Vowing to Seek the Sancgreall *(1870), one of H.H. Armstead's bas-relief panels for the Queen's Robing Room, Westminster (right).*

From 1859 to 1891, Tennyson composed and edited twelve Arthurian poems, published collectively as *Idylls of the King*. His verse epic was framed with a dedication to Prince Albert and an epilogue 'To the Queen'. From his dramatic birth, carried by a great ocean wave to Merlin's feet, to his equally dramatic departure for Avalon, Tennyson's Arthur is 'Ideal manhood closed in real man'. Victorian virtues are given human form in Arthur – superhuman form in Galahad – while modern sins can be glimpsed in the actions of Guinevere and Gawain. Lacking the cohesion of a classical verse epic, the *Idylls* are nonetheless compelling, complex and full of some of the most beautiful poetry in the English language. Their failure to appeal to many modern readers should not obscure the fact that they were enormously popular with Victorian audiences and envied by contemporaries such as Robert Browning.

The Pre-Raphaelites

The popularity of both Tennyson's Arthurian poems and the many new editions of Malory created a market for Arthurian illustration.

The Lady of Shalott

Sweet is true love tho' given in vain, in vain;
And sweet is death who puts an end to pain.
Alfred Tennyson, 'Lancelot and Elaine' from *Idylls of the King*

ONE OF THE MOST popular Arthurian characters in modern art and poetry is Elaine, the Lady of Shalott. There are several women named Elaine in the Arthurian legends, including Lancelot's mother and Elaine of Corbenic, the mother of Sir Galahad. The most intriguing story belongs to Elaine the White, daughter of Bernard of Astolat and tragic heroine of Tennyson's famous poem 'The Lady of Shalott'. The 'Fair Maid of Astolat' was kept a virtual prisoner in a tower by her father, who did not want her to see the corruptive beauty of the world outside. She could only glimpse the world's reflection in a mirror in her chamber, and dared not look directly out of the window for fear of the curse that said such sights would kill her. One day, Sir Lancelot came riding in full armour to the Castle of Astolat. Elaine could not help but look directly upon the splendid knight riding on the riverbank below. Her mirror cracked and she became entangled in her loom, a sign that the curse was indeed upon her. She came down, nevertheless, beside her father to greet the great Lancelot. On hearing that he was to fight in a tournament nearby, she asked him to wear her token. Lancelot, wishing to fight anonymously, received the token – a red sleeve – thinking only that, since he never wore such a device, the other knights would not recognize him. Elaine, however, took it as a sign that he returned her love and gladly received his shield for safekeeping. Lancelot won the tournament but was severely injured, and Elaine sought him out in order to tend his wounds. Later, he offered her a gift to thank her for nursing him back to health, but she said she wanted only to be his wife or paramour. Thinking of Guinevere, he told her, regretfully, that this could never be, and took his shield and his leave of her. Elaine returned to her tower in grief, and felt death coming upon her. Lancelot returned to Camelot only to encounter a jealous queen who had seen him wearing Elaine's token. Guinevere cast the sleeve into the river just as a barge floated by bearing the body of the Fair Maid of Astolat. In her hand was a letter addressed to Lancelot, announcing to all that she had died out of love for the great knight and asking the queen and the ladies of Camelot to pray for her soul. Lancelot read it and wept bitterly.

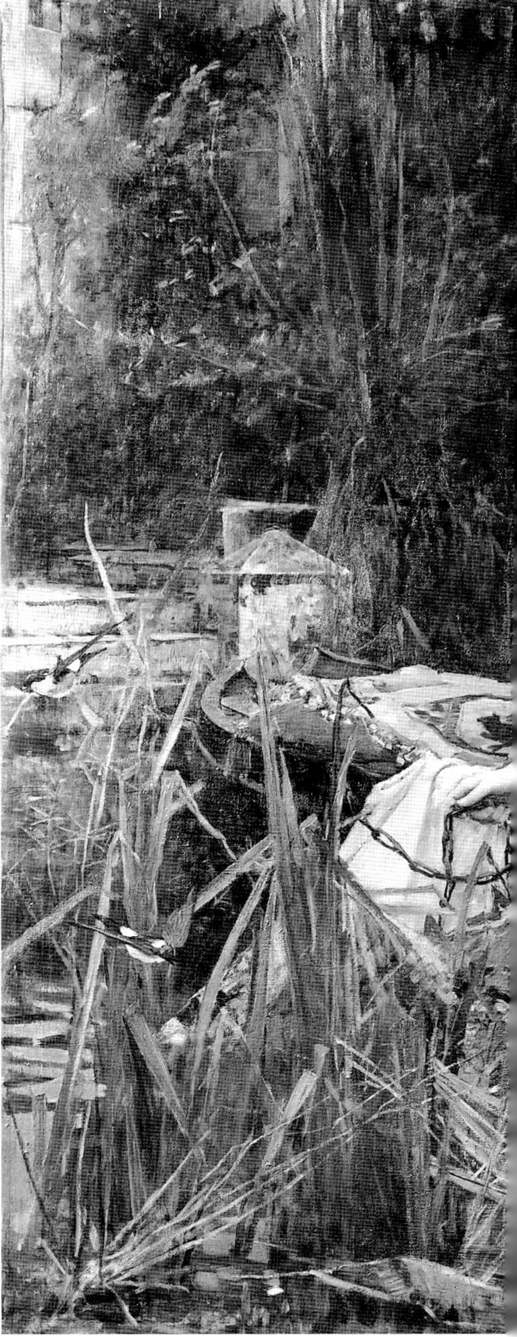

J.W. Waterhouse, The Lady of Shalott *(1883)*.

Artists of the stature of Dante Gabriel Rossetti, William Holman Hunt, Gustave Doré, Aubrey Beardsley, Howard Pyle and N.C. Wyeth contributed illustrations to Arthurian works over the next hundred years. But the most spectacular impact of Arthur on the visual arts can be seen in the Pre-Raphaelite movement. Formed in 1848, the PRB (Pre-Raphaelite Brotherhood) consisted of three rebellious young painters from the Royal Academy in London: Rossetti, Holman Hunt and John Everett Millais. Others were soon invited into the Brotherhood, including sculptors and writers who followed the method and philosophy of the founders. Pre-Raphaelites, either formal or by association, eventually included Christina Rossetti, Ford Madox Brown, Arthur Hughes, John Ruskin, Sir Joseph Noel Paton, William Morris, Sir Edward Burne-Jones, Frederick Sandys and John William Waterhouse.

Rebelling against the rigid rules and classicism of the Academy establishment, the Pre-Raphaelites were romantics who lived and breathed the Middle Ages and made its aesthetics and morality relevant to the Victorian age. Figures from Dante, Chaucer, Malory and Ten-

William Holman Hunt, The Lady of Shalott *(1886–1905).*

Bühnenfestspielhaus Bayreuth.

Am 26. und 28. Juli

für die Mitglieder des Patronat-Vereins,

am 30. Juli, 1. 4. 6. 8. 11. 13. 15. 18. 20. 22. 25. 27. 29. Aug. 1882

öffentliche Aufführungen des

PARSIFAL.

Ein Bühnenweihfestspiel von RICHARD WAGNER.

Personen der Handlung in drei Aufzügen:

Amfortas . . . . . . Herr Reichmann.
Titurel . . . . . . „ Kindermann.
Gurnemanz . . . . . . „ Scaria. „ Siehr.
Parsifal . . . . . . „ Winkelmann. „ Gudehus. „ Jäger.
Klingsor . . . . . . „ Hill. „ Fuchs.
Kundry . . . . . . Frau Materna. Fräulein Brandt. „ Malten.
Erster / Zweiter Gralsritter — Herr Fuchs. „ Stumpf.
Erster / Zweiter / Dritter / Vierter Knappe — Fräulein Galfy. „ Keil. Herr Mikorey. „ v. Hübbenet.

Klingsor's Zaubermädchen:
Sechs Einzel-Sängerinnen:
I. Gruppe — Fräulein Horson. „ Meta. „ Pringle.
II. Gruppe — „ André. „ Galfy. „ Belce.
und Sopran und Alt in zwei Chören, 24 Damen.
Die Brüderschaft der Gralsritter, Jünglinge und Knaben.

Ort der Handlung:

Auf dem Gebiete und in der Burg der Gralshüter „Monsalvat"; Gegend im Charakter der nördlichen Gebirge des gothischen Spaniens. — Sodann: Klingsor's Zauberschloss, am Südabhange derselben Gebirge, dem arabischen Spanien zugewandt anzunehmen.

Beginn des ersten Aufzugs 4 Uhr.
„ „ zweiten „ 6½ „
„ „ dritten „ 8½ „

(Right, top) Two costume designs by Paul von Joukowsky for the 1882 performance of Richard Wagner's Parsifal. *(Right, below) Poster announcing the premier of Wagner's* Parsifal *at Bayreuth, July–August 1882.*

nyson dominate their paintings, shaping the way many of us visualize Arthur, Merlin, Guinevere and the Lady of Shalott. While forming only part of the greater Romantic and neo-Gothic movements, Pre-Raphaelite artists made the most significant contribution of any group of English painters since J.M.W. Turner (d. 1851).

One of the later Pre-Raphaelites, William Morris, became better known for his interior designs and for an Arthurian poem called 'The Defence of Guenevere'. At her trial for treason, Morris's Guenevere defends herself, to an accusing Gawain, with the assertiveness of a modern heroine:

> She said that Gauwaine lied, then her voice sunk;
> And her great eyes began to fill.
> Though still she stood right up, and never shrunk,
> But spoke on bravely, glorious lady fair!

This modernization of the legend marked a trend in Arthurian literature that would recur for the next hundred years. In Germany, the most acclaimed composer of his time turned to Arthurian subjects for his experimental operas: Richard Wagner (p. 173) virtually defined modern classical music and brought opera to new heights in the nineteenth century, and he did so through reviving the medieval German tales of Tristan and Parsifal.

In America, which had no medieval era to sentimentalize, the Arthurian legend might have languished as little more than an 'olde curiositie' were it not for Missouri's Samuel Clemens, better known to the world as novelist Mark Twain. Whereas Tennyson saw Arthur as part of his own tradition and relevant to a progressive society, Twain saw Arthur merely as a symbol of the decadent *ancien régime* of a Europe pulling itself too slowly out of feudalism and serfdom. In his *A Connecticut Yankee in King Arthur's Court*, Twain used the residents of Camelot as material for satire, juxtaposing Yankee ingenuity with the outmoded *noblesse oblige* still resonating with many in Victorian England.

Twain, nevertheless, also used the Arthurian legend to make serious criticisms of the modern industrialized world. At the close of the nineteenth century, the very fact that an American literary icon, not to mention a British poet laureate and a German musical giant, chose Arthur as the subject of serious and substantial works, gave a certain validation to this medieval tradition and ensured that the twentieth century, for all its technological modernity, would do the same.

(Above) William Morris, Queen Guinevere *(1858). An alternative title,* La Belle Iseult, *is suggested by the little dog sleeping on the rumpled bed (Tristan had given Iseult a dog as a gift).*

Mark Twain (1835–1910) is responsible for the most significant American contribution to Arthurian literature, A Connecticut Yankee in King Arthur's Court *(1889).*

VII
THE QUEST FOR CAMELOT

King Alfred ought never to be confused with King Arthur, equally memorable but probably nonexistent and therefore perhaps less important historically (unless he did exist).

W.C. Sellar and R.J. Yeatman, *1066 and All That*

FOR MANY PEOPLE, both medieval and modern, Arthur was, and for ever will be, a purely literary figure. Countless singers, writers and actors have made a living over the centuries by creating and recreating his story. But to others, the literary manifestations of Arthur are merely branches of a great tree whose trunk is of solid history. To these, Arthur was an historical person, and the real charm of his legend is the possibility of untangling all the later traditions and finding the 'real' Arthur.

Just as the many candidates for the 'real' Arthur differ in complexion, so too do the motivations of those seeking him. Over the years, the historical Arthur has been sought by kings needing a symbol (or prestigious ancestor) for their monarchy, by oppressed peoples needing a military messiah, by authors looking to sell copies of their books and, most recently, by tourist agencies trying to help out the local economy. Still, there are many serious historians, including some academics, who have attempted to piece together scattered bits of evidence to construct a case for the existence not just of Arthur, but also of Merlin and the Holy Grail.

This quest for the historical Camelot continues unabated to this day. It is now nearly impossible to keep up with all the new – or reheated – theories professed in books and on Internet sites each year.

Still visible are the ditches and ramparts of the hillfort at South Cadbury, an ancient place of refuge which was refortified in the early Middle Ages. Excavations in the 1960s sought to reveal why this Somerset hill has, since the sixteenth century at least, been known to locals as Camelot.

THE HISTORICAL ARTHUR

(Right) King Arthur; illustration from a fourteenth-century manuscript of Peter of Langtoft's Chronicle. *The crowns at Arthur's feet represent the thirty kingdoms that reputedly paid tribute to the king.*

THE ONCE AND FUTURE King may have been revived in the nineteenth century, but he certainly had to fight his battles in the twentieth. Or rather, many battles were fought over him, in a century that witnessed an unparalleled interest in both proving and disproving the existence of Arthur. Amateur enthusiasts, popular writers and academics all weighed in with strong opinions on one side or the other. Presented here are the most prominent theories concerning the historicity of Arthur.

Leader of Battles

Since the time of the Tudor antiquarians, many scholars have expressed scepticism about the supposed activities of Arthur, but most have treated him as a real person of the early medieval period about whom we know little. Nineteenth-century historians, for the most part, saw Arthur as a petty king of the Britons during their desperate struggle against the Saxons.

In the early twentieth century, some scholars took a different view of Arthur's role in history. He was not a Celtic chieftain, they said, but rather a Roman (or Romanized) army officer, holding the title of *dux* or *comes* of Britain. The historian R.G. Collingwood saw Arthur as Count of Britain, responsible for leading a

THE LATE ROMAN 'KNIGHT'

In the later years of the Empire, the Romans utilized heavy cavalry called cataphractarii *or* clibanarii. *A military development of the Persians which spread westward in the third century, this mounted warrior carried a spear and wore a coat of heavy mail, as did his horse (right). Records show that some heavy cavalry units were stationed in Britain. The question is, were they still present and organized by a British commander against the Saxons in the fifth century? Many proponents of an historical Arthur have thought so.*

Graffito from Dura-Europos depicting a clibanarius *(second/third century).*

The Roman amphitheatre at Caerleon, known locally as Arthur's Table. Though the legionary fortress went out of use c.260, a small civilian occupation probably continued at Caerleon into the early Middle Ages.

mobile field army consisting of heavily armed cavalry who fought the Saxons to preserve 'the Roman character' of the island. This view of Arthur is based on the acceptance of two precepts, namely that Arthur's name derives from the Roman 'Artorius', and that his description in the *History of the Britons – dux bellorum* – is reminiscent of a formal Roman title. Since the *dux Britanniarum* had been in charge of a stationary frontier force, proponents of this theory say it is more likely that Arthur held a command like that of the more powerful and mobile *comes Britanniarum*.

This theory was further developed in 1971 by the archaeologist Leslie Alcock, who had just concluded the substantial excavations at South Cadbury in the previous year (p. 42) and who began to put his findings there, and at other British hillforts, into historical context. Alcock saw Arthur as a major warlord, a *magister militum* of the late fifth century whose military headquarters were the impressively refortified South Cadbury Castle. Alcock firmly backed the historicity of Badon and Camlann, attributing both battles to Arthur and dating them around 490 and 510 respectively.

Arthur the Emperor

This was the most Alcock was willing to say about Arthur, based on archaeological evidence and the Welsh 'historical' material. Just two years later, however, the historian John Morris went much further, recreating an historical scenario for Arthur more elaborate than anything since Geoffrey of Monmouth. Morris not only subscribed to the historicity of Arthur, he

THE CAREER OF RIOTHAMUS

We know a reasonable amount about this candidate for an historical Arthur. According to a near-contemporary historian, Jordanes, the western Roman emperor Anthemius sent to the Britons asking for their aid against the Visigoths. 'Riotimus, king of the Britons', came 'by way of Ocean' with 12,000 soldiers to protect Gaul. The Gallic aristocrat Sidonius Apollinaris sent this Riothamus a letter in around 470, and spoke of the great reputation of the Briton's character. Unfortunately, Riothamus's position was soon betrayed by the praetorian prefect of Gaul, and the Britons were routed by the Visigoths. They sought refuge among the Burgundians, but Gregory of Tours records that many of these Britons were slaughtered by the Goths near Bourges. We do not know the ultimate fate of their king.

Gallo-Roman bronze statue from Kerguilly, Brittany.

believed him to be the central figure of this entire period of British history. For Morris, Arthur is neither petty king nor subservient war leader, but 'the last Roman emperor in the west'.

In constructing this expansive narrative, Morris used a variety of written sources including Celtic genealogies and hagiography written, in many cases, several hundred years after the 'Arthurian' period. For this, especially, he has been attacked by numerous critics in reviews and specialist essays. The most significant was a 1977 article by David Dumville, a Cambridge textual historian. Dumville, drawing upon the recent work of many Celticists, took both Alcock and Morris to task for using late and unreliable source materials to write the history of sub-Roman Britain and, above all, for using Arthur in the titles of scholarly history books. 'The fact of the matter,' states Dumville bluntly, 'is that there is no historical evidence about Arthur.'

Riothamus

Dumville's important critique started a trend of Arthurian scepticism in academe, scaring most historians away from the period and feeding the distrust of written sources already felt by many archaeologists. Even Alcock became agnostic on the matter of Arthur. Many supporters of an historical Arthur felt that, after such serious doubts had been cast upon the 'Welsh material', a new direction of inquiry was needed.

The first truly intriguing possibility was put forward by Geoffrey Ashe. A professional writer and lecturer on British history and mythology, Ashe had followed traditional thinking on Arthur until, in the early 1980s, he proposed a new and unexpected candidate for Arthur: he was Riothamus. Although this identity was first put forward as a possibility by the historian Sharon Turner in the late eighteenth century, no one had given much thought to a relationship between Arthur and this obscure British war-leader. Ashe points out that we have in Riothamus an historically attested figure, a king of the Britons, who did many things later attributed to Arthur: he fought in Gaul, was betrayed by a treasonous deputy and his death is uncertain (he disappeared near Avallon in Burgundy). Geoffrey of Monmouth, thought by most modern scholars to be completely untrustworthy, said that Arthur did all of these things. Ashe proposed that we believe Geoffrey, that he really was copying from 'an ancient book in the British tongue', or at least from something like it.

Furthermore, the *Legend of St Goeznovius* (which Ashe believes was composed in 1019, some time before Geoffrey's *History*) states that Arthur fought in Gaul and implies that his death was mysterious. Ashe asks us to consider that both Geoffrey and the author of the *Legend of St Goeznovius* (p. 99) were drawing from the same (now lost) historical tradition concerning Arthur. This need not have been the only tradition that attached itself to Arthur. Indeed, if Riothamus died *c.*470, it must have been someone else who fought at Badon *c.*500. It is likely that Geoffrey's Arthur was a composite figure. But how do we move linguistically from Riothamus to Arthur? Riothamus (Brittonic *Rigotamos*), Ashe points out, translates as 'king-most' or 'supreme king'. Was this an actual title or honorific, like the *tyrannus superbus* that is used of Vortigern, given to a man whose personal name was Arthur?

Cornishman, Welshman or Scot?

The eminent Celtic linguist Kenneth Jackson has argued that Vortigern and Riothamus are not titles, but are indeed personal names with a royal element, which is common in both Celtic Britain and Gaul (Kentigern, for example) and akin to modern personal names such as Rex and Leroy. Whether or not a connection can be made between Riothamus and Arthur, Ashe has performed a service by reminding us of the very real and important activities of Riothamus and his Britons, whom many historians have dismissed as an obscure group of Bretons.

A Breton origin for Arthur is a possibility, but given the spectacular sub-Roman fortifications in Cornwall and the southwest many, including Ashe and Alcock, have located Arthur in this region of Britain. The landscape of Somerset, Devon and Cornwall is thick with Arthurian associations, at places such as Tintagel, South Cadbury and Glastonbury (see Gazetteer). There are, however, just as many Arthurian sites in Wales: Caerleon claims Arthur's Round Table, Carmarthen is taken to mean Merlin's Town (p. 157) and half a dozen Welsh megaliths are called 'Arthur's Stone'. But Arthur's Seat is, of course, in Scotland – a majestic hill overlooking Edinburgh's Royal Mile – and the Scots can make good claim to Arthur as well. A 'northern Arthur' theory suggests that Arthurian traditions appeared first in the north, probably in the British kingdom of Strathclyde, before filtering down into Wales.

While this theory does not require an historical Arthur to have been active in northern Britain, merely suggesting that the legend first formed there, many have proposed Scottish or north British candidates. The best is probably one Artuir, son of Áedán mac Gabráin, king of the Dalriada Scots. Though this Arthur is an historically attested figure, he is not a Briton, his short-lived career is not particularly noteworthy and his dates (he died *c.*590) may make him too late. What this Scottish example and later Welsh Arthurs do seem to indicate, however, is that for some reason Arthur was becoming a popular name for princes throughout Britain by the later sixth century.

The Narts of the Round Table

One explanation for the popularity of the name Arthur in post-Roman Britain is that a distinguished Roman had borne the name Artorius and that later Britons and Scots commemorated him by giving their male children vernacular forms of the name. The only Roman connected with Britain to bear the name was Lucius Artorius Castus, an accomplished but obscure army commander stationed in Britain in the late second century. Several modern writers have proposed that this man was the 'real' Arthur, with medieval chroniclers and poets borrowing from his story to add a distinguished hero to the later struggle between the Britons and the Saxons.

THE NAME 'ARTHUR'

Most etymologies of Arthur conclude that his name is somehow related to the word for 'bear'. Arth is the modern Welsh word for bear, and there are bear-deities named Artos or Artio throughout Indo-European mythology. Britain, however, has not yielded evidence of a bear god with a name similar to Arthur. This has led some to insist that Arthur is simply a vernacular (Brittonic or Welsh) form given to what was originally a Latin name, Artorius. Such transformations were common in the Brittonic Age, possibly suggesting an historical Arthur dating from this time. Whatever the case, Arthur was only occasionally used as a personal name in early medieval Wales and Scotland, but after c.1100 it became common not only in Celtic-speaking lands but throughout Europe. The survival of 'Arthur' and 'MacArthur' today must certainly be due to the widespread popularity of the Arthurian legends in the later Middle Ages.

Bronze statue of the bear goddess Artio from Muri, Switzerland (second/third century AD).

LUCIUS ARTORIUS CASTUS (c.140–200)

Inscriptions found in Croatia tell us something about this member of the Artorii clan. A long military career included commands in Judea, Macedonia, Britain and Armorica. We do not know what office Castus held in Britain, but he did leave as dux *of a force of cavalry sent to put down a local uprising in Armorica c.185. Scholars have speculated about Castus's role in Britain. Some have located him in the north where he may have served as* praefectus *(or prefect) of the Legio VI Victrix. It was to the northern frontier that a force of 5500 Sarmatian cavalry was sent c.175, and they left an inscription which shows that they had settled near the small cavalry fort of Bremetenacum Veteranorum (Ribchester, in Lancashire). These Sarmatian recruits were heavily armoured cavalry, possibly fighting under a dragon windsock standard similar to that depicted on this funeral stele (right) from Chester.*

The theory was first formally proposed by Kemp Malone in 1925. Malone pieced together the scattered evidence for Castus's career and pointed out the parallels with that of Arthur, mainly that both men led armies in the protection of Britain against the barbarians, and both men additionally took troops across the Channel to campaign in Gaul. As it turns out, there were many other similarities, not just between Arthur and Castus, but between the entire Arthurian legend and the ethnic folklore of one unit stationed in Britain under Castus, the Sarmatians.

This so-called 'Sarmatian connection' was first suggested in 1975 by Helmut Nickel, then Curator of Arms and Armor at the Metropolitan Museum of Art, who saw the Sarmatian heavy cavalry as proto-knights. At the same time the folklorist C. Scott Littleton began to notice similarities between the Arthurian legends and the (undated) sagas of the Ossetes – modern descendants of a Sarmatian tribe that still inhabits land south of the Caucasus mountains. The Ossetian tales concern a band of heroes called the Narts and, especially, their leader, Batraz. Like Arthur, Batraz has a magic sword that is thrown back into the sea just prior to his death. Littleton, with collaborators Anne C. Thomas and Linda A. Malcor, went on to identify several Ossetian parallels with Arthurian and Grail adventures.

Arthur the God

The Sarmatian connection was not the first attempt made to explain Arthur by looking at folklore. Many scholars have sought to avoid the historical issues by considering a mythological origin for Arthur and his legends. Beginning in the eighteenth century, those attracted to the pagan elements of the Arthurian tradition started to explore the possibility that Arthur was not a real person, but rather a literary manifestation of a deity or demi-god. But which god?

Most have looked for a Celtic deity. Both the Welsh material and the continental Grail traditions, steeped in the magical and supernatural, betray motifs obviously borrowed from Celtic mythology. These were explored in detail by Roger Sherman Loomis, one of the founders of the International Arthurian Society. After arguing that Arthur's knights were 'gods of sun and storm', Loomis concluded that Arthur's name was not recognizably mythological and that no mythological traits appear in his story until the creation of the Modena archivolt c.1120. Arthur 'was both man and god', starting as a real Roman Artorius and being elevated to the status of the Great Youths of the Celtic pantheon.

Loomis, like many others in the mid-twentieth century, considered an historical Arthur underlying the later legends to be quite plausible. Others have not. John Darrah, admitting to a complete disdain for the 'meagre chronicles of the Dark Ages' and the 'humdrum bric-à-brac' of excavated sub-Roman sites, searches for the 'proto-Arthur' beyond the Romans and the Celts, taking us back to Stonehenge and the Early Bronze Age. Adopting anthropological language, Darrah characterizes the Arthurian tradition as a 'sacred-king cult' in Britain, passed through folk memory to the Welsh and French poets of the Middle Ages.

Whereas Darrah refuses to address the historical Arthur debate, O.J. Padel tackles it head on. By starting the inquiry with the question 'Was there an historical Arthur?' we have, says Padel, predetermined the answer 'Yes, perhaps'. Contradicting Loomis, Padel does see a mythological Arthur in the earliest written sources: he argues that the giant boars and magic graves in the early Arthurian poems indicate a pre-existent mythological Arthur. The portrait of Arthur that emerges is of a leader (perhaps a giant) of a band of heroes living outside society, in wild places inhabited by magnificent creatures and imbued with magic. By the ninth century, this folkloric Arthur had attracted the names of battles originally fought by other – historical – leaders. The closest parallel, Padel suggests, is the body of Irish stories that attached themselves to the god Fionn. In both cases, the *legendary* figure was *historicized*, rather than the other way around.

As Geoffrey Ashe has pointed out, however, there is no British parallel, no Welsh deity become human, no Welsh demi-god with Arthurian characteristics. Marvellous stories and features in the landscape can just as easily proceed from the reputation of an historical figure as a mythological one. Either way we are dealing with a time when both written records and material remains are scant. As both Kenneth Jackson and Thomas Charles-Edwards have warned us, the nature of the evidence is such that proof – by the standards of modern academic historians – is impossible.

Such a statement should not, and, indeed, will not, end the search for an historical Arthur. It is possible that some compelling evidence for Arthur, literary or archaeological, will be uncovered. But even if we never find the bones of the king, asking questions about Arthur's historicity can lead to a better understanding of historical methodology and of the period which produced the Matter of Britain.

Arthur carrying a cross on his shoulders before his victorious troops at Badon. Artist's illustration for the entry in the Annales Cambriae.

The Battle of Camlann

BY THE END of the Grail Quest, the fellowship of the Round Table had thinned, and many of the knights who returned to Camelot were bitter and disillusioned. Pellinore, Lamorak, Tristan, Bagdemagus and Galahad were all dead, Perceval was living his days out as a hermit in the Holy Land and Bors and Lancelot returned only slowly and with some regret. The younger knights at court had not seen the struggles of Arthur in building Camelot, only the luxury and decadence it now offered. Their leader was Mordred, youngest son of Queen Morgause of Orkney and, it was rumoured, of her half-brother Arthur. Mordred and his brother Agravaine plotted to expose the affair of Lancelot and Guinevere, which had resumed after Lancelot returned from the Grail Quest. The two were successful, catching Lancelot in the queen's chambers, but Agravaine fell to Lancelot's sword as the latter fled from Camelot. Guinevere was presented to Arthur as a traitor to the realm and, by his own laws, he was forced to call for her execution. Lancelot's rescue of the queen at the stake caused only more misery, as Gareth, Gaheris and other innocent knights were slain by Lancelot's party. Gawain, seeking vengeance for his brothers' deaths, convinced Arthur to wage war on Lancelot, but while the former friends Gawain and Lancelot traded blows in France, Mordred usurped the throne at Camelot and captured Guinevere, whom Lancelot had returned to Arthur. Arthur and Gawain raced back to Britain, but Gawain died shortly afterwards from the wounds inflicted by Lancelot, and Arthur was left with only a handful of Round Table knights to resist Mordred. The two sides faced each other at Camlann, and Arthur hoped to make peace as he met Mordred in the middle of the field. But a snake bit one of the knights, who flashed his sword and unwittingly gave the signal to commence fighting. Before the day was over almost every knight on both sides had been slain. Arthur killed Mordred himself, but not until the traitor had inflicted a serious head wound on the king.

Arthur Rackham, 'How Mordred was slain by Arthur, and How by Him Arthur was Hurt to Death', from A.W. Pollard's 1917 abridgement of Malory, The Romance of King Arthur and His Knights of the Round Table.

Merlin and Myrddin

The Birth of Merlin, from a fourteenth-century Italian manuscript of The History of Merlin.

DID MERLIN EXIST as an historical person? Fewer people have asked this question of Merlin than of Arthur. After all, Merlin's legend depicts him as otherworldly, a seer sired by a demon, gifted with magical abilities such as shape-changing and being able to predict the future. Yet Merlin's legend is at least as old as Arthur's, while the reputation of Merlin's prophecies was as widespread in medieval Europe as was Arthur's martial fame. Perhaps most surprising of all, the association of Merlin with Arthur, which has become so much a part of modern Arthuriana, is not quite as ancient as one might think.

The Wild Man of the Wood

Merlin does not actually appear with that name until Geoffrey of Monmouth's *History of the Kings of Britain*, finished in 1136. But it is clear from his later work, the *Vita Merlini* (Life of Merlin), that Geoffrey was using this Latin name to describe a well-known Welsh bard called Myrddin. He was the subject of several early Welsh tales which associate him with King Rhydderch of Strathclyde and the Battle of Arderydd (p. 95). These historical references place Myrddin at the very end of the sixth century. But since the tales themselves were written down much later, this does not constitute proof of an historical Merlin.

Beginning in the 1960s, A.O.H. Jarman was the first scholar to conduct extensive research into the origins of the Merlin legend. He traced the Merlin path to the Scottish Lowlands, where from prehistoric times there existed tales concerning an unnamed Wild Man who had been driven, by some traumatic event, deep into the forest and dwelt there with the wild animals. Over time, this Wild Man acquired prophetic abilities as well as a name – Lailoken – and his story was linked to historical events of the sixth and seventh centuries in the kingdoms of the northern Britons. In the eighth or ninth centuries the story was carried to North Wales, where it took on a Welsh setting. At this time the Wild Man's name, according to Jarman, was changed to Myrddin, probably because this eponymous founder of Carmarthen (in Welsh, Caerfyrddin) had by then acquired a reputation for prophecy.

Jarman also found parallels with the name Lailoken and elements of his story: the Scottish name Lailoken appears in Welsh poetry as *llallogan* and *llallawc*, both used as epithets for Myrddin (p. 157). In Ireland it appears as Lallóc, and the Irish tales of Suibhne Geilt ('Sweeney the Wild Man') have similarities with both the Scottish Lailoken story and the Welsh Myrddin tradition.

The Prophetic Boy

Circulating in Wales at the same time (the eighth and ninth centuries), was the story of another British prophet. The *Historia Brittonum* tells the story of the 'boy without a father' who is brought for sacrifice to the tower of King

William Goscombe John, bronze figures, Merlin and the Child Arthur *(c.1902).*

From Myrddin to Merlin

Many scholars believe that the character Merlin derives from a northern bard named Myrddin. The chart below illustrates Nikolai Tolstoy's theory (see p. 157) on how this transition occurred

Northern Britain

Myrrdin, bard of the Cumbrian king Gwenddolau ap Ceido.

↓

The story of Myrddin's exile in the Caledonian Wood is told in verse.

↓ (branches to Northern Britain and Wales)

Northern Britain: Myrddin's story becomes attached to the hagiography of St Kentigern, where the name 'Lailoken' is substituted (either to connote affection or to avoid the Latin *Merdinus*).

↓

The Church of Glasgow includes the Lailoken tales in its Kentigern hagiography. Some manuscripts call Lailoken 'Merlin'.

Wales

Britons migrating from Cumbria to Wales in the seventh and eighth centuries bring with them stories of Myrddin, whose name is noticeably similar to that of the Welsh town Carmarthen (Caerfyrddin).

↓

The Welsh tales of Myrddin are written down.

⋮ (both lines converge)

Geoffrey of Monmouth discovers the Welsh tales of Myrddin and the identification of this figure with Merlin, prompting him to write his *Vita Merlini*.

(Left) Dinas Emrys, near Beddgelert, Gwynedd. Excavations have shown that this hillfort was occupied in both the Roman and early medieval periods.

Vortigern. After revealing two 'worms' fighting in a hidden pool beneath the tower, the boy utters a prophecy concerning Vortigern's own fate and the conflict between the Britons and the Saxons (represented by the worms) for which he is responsible. Finally the boy tells Vortigern his name – Ambrosius (in Welsh, Emrys) – and the fortification is given to the boy, hence its name, Dinas Emrys.

Geoffrey of Monmouth takes up this story in the early twelfth century and elaborates upon it. In his version, he identifies the boy as 'Merlin, who was also called Ambrosius', and elsewhere as Merlin Ambrosius. Here, Merlin is found by Vortigern's messengers in 'a town which was afterwards called Kaermerdin', implying that it was renamed in honour of the prophet. Geoffrey also takes the brief prophecy found in the *Historia Brittonum* and transforms it into the voluminous *Prophecies of Merlin*, written separately but eventually incorporated into his *History of the Kings of Britain*. The *Prophecies* allude to political events in Geoffrey's own world, but they also allow him to make Merlin predict Arthur's future greatness. This is the first appearance, in writing, of a link between Arthur and Merlin.

The second comes just a few chapters later, when the king, Uther Pendragon, calls for 'the prophet Merlin' to help him win Ygerna (Igraine), the wife of Duke Gorlois of Cornwall. Merlin gives Uther drugs that transform his appearance into that of Gorlois, allowing him access to Ygerna's bed, where Arthur is conceived. No more is said of Merlin. But Merlin's potent 'drugs', together with the earlier reference to his skills in transporting the Giant's Ring (Stonehenge) from Ireland to Salisbury, are the first hint of Merlin possessing magical abilities as well as the gift of prophecy.

After Geoffrey's *History* was completed he discovered more of the Welsh legends concerning Myrddin, specifically those which depict him as the Wild Man of the Wood. So, in 1150, Geoffrey wrote a long Latin poem called the *Vita Merlini* in which Merlin appears as a king and prophet of Dyfed in the late sixth century who, after a battle against the king of Scotland, becomes mad with grief and retreats into the Caledonian Wood. This is a strange poem, quite unlike the *History*, based on the entirely different Myrddin tradition which Geoffrey discovered well after his original depiction of Merlin. Geoffrey tries to reconcile the two traditions – not an easy task, considering that an adult Merlin in the *History* disappears well before Arthur's death, given as 542, while his exploits in the *Vita* concern events at the end of the sixth century. Undaunted, Geoffrey's Merlin explains in the *Vita* that he has 'lived long and seen much', after which the prophet recounts the deeds of Vortigern, Uther and Arthur just as Geoffrey had described them in the *History*.

Artist's impression of an episode from the Vita Merlini, *in which an enraged Merlin rides a stag to court to prevent the wife he had abandoned from remarrying.*

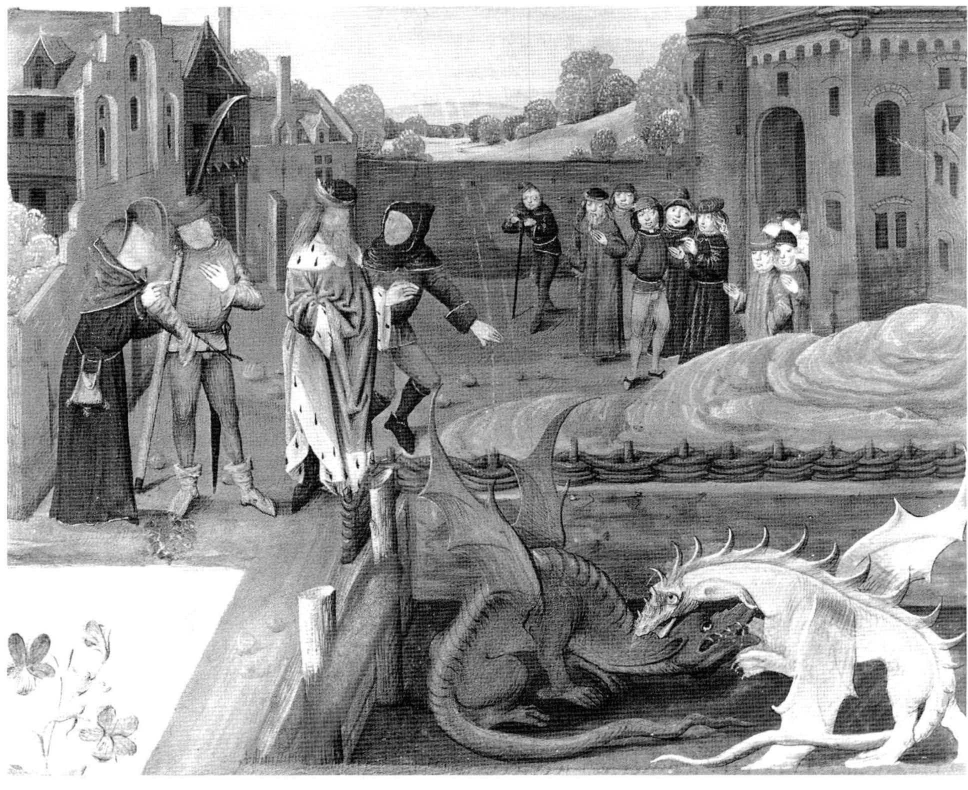

The prophetic boy reveals to Vortigern the fight of the Red and White Dragons. Illustration from a fifteenth-century English manuscript.

Ygerna, Uther and Merlin, in a fourteenth-century English manuscript.

Merlin's prophecies in the Middle Ages

In both the *History* and the *Vita*, Geoffrey attributes a great deal of political prophecy to Merlin. Although some of his predictions about Arthur's future deeds serve as a plot device, many of the prophecies can be linked to actual events in twelfth-century Britain and France (the death of Henry I's son in the White Ship tragedy is just one). Readers accepted this as genuine ancient prophecy and Geoffrey's Merlinic prophecies were soon translated into several European languages. By the end of the twelfth century, five systematic commentaries had been produced. In the medieval Celtic fringe, several attempts were made to use Merlin's prophecies – especially the one concerning Arthur's return – to incite rebellion against the English (see box, opposite).

The historical Merlin?

As in the case of Arthur, Merlin was believed to have been an historical figure by most of the medieval writers and rulers who were recalling his prophecies. Many medieval scholars, however, had doubts about the authenticity of the prophecies as well as the wonder-working abilities ascribed to him in the contemporary romances. One of the earliest critics was Gerald of Wales (1146–1220), who, though not doubting Merlin's historicity, observed in his *Itinerary of Wales* that Geoffrey of Monmouth must have combined two separate Merlins – Merlin Ambrosius and Merlin Caledonius (or Merlin 'Sylvester', that is, 'of the wood') –

in his writings to reconcile two prophetic figures who lived more than a century apart.

Gerald's theory of a 'composite Merlin' has influenced much modern thinking on the subject of Merlin's origins, including the work of Celticist Rachel Bromwich. The most exhaustive examination of Merlin's historicity, however, was done by Nikolai Tolstoy in the 1980s. Tolstoy, great-nephew of Leo Tolstoi, elaborates (p. 154) on Bromwich's theory and argues, against Jarman, that it was not a local Welsh tradition that invented Myrddin to explain the name Caerfyrddin (Carmarthen). Rather, both Myrddin and Caerfyrddin (which mean 'sea-fortress' and 'fort of the sea-fortress' respectively) derive ultimately from Clas Myrddin (Myrddin's Close) which one of the Welsh Triads claims was an early name for the island of Britain. In other words, both the prophet and the town were named after Britain itself.

Tolstoy then poses the question that if Myrddin really was the name of the historical bard of northern Britain, why do the records from Scotland (the hagiography of St Kentigern) call him Lailoken? Given that the Welsh form *llallogan* means 'dear friend', Tolstoy suggests that perhaps Lailoken was an epithet accompanying the name Myrddin rather than itself a personal name. Furthermore, some of the *vitae* which connect Lailoken to St Kentigern do indeed call the former 'Merlin'. It has been assumed that Geoffrey created the name Merlinus, choosing this Latin form for Myrddin over Merdinus (in French, *merde*) because of the scatological connotations of the latter. But there may have been, as Tolstoy postulates, a version of the Lailoken/Myrddin story circulating in the Glasgow area in the late twelfth century which was not influenced by Geoffrey's *Vita Merlini*, whose hero, nevertheless, was called Merlin.

Tolstoy takes this 'historical' basis and investigates sites in the Scottish Lowlands associated with the Myrddin/Lailoken stories. He also looks at comparative mythology, finding Irish parallels with the British Wild Man, and explores the possibility that Myrddin was a Celtic shaman, perhaps the last representative of the British order of Druids.

As with the theories about an historical Arthur, much of this is circumstantial evidence. With no contemporary accounts to verify either Lailoken or Myrddin, a convincing case for Merlin's historicity is difficult to make. It is perhaps appropriate that the shape-changing – and seemingly name-changing – seer continues to elude the grasp of rational detection. Modern historical method has proven, so far, to be a sorry way of trapping the ethereal Merlin.

Louis Rhead, 'Merlin the Enchanter', illustration for the 1923 edition of King Arthur and his Knights, *by Sir James Knowles.*

Merlin and Medieval Celtic Politics

'The soothsayer Merlin . . . foretold that the mad people [the English] should be expelled. . . . If our valiant predecessor, King Arthur, had been now alive, I am sure not one of the Saxon walls would have resisted him. . . . May the Omnipotent procure him a successor only similar to him, I would not desire a better, who may deliver the Britons from their old grievances, and restore to them their country and their country's glory.'

From *The Song of the Welsh*, an anonymous Latin poem written during the time of the Baronial War (1263–65) to justify Llywelyn the Great's recent assumption of the title 'Prince of all Wales'

'The people believe that [Robert] Bruce will carry all before him, exhorted by false preachers from Bruce's army. . . . For these preachers have told the people that they have found a prophecy of Merlin, that after the death of "le Roy Coveytous" [Edward I] the people of Scotland and the Welsh shall band together and have full lordship and live in peace together to the end of the world.'

Report to Edward II during Robert the Bruce's rebellion in Scotland, 1307

'You are descended in a direct line from Albanactus . . . [while] the descendants of Kamber reigned as kings until Cadwaladr. . . . I, dear cousin, am descended directly from Cadwaladr. . . . The prophecy [of Merlin] says that I will be delivered from the oppressions and bondages [of the English] by your aid.'

'Seeing that it is commonly reported by the prophecy that, before we can have the upper hand [against the English], you and yours, our well-beloved cousins in Ireland, must stretch forth hereto a helping hand.'

Letters from Owain Glyndŵr to Robert III of Scotland (1401) and the lords of Ireland (1402)

'Sometimes [Glendower] angers me/with telling me . . ./Of the dreamer Merlin and his prophecies.'

Hotspur, in William Shakespeare's *Henry IV, Part I*

(Left) The Red Dragon of the Britons, which now graces the Welsh national flag, was an emblem used by both Owain Glyndŵr and Henry VII.

In Search of the Holy Grail

Many medieval writers depicted the Grail as a large ornate bowl or chalice used to serve the Eucharist. Perhaps the finest extant example of such a vessel is the Ardagh Chalice, crafted for an eighth-century Irish monastery.

AS WE HAVE SEEN, people have long been fascinated by the existential ambiguity surrounding Arthur, Merlin and the other denizens of Camelot. There has also been some curiosity regarding the existence of the magical objects associated with Arthur and his court: Richard the Lionheart claimed that he possessed the real Excalibur, and the Plantagenet kings who came after him counted Arthurian objects as part of the royal regalia. But it was the Holy Grail that elicited the most interest throughout medieval Christendom, and it is this object that continues to draw people into its mysteries to the present day.

Chrétien's Grail

The Grail makes its first literary appearance in *Perceval*, or *Le Conte del Graal*, written by Chrétien de Troyes c.1190 (p. 107). In a procession passing before Perceval and the Fisher King, a young maiden carries '*un graal*' of fine gold, set with precious stones, that was large enough to hold a whole salmon but instead bore only a single Mass wafer that would sustain the aged king. The Old French word *graal* (from the Latin *gradale*) was often used to describe a fine, deep dish used at certain stages of a formal meal to serve meats or other substantial foods. Chrétien does not elaborate on the origin or use of his *graal*, and since the *Perceval* remained unfinished upon the poet's death there was a certain mystery that lingered about this intriguing item.

The Celtic myth

Several poets took up the task of finishing Chrétien's story, explaining to an eager public the true meaning of the Grail (p. 110). In the *First Continuation*, the 'Rich Grail' floats about the hall and provides food and drink to all in attendance. In Wolfram von Eschenbach's *Parzifal*, the Grail is a stone that produces an abundance of savoury foods. Many scholars have seen in these stories the pagan, probably Celtic, motif of the magic food-providing vessel, akin to the cornucopia. Was Chrétien drawing upon some ancient, pre-Christian tradition borrowed, like other magical elements in the French Arthurian romances, from the bards of the Celtic fringe?

The Grail Procession, miniature from a fourteenth-century Flemish manuscript of the Quest del Saint Graal.

The Christian myth

The *Perceval* continuators were not all in agreement over the nature of the Grail: in Robert de Boron's verse trilogy (p. 112) the Grail is placed in the Christian tradition, specifically identified as the cup used by Jesus and the disciples at the Last Supper. Following apocryphal traditions (especially 'The Gospel of Nicodemus'), Robert narrates the adventures of the Grail from its passing to Joseph of Arimathea, who used it to catch Christ's blood at the Cross, to its arrival in Britain with Joseph's son, Josephus. The family of Josephus, he tells us, hold round-table services with the Grail and become its keepers down to the Fisher King and to Arthurian times. In addition to the Grail, Josephus brings to Britain the Spear of Longinus, which pierced Christ's side on the Cross and came to be equated with the Bleeding Lance of the Fisher King.

For obvious reasons, this thoroughly Christian version of the Grail story became the most popular in medieval Europe. It was retold, in prose, in the Vulgate Lancelot cycle of romances that, in turn, inspired the Grail adventures in Malory's *Le Morte d'Arthur*. The enigmatic *graal* becomes, in these works, *Sangraal* (in Malory, *Sangreal*) – the Holy Grail. This literary transformation also launched very real investigations, in

St Joseph of Arimathea, the 'secret disciple' who entombed the body of Jesus and came to possess the Holy Grail. Icon by a monk of the Brotherhood of St Seraphim of Sarov, England (1978).

Edwin Austin Abbey, 'The Golden Tree and the Achievement of the Grail' (1895), panel XV of the Quest of the Holy Grail *murals. Depicted here, the moment when Galahad, having achieved the Grail, has the Christian mysteries revealed to him.*

the Middle Ages, into chalice-like relics in the hope of finding the actual Grail. In Glastonbury, moreover, a tradition dating from the thirteenth century claims Joseph of Arimathea as founder of the famous Abbey and the romance *Perlesvaus* (*c*.1200) links Glastonbury with Avalon (Robert de Boron wrote that the Grail was conveyed to 'Avaron'). Subsequently, local features came to be called Chalice Hill and Chalice Well.

The Fisher King is pierced through the thigh, illustration from a fourteenth-century French manuscript of Le Roman du Saint-Graal.

Modern theory

Modern quests for the Holy Grail take many forms (see box, below), but most have been influenced by two scholarly works: James Frazer's *The Golden Bough* (1890) and Jessie L. Weston's *From Ritual to Romance* (1920). Frazer's theory (that a prehistoric ritual – the sacrifice of the vegetation god – lay behind much Western myth, including that of the maimed Fisher King) inspired Weston and generations of Grail seekers. Weston traced the origins of the Grail back to the prehistoric ritual later represented in the classical myth of Adonis, the handsome youth who dies from a thigh wound but whom Zeus brings back to life, though only for the spring and summer months. She equates Adonis with the later figure of the Fisher King, whose own wound brought desolation to his land (henceforward know as the Wasteland), and proposes that the Grail and Lance represent female and male sexual symbols used in a fertility ritual celebrating the rebirth/healing of the god/king. Gnostic texts, she asserts, delivered this fertility myth to medieval Christians who, in turn, transformed it into the Grail romances. Thus, the Grail Quest, despite its pagan fertility-cult origins, can be likened to a Gnostic striving for oneness with God.

GLASTONBURY: LEY-LINES, THE ZODIAC AND THE GRAIL

*Glastonbury, a small town nestling in the tranquil plains of Somerset, has become in recent years a Mecca for Grail-seekers, Arthurian tourists and a variety of New Age enthusiasts. Many believe that Glastonbury Tor – an impressive feature thrusting upward from the flat landscape, with man-made terraces looping in a maze-like pattern – to be a centre of preternatural power. One of the first to identify Glastonbury as an energy-centre was the neo-mystic Dion Fortune (*née *Violet Firth in 1891). Revivalist Druid orders make pilgrimages to Glastonbury Tor because they believe it to be one of their ancient shrines. Others have claimed Glastonbury as one feature in a Zodiac circle spanning some 10 miles (17 km) of Somerset terrain. While proponents of such astrological theories turn to Nostradamus for proof, advocates of the ley-line theory – that Glastonbury and other prehistoric monuments lie along straight lines of great terrestrial force – appeal for corroboration to everything from Feng Shui and dowsing rods to UFO sightings. Perhaps less mystical were the groups of young people, labelled 'hippies' by the locals, who, from 1971 onward, have travelled frequently to Glastonbury for rock music festivals and other 'alternative' entertainments.*

Glastonbury from the air, with the Tor's looping terraces visible in the upper left of the photograph.

(Left, and below left) Chalice Well Gardens, in Glastonbury. A beautiful and serene spot where modern pilgrims come to taste the healing waters that spring, some say, from the Grail buried deep below. The vesica piscis symbol, which has both Christian and pre-Christian associations, adorns the well cover and lends its shape to the pool at the foot of the garden.

This seemingly radical reappraisal of the Grail myth has appealed to many, and most notably to T.S. Eliot who claimed Weston's work was a great inspiration for his poem *The Waste Land* (1922). It also won over many scholars, including R.S. Loomis. But many of Weston's speculations are now judged to have been unsubstantiated, and Loomis eventually recanted his allegiance to the theory. He, like many other literary scholars of the twentieth century, chose to focus on the 'Celtic' origins of the Grail myth. The Grail, the Grail Procession, the Question Test ('Whom does the Grail serve?'), the Fisher King, the Broken Sword – all these elements have parallels in Irish and Welsh myths. Given the location of these stories in Britain, and the existence of an early Welsh Grail story in *Peredur*, many continue to follow Loomis in tracing the Grail's ultimate origin to a Celtic tradition that has mortals visiting the Otherworld, where magical vessels and other marvels abound.

At the end of *From Ritual to Romance*, Weston cautions Celticists not to attribute every Grail motif to 'Celtic Fairy-lore'. The visit to the Otherworld, she protests, is a much older and more serious 'mystery tradition': 'The Otherworld is not a myth, but a reality, and in all ages there have been souls who have been willing to brave the great adventure, and to risk all for the chance to bring back with them some assurance of the future life.' Such powerful prose proved to contain a challenge too good to pass up, and has led to the modern interest in the Grail as an occult object. But it also proves the point that, for some, the Grail – like Arthur and Merlin – can have a supra-historical dimension, addressing spiritual, psychological or philosophical truths that are greater than mere historical facts. The Grail is much like Arthur in that it takes on an appearance to suit whoever is looking for it. For many this ambiguity is unsettling, for others most appealing.

Detail from Angel of the Holy Grail *by Frederick Shields (c.1875).*

THE ISLE OF AVALON

ONLY A FEW Knights of the Round Table survived the Battle of Camlann. After the battle Sir Bedivere, the Cupbearer, and Sir Lucan, the Butler, carried a wounded King Arthur from the field. Lucan died in this service to his king, leaving the loyal Bedivere to tend to Arthur. The king instructed his knight to throw his magical sword Excalibur back into the watery depths from which it had come. Bedivere walked to the edge of a great lake as Arthur instructed, but he could not bring himself to throw Excalibur into the water, so he hid the sword and returned to the king. When Arthur asked him what he had seen when he discarded the sword, the king realized that Bedivere had not carried out his instructions. Scolded, Bedivere returned to the water to discharge his duty. When he finally hurled Excalibur out into the lake a woman's had emerged, draped in the purest white samite, and caught the sword. After brandishing it thrice, the hand drew Excalibur back into the water and it was never seen again. As Bedivere was returning to Arthur he saw a mysterious ship approaching the shore. It bore four queens – one of whom is said to have been Morgan le Fay – as well as the Lady of the Lake. These noble women received Arthur on board and then set sail for Avalon, where the king's wounds could be healed. Later, on his travels, Bedivere came to a monastery at Glastonbury where he saw a fresh grave and a lead cross that bore a Latin inscription. The earliest accounts say that the inscription read 'Here lies the famous King Arthur in the Isle of Avalon'. Later writers, such as Thomas Malory and T.H. White, say that the inscription read simply 'Here lies Arthur, the Once and Future King'. Medieval romances and prophecies alike upheld the belief in Arthur's immortality, stating that one day, when Britain needs his leadership most, King Arthur will indeed return.

Joseph Noel Paton, The Death Barge of Arthur *(1862)*.

VIII

Conclusion: An Age of Arthur

Don't let it be forgot,
That once there was a spot,
For one brief shining moment,
That was known as Camelot.
Alan Jay Lerner and Frederick Loewe, *Camelot*

THE SEARCH FOR the historical origins of Arthur, Merlin and the Holy Grail is just one aspect of the modern age's great fascination with the Arthurian myth. The Once and Future King has truly returned to reign over almost every aspect of contemporary culture. While remaining a literary favourite, the king has certainly seen his portfolio diversify in our times. Hardly is a new medium created before someone thinks to link it to Camelot, adding to that vast body of what scholars have termed 'Arthuriana'. Are we, it is fair to ask, living in another 'Age of Arthur'?

The final chapter of this book examines the diverse manifestations of the Arthurian tradition as it appeared in the last century, with a glimpse at what form the king may assume in the future. In doing so we leave behind archaeological artifacts and ancient texts and turn to the brave new world of moving pictures and the information superhighway. Camelot has now become, in the English vocabulary, a common synonym for Utopia, and Arthur, Gwen and Lance have become common personal names. We have corporate 'round tables' and Excalibur limousines, and 'Merlin' has been used as an appellation for telephones and electronic games.

In the world of arts and letters, you are now just as likely to find our king riding a commuter train or fighting Martians as performing noble acts of chivalry. Indeed, postmodernism, feminism and New Age spirituality have in many instances replaced chivalry and Christianity in contemporary retellings of the Arthurian saga. This only proves, however, that our times are not so different from the twelfth or the sixteenth centuries. For, once again, Arthur has arisen to speak to a new generation, and again he speaks in their own language.

An Arthur for an irreverent age: (left to right) Graham Chapman, Terry Gilliam, Terry Jones and Michael Palin in a scene from the film comedy Monty Python and the Holy Grail *(1975).*

ARTHURIAN THEMES still occasionally appeared in poetry and novels in the early twentieth century, but not with the vitality that they had in the Victorian Age. *Fin de siècle* anxieties, culminating in the mass destruction and terror of World War I and the Russian Revolution, hardly required expression through a medieval and aristocratic myth. Even an outburst of Arthurian drama, which included plays by Thomas Hardy (1840–1928) and John Masefield (1878–1967), were characterized by relentless tragedy and a sentimental yearning for a distant past.

The cover of Marion Zimmer Bradley's best-selling Arthurian fantasy novel, The Mists of Avalon *(1982).*

The 1920s and 1930s, however, saw major original contributions to the Arthurian tradition in both prose and verse. T.S Eliot's lauded poem *The Waste Land* (1922) and Edward Arlington Robinson's Arthurian verse trilogy (*Merlin*, 1917; *Lancelot*, 1920; *Tristram*, 1927) continued the trend of tragedy and desolation, but their use of imagery and metaphor made these poems the most significant Arthurian verse since Tennyson. As complex as Eliot's *The Waste Land*, but not nearly as well known are two collections of Arthurian poems by Charles Williams – *Taliessin Through Logres* (1938) and *Region of the Summer Stars* (1944). Though difficult for many readers (Williams's friend C.S. Lewis published a useful guide accompanying the poems), these are powerful vignettes of the Arthurian/Grail saga with unforgettable images and a mystic vision that is incomparable to anything before or since.

Williams and C.S. Lewis also produced novels that brought Arthurian themes into modern settings (a practice followed by many twentieth-century novelists). Williams's *War in Heaven* (1930) concerns the reappearance of the Holy Grail, while Lewis's *That Hideous Strength* (1945, the final volume in his 'Space Trilogy') resurrects Merlin. Serious and often compelling, neither novel earned the attention or devotion engendered by the *Lord of the Rings* novels of their friend and Oxford colleague, J.R.R. Tolkien. Many have seen, however, a bit of Merlin in Tolkien's wizard Gandalf.

These three, together with other Oxford academics and friends, earned for themselves the nickname The Inklings. While they taught and lectured in Oxford, at rival Cambridge a student named Terence Hanbury White was finishing his undergraduate dissertation on Thomas Malory. In 1938 he dedicated his novel *The Sword in the Stone* to Malory, and twenty years later this book was incorporated into his Malorean tragedy, *The Once and Future King* (1958). The former, with its original and touching scenes of Merlyn's education of 'the Wart' (Arthur's boyhood name), would endear generations of readers and become the basis of an animated Disney film. The later novel, which itself served as the basis for the Broadway play and movie *Camelot*,

Oxford medievalist and novelist J.R.R. Tolkien (1892–1973). The modern fantasy novel industry owes a great debt to Tolkien and his colleague C.S. Lewis.

was to become, after Malory, the most widely known version of the Arthurian saga.

Though he conceives Arthur's story as an Aristotelian tragedy, White infuses *The Once and Future King* with humour, satire, slapstick, romance and political philosophy. Himself something of an expert on falconry and medieval sport, White conjures up an Arthurian world that juxtaposes late medieval chivalry with Edwardian society. Writing at the outbreak of World War II, White places Arthur's chivalric worldview against Nazism and Communism, initiating a serious discussion of human nature. For better or worse (the book received many negative reviews), this discussion spilled over into *The Book of Merlyn*, written c.1940 but only published posthumously, in 1977. Fighting to replace tyranny – 'Might makes Right' – with chivalry – 'Might for Right' – the tired King Arthur must, in the end, recognize the limits of the human beings he has used in his Utopian experiment.

In one sense, T.H. White's novels are retellings of the 'traditional' Arthurian legend, as defined by Malory. The twentieth century witnessed many such retellings of Malory, from Howard Pyle's illustrated series of juvenile fiction to John Steinbeck's unfinished *The Acts of King Arthur and His Noble Knights* (written in 1958–59 and published posthumously in 1976). Most are set unspecifically in the High Middle Ages, making use of castles and heraldry. Phyllis Ann Karr's murder-mystery *The Idylls of the Queen* (1982) focuses on one episode from Malory (Guinevere and the poisoned apple), while Thomas Berger's *Arthur Rex* (1978) brings in material from *Sir Gawain and the Green Knight* and uses mock-archaic language to puncture Arthurian characters and conventions.

A more recent and popular trend amongst novelists is to place the Arthurian saga in its 'proper' historical context, that is, the fifth and sixth centuries AD. The trend really began with Rosemary Sutcliff's *Sword at Sunset* (1963), which tells of the Romano-British warleader Artos and his long-suffering wife Guenhumara. (Sutcliff also began the mini-trend of having Bedwyr as the queen's lover rather than Lancelot.) Post-Roman political intrigue is also explored in the novels of Mary Stewart, whose *The Crystal Cave* (1970) is remembered for its vivid and original portrait of Merlin. Arthurian women come into their own in many of these Dark Age dramas, notably in Marion Zimmer Bradley's *The Mists of Avalon* (1982). This best-seller features as an unlikely heroine Morgan, a proto-feminist priestess of Avalon (identified as Glastonbury) battling the evil forces of Christianity. Morgan is also portrayed as Arthur's first and truest love (though also his half-sister), as she is in a similar portrayal in Parke Godwin's *Firelord* (1980). But, of all the Arthurian women, it is Guinevere who has attracted most modern writers, whether appearing in Roman guise in the trilogy of Sharan Newman, or as a Celtic princess in that of Persia Woolley.

Even novelists less concerned with historical accuracy often prefer to draw on older pagan and Celtic themes in their Arthurian works. Gillian Bradshaw's 'Gwalchmai' trilogy draws on Celtic myths in its depiction of Gwalchmai as the original Gawain. Stephen Lawhead's *Taliesin* (1987) draws together Welsh traditions and the myth of Atlantis to explain the supernatural qualities of Avalon and Camelot, depicting the bard Taliesin as Merlin's father. Unlike most late-twentieth-century versions of the legends, Lawhead's Arthurian novels bring Britain's pagan Celtic past into harmony with the new Christian religion that dominates Arthur's court.

The preoccupation with archaeology and historical realism shown by many of these novels follows the explosion of interest in an 'historical' Arthur. But other modern novelists prefer to bring Arthurian characters and themes into the present. Following in the tradition of Lewis's *That Hideous Strength* are Sanders Anne Laubenthal's *Excalibur* (1973), Susan Cooper's *The Dark is Rising* (1973) and Donald Barthelme's *The King* (1990). More subtle is Bernard Malamud's transporting of the story of Perceval and the Grail on to the baseball diamond in his 1952 classic *The Natural*. Similarly, John Cowper

'The young Arthur and his tutor, Merlyn'. Drawing by T.H. White for his novel The Sword in the Stone *(1938).*

In Charles Williams's poem 'The Son of Lancelot', Lancelot goes mad 'in a delirium of lycanthropy' when he discovers that he has been tricked into sleeping with Helayne. At the resulting birth of his son Galahad, Lancelot tries literally to devour his sin ('he was hungry for his son'), but is intercepted by Merlin who had changed into a white wolf.

Powys's *A Glastonbury Romance* (1932), James Joyce's *Finnegans Wake* (1939) and Walker Percy's *Lancelot* (1978) all use elements of the Arthurian tradition to give structure and deeper meaning to contemporary stories.

Though the greatest production was of English-language novels, Arthur remained alluring to continental writers of the twentieth century, with both French and German novelists showing the influence of Wagner in their Arthurian works. Joseph Bédier's *Le Roman de Tristan et Iseut* (1900), a straightforward working of the Tristan story, was translated into several languages and influenced many succeeding treatments of the legend. Merlin also attracted many French and German authors, most notably René Barjavel in *L'Enchanteur* (1984) and Nobel Prize-winner Gerhart Hauptmann in 'Merlins Geburt' (The Birth of Merlin), the first chapter of his unfinished novel *Der neue Christophorus* (1917–44). And Italian postmodernist Italo Calvino made a unique contribution to Arthuriana with his 1959 novel *Il cavaliere inesistente*, featuring automaton Knights of the Grail.

Arthur in the Comics

Some modern novelists have projected Arthur and his knights into the future to do battle for the forces of good. At bookstores today, science fiction and fantasy sections are usually swollen with Arthurian titles. Not to be overlooked is the comic section, where comic books and graphic novels have taken a similar approach to Arthur. Mike Barr and Brian Bollund's Camelot 3000, *originally published as a series of comic books (1982–85) and later as a graphic novel, brings Arthur back to life in* AD *3000 to save the world from a Martian invasion unleashed by Morgan le Fay. While Arthur and Merlin appear as their immortal selves, Guinevere and the knights are reincarnated in some unlikely bodies (Gawain is an African-American, Galahad a Samurai, Tristan a woman, Percival a nuclear mutant). Matt Wagner's* Mage *(1984) follows a similar reincarnation theme.*

The father of Arthurian comics is, of course, Hal Foster. His comic strip Prince Valiant *began appearing in American newspapers in 1937 and continues, with new authors, to this day. The weekly story of the exiled prince of Thule has inspired games, novels and movies; it even brought back the page-boy haircut. Many American and British comic books followed upon the success of* Prince Valiant. *In Germany, the* Sir Roland the Lionhearted *series of comic books relocates Arthur and Camelot in the Odenwald, drawing also upon other legend traditions.*

Arthur fights an alien in Camelot 3000.

COMIC STRIPS, TELEVISION and films have provided artists with powerful new media to bring their vision of Camelot to an even larger public. Cinema in particular has produced many original and provocative versions of the Arthurian legends – as well as some of the most forgettable.

The earliest cinematic forays into Arthuriana were attempts to bring Wagner's operas (p. 173) and Tennyson's poems to the silver screen. For American movie studios, however, the most appealing and approachable Arthurian text was Twain's *A Connecticut Yankee in King Arthur's Court*, which continues to spawn television and film versions every few years. Twentieth Century Fox began the trend with a silent version in 1921, followed ten years later by a 'talkie' starring Will Rogers and Myrna Loy. Paramount countered in 1949 with *A Connecticut Yankee in King Arthur's Court*, starring Bing Crosby as a singing Hank Morgan, while Disney sent a Yankee astronaut to Camelot in *The Unidentified Flying Oddball* (1979).

While occasionally they have their moments, none of these films rates as a critical success nor do they offer much to the modern Arthurian tradition. Hollywood at first used Arthur, like Robin Hood, as an excuse for swash-buckling and as a vehicle for leading men. MGM's *Knights of the Round Table* (1953) featured Robert Taylor and Ava Gardner as a rather stoical Lancelot and Guinevere, the same year that Twentieth Century Fox premiered a Technicolor version of

The boy Arthur, known affectionately as the Wart, pulls the sword from the stone. Movie still from Disney's The Sword in the Stone *(1965).*

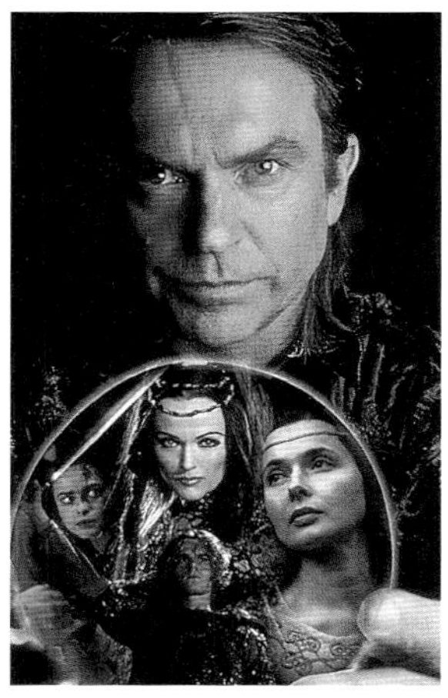

(Above) Sam Neill starred in the title role of the NBC mini-series Merlin *(1998). (Left) Arthur, played by Richard Harris, gathers his knights at the Round Table in a scene from* Camelot *(1967).*

Robert Taylor starred as Lancelot in the MGM film Knights of the Round Table *(1953), filmed on location at Tintagel.*

Prince Valiant with Robert Wagner wearing the page-boy haircut. Even the directing of Cornel Wilde could not breathe much life into 1963's *The Sword of Lancelot*. Disney animation, rather than either plot or music, has made a classic out of the 1965 screen version of T.H. White's *The Sword in the Stone*, the most famous animated adaptation of the legends.

From the late 1960s onwards, American and British films turned to more serious treatments of the Arthurian legends. *Camelot* (1967), starring Richard Harris and Vanessa Redgrave, brought the successful Broadway musical to the cinema – with mixed results. *Camelot* narrows the scope of the story by focusing on the Arthur–Guinevere–Lancelot love triangle, a strategy adopted with much less success by director Jerry Zucker in *First Knight* (1995), which cast Sean Connery, Julia Ormond and Richard Gere in the lovers' roles. John Boorman's *Excalibur* (1981) attempted broad coverage of the Arthur saga by following Malory, albeit loosely. The result is an engaging, though overly ambitious, fantasy with some powerful moments made memorable by a score that includes music by Wagner and Carl Orff.

For many filmgoers, the most entertaining cinematic treatment of Arthur is the cult-comedy classic *Monty Python and the Holy Grail* (1975). With an impressive knowledge of the Arthurian legend and obscure medieval detail, the Python troupe offer a vision of Camelot full of silly slapstick, satire and high-brow humour. Co-director Terry Gilliam returned to the Arthurian legends in 1991's *The Fisher King*, a story of Perceval-like redemption with Jeff Bridges and Robin Williams in the quest for a modern Grail. Another commercially successful and loose adaptation of the Grail story is Stephen Spielberg's *Indiana Jones and the Last Crusade* (1989), where the roles of knight and maimed king are assumed by Harrison Ford and Sean Connery (playing the medievalist Dr Henry Jones).

European films have usually fared better with critics than these big Hollywood productions. *L'Éternel Retour* (1943), filmed in Nazi-occupied France with a screenplay by Jean Cocteau, introduces the story of Tristan and Isolde into a sinister part of the twentieth century. Director Robert Bresson's award-winning *Lancelot du Lac* (1974) follows the plot of the *Mort Artu* but

uses eccentric camera work to explore the passion of medieval battles and Lancelot's own inner turmoil. The Arthurian film most faithful to its medieval text is Eric Rohmer's *Perceval le Gallois* (1978), a visually stunning adaptation of Chrétien's *Perceval*. Not surprisingly, German filmmakers have displayed most interest in adapting German texts and music. Richard Blank's *Parzifal* (1980) brought Wolfram von Eschenbach's story to German television, while Hans-Jürgen Syberberg's *Parsifal* (1981–82) was an acclaimed and controversial film adaptation of Wagner's last opera.

British radio and television have produced Arthurian 'serials', but a seriously Arthurian series has eluded American television. Animated series, single episodes and made-for-television movies have featured Arthurian characters and themes. Of the latter, CBS's *Arthur the King* which aired in 1985 featured Malcolm McDowell and Candice Bergen, miscast as Arthur and Morgan le Fay (though this show did offer the rarely seen 'Gawain and the Loathly Lady' plot). More ambitious was the 1998 NBC mini-series *Merlin*, with Sam Neill in the lead role, which was seen by a large viewing audience in America and which also won several awards for special effects and cinematography. The screenplay, however, was a very loose adaptation of the Merlin–Nimuë 'romance' with the fairy Queen Mab (a character from Irish and English folklore not heretofore an Arthurian figure) inexplicably inserted as the villainess.

(Above) Robert Bresson's film Lancelot du Lac *won the 1974 International Critics' Prize.*

In the French film Perceval le Gallois *(1978), sets were used to represent medieval manuscript illumination.*

Arthurian Music

(Right) The modern bard Robin Williamson has used Arthurian characters and themes in his music, part of the resurgence of 'Celtic' music that began to have an impact on folk and rock in the 1970s.

ADAPTATIONS FOR TELEVISION and film have relied upon grandiose musical scores to add to the power and drama of the Arthurian saga. In the medieval and Renaissance periods, Arthurian music tended to be 'light entertainment', from lyrical troubadour ballads to Italian *cantari* and English masques. With the advent of opera, however, Arthurian music became more serious and ambitious. Henry Purcell's opera *King Arthur* (1691) is a mere 'trifle' (to use the poet John Dryden's description – he wrote the libretto) compared to the grand Arthurian projects of the nineteenth century, while the Arthurian operas of the twentieth century failed to garner much attention (the exception being the 1991 premiere of Sir Harrison Birtwistle's *Sir Gawain and the Green Knight*, which featured nude performers).

Of course, Richard Wagner's Arthurian operas tower above all modern Arthurian musical projects. Wagner showed his interest in the Grail in *Lohengrin* (1848), explored the destructive nature of passion (and new musical frontiers) in *Tristan und Isolde* (1859) and attempted an ambitious work of Christian mysticism and ritual with *Parsifal* (1882). As with his Ring cycle, Wagner turned in his Arthurian operas to early medieval myth – and to German authors Gottfried von Strassburg and Wolfram von Eschenbach – freely reworking the stories to emphasize romance and ritual in his librettos. So compelling has this music remained that, a century later, John Boorman chose selections from *Tristan* and *Parsifal* along with 'Siegfried's Funeral Music' to add an aural punch to his film *Excalibur*.

For most people, however, the Arthurian music with which they most connect is more middle-brow and a bit less complex. *Camelot*, based on T.H. White's *The Once and Future King*, became a hit Broadway musical in 1960 with music by Frederick Loewe and lyrics by Alan Jay Lerner. Julie Andrews, Robert Goulet and thousands of community theatre players since, have ushered these Lerner and Loewe songs – especially the title track – into the American musical repertoire. *Camelot* was a favourite of President John F. Kennedy, and was made into a film in 1967. Less well-known is the music written by Benjamin Britten for a BBC radio play of White's *The Sword in the Stone* (1938), as well as the several musical versions of Mark Twain's *Connecticut Yankee*.

Arthurian Ballads

'King Arthur had three sons,
Big rogues as ever did swing,
He had three sons of whores
And he kicked them all three
out-of-doors
Because they could not sing.'
From 'King Arthur'
(English, traditional)

'Where shall we find King
Arthur?
His place is sought in vain,
Yet dead he is not, but alive,
And he shall come again!
From 'He Shall Come Again'
(Cornish, traditional)

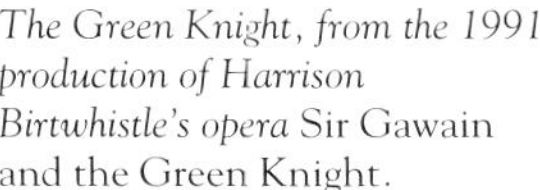

The Green Knight, from the 1991 production of Harrison Birtwhistle's opera Sir Gawain and the Green Knight.

Most recently, rock and popular music have occasionally made use of Arthurian stories and characters. The most substantial rock piece is Rick Wakeman's *The Myths and Legends of King Arthur and the Knights of the Round Table* (1975), which synthesizes Wakeman's keyboard creations with narration, choirs and electric guitars. Arthurian themes have long been part of the folk music of the Celtic fringe. In the late twentieth-century, however, enthusiasm for 'Celtic' music helped to draw attention to the music of artists such as Alan Stivell and Robin Williamson, who have woven their own musical tales of Avalon and Merlin.

Wagner and the Matter of Britain

The German composer Richard Wagner (1813–83) is duly credited with pioneering new musical forms in the Late Romantic period. But he is best known for creating grand operatic sagas, including two Arthurian works, Tristan und Isolde *(completed in 1859 and performed 1865) and* Parsifal *(1882). Having studied medieval literature at Dresden, Wagner probably became acquainted early on with the works of the great German poets Gottfried von Strassburg and Wolfram von Eschenbach. As early as 1848 he displayed his fascination for Arthurian romance in his opera* Lohengrin *(performed in 1850), which follows the adventures of Parsifal's son (here depicted as the Swan Knight) and is interwoven with Grail themes.*

A more mature composer, who had drunk deeply of modern German philosophy and begun to apply it to musical theory, Wagner returned to the Matter of Britain with the opera Tristan und Isolde. *Condensing Gottfried's plot into three cohesive acts, Wagner wrote some of his most powerful music to communicate a tale of all-consuming love. Here, Isolde loves Tristan from the beginning, but because of his seeming rejection of her she gives him the potion, which she thinks is poison, and both drink in expectation of death. Of course it is really a love potion, and after the two drink they lose all sense of reason in being consumed by passion. As the opera moves to its conclusion the orchestra and voices move closer together until they are one. The sensual but incidental music of the 'Prelude' returns with the despairing 'Liebestod' (Love-Death), a powerful aria in which Isolde, in a final consummation of her love for Tristan, gives up her life at his deathbed.*

Wagner's musical philosophy continued to develop in a bold and ambitious direction when, just one year before his death, he completed Parsifal. *This long opera was an attempt at* Gesamtkunstwerk *('a total work of art'), in which music, words and staging form a seamless unit (the opera was specifically intended to realize the potential of the Festspielhaus at Bayreuth, the opera house in Bavaria which Wagner himself designed). Wagner takes his plot mainly from von Eschenbach, but reworks it so that the Grail is the cup of the Last Supper and is surrounded by specifically Christian rituals, while the maimed king Amfortas is wounded in the side, like Christ. The opera is ripe with ritual and symbolism, illustrated more often by the music than the words. Much of the opera's music is discordant and filled with deceptive cadences, but Parsifal's actions in the final act – including the healing of Amfortas – bring harmony to the discord.*

Parsifal *is a complex work and not nearly as well known as* Tristan, *or the* Ring *cycle. It was, however, Wagner's last musical statement, and an admirable attempt at using an Arthurian tale to illustrate the universal themes of purity and compassion. Though Wagner never made use of King Arthur himself (perhaps, though not necessarily, for nationalistic reasons), he made one of the most significant modern contributions to the Arthurian tradition.*

The stage setting for Act III of Wieland Wagner's 1966 production of Tristan und Isolde *at Bayreuth.*

Guinevere (Cherie Lunghi) and Lancelot (Nicholas Clay) unleash their passions in this scene from the film Excalibur *(1981). In the late twentieth century, movies and novels continued to focus on this tragic love affair.*

KING ARTHUR HAS, in recent times, manifested himself equally in high and popular culture. He has reached new audiences, especially the youth market, and will probably survive the twenty-first century with no loss of allure.

One reason for Arthur's appeal in our time has been the boom, beginning in the 1970s, of the science fiction and fantasy market. Many 'Generation-Xers' were introduced to Arthurian and other medieval myths through such novels and through the popular 'Dungeons & Dragons' role-playing games created by E. Gary Gygax. Players can assume the identity of a Knight of the Round Table or encounter Merlin in one of many Arthurian scenarios in Dungeons & Dragons. Or they can opt for a specifically Arthurian role-playing game such as *King Arthur Pendragon* (1985), designed by Greg Stafford with a supplementary book, *The King Arthur Companion*, by novelist Phyllis Ann Karr.

Arthur on the Internet

Role-playing and fantasy adventure games such as these made a smooth transition to the computer screen in the 1980s. Now, gaming enthusiasts can find Arthurian games on the Internet. Even before the advent of the graphics-dominated World Wide Web, Arthurian buffs could communicate their mutual enthusiasm in chat groups, listservs and e-mail correspondence on the Internet. There are presently dozens of websites dedicated to Arthuriana, of both the academic and popular varieties. The casual browser can, like a VR (Virtual Reality) Merlin, conjure up images from medieval manuscripts, commentaries on Malory and clips from *Monty Python and the Holy Grail* with just a few clicks of a mouse-button. Never before have so many Arthurian resources been this accessible, and never before has it been so difficult to steer a safe path through the clutter.

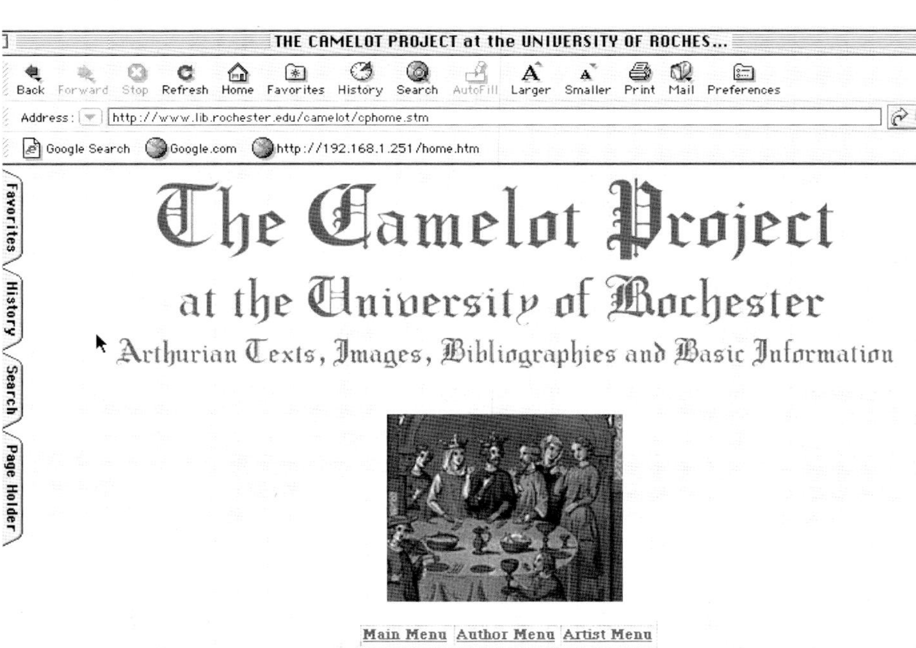

The World Wide Web includes dozens of Arthurian sites, both academic and amateur. The Camelot Project *(right), one of the top academic sites, offers medieval texts and images as well as bibliographies of Arthurian scholarship.*

THE KENNEDY-CAMELOT MYTH

In December 1960, president-elect John F. Kennedy and his wife Jacqueline attended the opening of the Broadway musical Camelot, based on T.H. White's novel The Once and Future King. Resonating with legends he had read earlier in life, the play became one of Kennedy's favourites and its themes seemed appropriate for what he was trying to achieve in America. Shortly after his assassination in Dallas in 1963, journalists began to describe the presidency of J.F.K. as 'the Camelot years', a characterization largely suggested by the First Lady in an interview with the writer Theodore H. White. Thus was born the Kennedy-Camelot myth, which has been constantly revived by the American media in order either to sentimentalize that 'brief shining moment' (to borrow a line from the musical) or to shoot holes in it – 'the myth of Camelot' – by exposing Kennedy's adulterous behaviour and political intrigues.

But to some, there is more to the Kennedy-Camelot myth than this. The mysterious circumstances surrounding the assassination have led to several conspiracy theories. In an early example, Kennedy was alleged to have survived the shooting but remained in a vegetative state while his wife, having married Aristotle Onassis, carried J.F.K. away on one of her new husband's ships to some secret island for convalescence. The Once and Future President never returned from his Avalon, but some transferred their hopes to his handsome young son, John F. Kennedy, Jr. The untimely death of J.F.K., Jr, in July 1999, when the plane he was piloting plummeted into the Atlantic, revived (in the news media at least) talk of the Kennedy-Camelot myth. One television network, broadcasting J.F.K., Jr's burial at sea, played a voice-over in which President Kennedy spoke eloquently of his family's love for the sea: his words conveyed the message that we are all born of the sea, as the salt in our blood attests, and we shall all one day return to it. Like Bedivere in Tennyson's poem 'The Passing of Arthur', many of us no doubt heard in this speech the faint echoing cry, 'From the great deep to the great deep he goes'.

President John F. Kennedy and the First Lady arrive in Dallas on 22 November 1963, just hours before J.F.K.'s assassination. Like Arthur, Kennedy received a fatal head wound.

KING ARTHUR

ARMOR CLASS: *0*
MOVE: *12" (6" in armor)*
HIT POINTS: *123*
NO. OF ATTACKS: 2
DAMAGE/ATTACK: *By weapon type*
SPECIAL ATTACKS: *Magic sword (see below)*
SPECIAL DEFENSES: *Magic scabbard (see below)*
MAGIC RESISTANCE: *Standard*
SIZE: *M (6')*
ALIGNMENT: *Lawful good*
CLERIC/DRUID: *Nil*
FIGHTER: *14th level paladin*
MAGIC-USER/ILLUSIONIST: *Nil*
THIEF/ASSASSIN: *Nil*
MONK/BARD: *5th level bard*
PSIONIC ABILITY: *Nil*
Attack/Defense Modes: *Nil*
S: *18 (52) (+2, +3)* I: *18* W: *19* D: *16* C: *18* CH: *18*

The entry for Arthur in the Advanced Dungeons & Dragons *book,* Deities and Demigods *(1980). Arthur's attributes (left) are superhuman, making him a formidable opponent in D&D combat.*

Craig-y-Ddinas, near Pontneddfechan, South Wales, where King Arthur and his warriors are said to lie sleeping in a cave.

SERIOUS ENTERTAINMENTS

For some people, taking a step beyond Dungeons & Dragons *means joining one of a growing number of medieval re-enactment groups. The* Society for Creative Anachronism *(or SCA), founded in 1966 by a group of science fiction and fantasy fans in* Berkeley, California, *has become an international subculture where those sharing medieval interests can gather – for an 'encampment' or for combat – and assume a chosen identity ranging from lady-in-waiting to Knight Templar. The SCA's 20,000 members run the gamut, from neo-pagan to* Christian *and from weekend dabbler to serious student of the minutiae of medieval material culture. In the United Kingdom, the re-enactment group* Britannia *(pictured right) specializes in* Roman *and 'Arthurian' combats, and their members have been featured in such films as* Braveheart *and* Robin Hood: Prince of Thieves.

In the US the last decade of the twentieth century witnessed an explosion of Renaissance Faires, commercial entertainments that combine elements from the theme park with those of a county fair. Jousting and late medieval costumes draw hundreds of thousands of visitors to these Faires each year, and provide full-time employment for legions of modern minstrels and armourers. For a less commercial and (usually) more historically accurate experience, one can visit events sponsored by the hundreds of 'living history' groups in the US and Europe. Less about combat than about recreating a total living experience, these groups make educating the public about Roman legions and medieval villages a top priority. And there are also the students, at Oxford and other universities, who have formed Arthurian societies for both social and academic pursuits.

Members of Britannia re-enact a battle between Romano-British soldiers and Pictish warriors at Portchester Castle in 1997.

'It is all true . . .'

The future for Arthuriana would be difficult for even Merlin to predict. There are, however, no apparent signs of decline, judging from the number of books, videos and websites that have appeared in the last few years. Camelot still speaks to us. It is not a dead myth, a utopian sentiment belonging only to past generations – despite occasional examples of journalistic nostalgia when it comes to describing John F. Kennedy's presidency as 'the Camelot years'. Rather it is, as Winston Churchill asserted, a lasting and important part of our western cultural inheritance, like the stories of Homer and the Bible, to be drawn upon whenever we want to express our societal hopes and fears. 'It is all true,' wrote Churchill of the Arthurian legends, 'or it ought to be'.

Historians and archaeologists may never produce definitive evidence for Arthur's existence. But they will continue to discover more about the medieval world in which he may have lived, and in which his legend certainly germinated. Scholars will also continue to elucidate the 'texts', from medieval romances to modern films, which portray his story. And new readers will continue to be enchanted by the old and timeless tales of Camelot. In this sense it is all true. Here lies Arthur, the Once and Future King.

Gustave Doré, 'Edyrn comes to Arthur's court at Caerleon-in-Usk', illustration for Tennyson's Idylls of the King *(1868).*

Directory of Organizations

The following list includes both academic and popular organizations with Arthurian, Celtic and/or medieval interests.

ArthurNet
The leading Arthurian discussion list on the Internet.
www.clas.ufl.edu/users/jshoaf/Arthurnet.htm

Britannia: The Arthurian Re-enactment Society
Formed in 1990 for the purposes of research and re-enactment of fifth- and sixth-century AD Britain and for the promotion of Arthur as an historical figure.
c/o Dan Shadrake
13 Ardleigh
Basildon, Essex
England, SS16 5RA
www.arthurian.freeuk.com

The Camelot Project
An electronic database of Arthurian texts, images, bibliographies.
c/o Alan Lupack, Curator
The Robbins Library
Room 416, Rush Rhees Library
University of Rochester
Rochester, New York, NY 14627-0055
www.lib.rochester.edu/camelot/cphome.stm

The Cardiff Arthurian Society (Llys y Brenin Arthur yng Ngaerdydd)
A student society whose stated aim is to promote medieval history, especially the legends surrounding King Arthur and his Knights of the Round Table.
www.cf.ac.uk/uwcc/archi/howshall/arthurm/index.html

The Charrette Project
A scholarly multi-media electronic archive containing a medieval manuscript tradition – that of Chrétien de Troyes' *Le Chevalier de la Charrette*.
www.princeton.edu/~lancelot/

CSANA (Celtic Studies Association of North America)
The major professional association for Celtic Studies in North America. CSANA sponsors a newsletter, a bibliography and an annual conference, and is open to academics and independent scholars.
Professor Ellissa R. Henken (membership information)
Department of English
Park Hall
University of Georgia
Athens, Georgia, GA 30602
www.cis.upenn.edu/~csana/

Garland Publishing
The major publisher of scholarly books on King Arthur in literature and the arts.
100A Sherman Avenue
Hamden, Connecticut, CT 06514
www.garlandpub.com

The International Arthurian Society
A scholarly society welcoming anyone interested in the study of King Arthur and the literature of the Round Table. Publishes, quarterly, the journal *Arthuriana*.
North American Branch:
Professor Joan Grimbert (Treasurer)
Department of Modern Languages and Literatures
Catholic University
Washington, DC 20064
dc.smu.edu/Arthuriana/ias.html

The International Courtly Literature Society
Promotes the study and criticism of the literature of courts and court-oriented cultures, particularly the medieval literature of western Europe.
Professor Leslie Zarker Morgan (Membership, North American Branch)
Department of Modern Languages and Literatures
Loyola College
Baltimore, Maryland, MD 21210
www-dept.usm.edu/~engdept/icls/iclsnab.htm

The International Marie de France Society
Its mission is to establish friendly and productive exchanges between those persons – academics, independent scholars and students – interested in Marie de France and the anonymous lays.
c/o Dr Chantal Maréchal
P.O. Box 7438
Richmond, Virginia, VA 23221
saturn.vcu.edu/~cmarecha/mdf.html

The Labyrinth: Resources for Medieval Studies
Provides free access to reliable electronic resources in medieval studies through a World Wide Web server at Georgetown University, facilitating connections to databases, services, texts and images on other servers around the world.
www.georgetown.edu/labyrinth/

The Medieval Academy of America
The oldest and largest association of medievalists in North America, it publishes the quarterly journal *Speculum* and sponsors an annual academic conference. Anyone interested in the Middle Ages is welcome to join.
1430 Massachusetts Avenue
Cambridge, Massachusetts, MA 02138
www.georgetown.edu/MedievalAcademy/

The Medieval Institute
Best known for its annual conference which draws about 3000 medievalists and includes many Arthurian sessions.
Western Michigan University
Kalamazoo, MI 49008-3801
www.wmich.edu/medieval/index.html

ORB (On-line Reference Book for Medieval Studies)
ORB is a co-operative effort on the part of scholars across the Internet to establish an on-line textbook source for medieval studies.
Professor Carolyn Schriber, Editor
Department of History
Rhodes College
2000 North Parkway
Memphis, Tennessee, TN 381112
orb.rhodes.edu/

The Oxford Arthurian Society
Founded by Oxford University students to explore King Arthur in history, literature and legend. It sponsors a magazine, banquets and speakers.
users.ox.ac.uk/~arthsoc/

The Pendragon Society
Founded in Winchester in 1959 to stimulate interest in Arthur and to investigate the history and archaeology of the Matter of Britain.
c/o John Ford
41 Ridge Street
Watford, Hertfordshire
England, WD2 5BL
www.pendragon.mcmail.com/index.htm

TEAMS (The Consortium for the Teaching of the Middle Ages)
The TEAMS Middle English text series makes available (in print and on-line) to teachers and students Arthurian texts which occupy an important place in the literary and cultural canon but which are not readily available in student editions.
www.lib.rochester.edu/camelot/teams/tmsmenu.htm

Glossary

adventus Saxonum The 'coming of the Saxons', referring to the first Anglo-Saxon settlements in Britain in the fifth century.

Age of Arthur and the **'Arthurian' age** Popularly used as labels for Britain in the fifth and sixth centuries. Synonymous with my term **Brittonic Age**. Most historians and archaeologists now avoid naming the period after Arthur, but in a supra-historical sense it is entirely appropriate.

Alba and **Albany** Medieval names for Scotland.

Albion Ancient name for Britain, first used by Greek explorers.

Anglo-Saxon An old but still commonly used term used to describe various Germanic-speaking peoples (and their cultures) who settled in Britain in the early medieval period. 'English' is usually synonymous, though it too oversimplifies.

Arthuriana A term used by modern scholars to describe the total Arthurian experience, meaning the appearance of Arthur or Arthurian figures in history, literature, the arts, music, film, television and electronic media.

barbarians The Greek, and later-Roman, term for peoples outside their culture, whose language sounded to their civilized ears like 'bar-bar'. Late imperial and Christian writers use the term barbarian to refer to a variety of Celtic, Germanic and Hunnic peoples originating outside the borders of the Empire, continuing to use it even after some of these peoples had settled in Roman territory.

bards Ubiquitous in Celtic-speaking lands in the Middle Ages, bards were both entertainers and oral historians. Wealthy courts had resident bards, though most were itinerant.

Brittonic Age My term for Britain during the fifth and sixth centuries. An alternative to the label **sub-Roman Britain** and synonymous with the **Age of Arthur**.

Brut A generic term for a history or chronicle of the ancient Britons. From Brutus, the legendary founder of Britain.

Caledonia Roman name for Scotland.

cives The term means 'citizens', which could either denote Roman citizenship, citizenship in a town, or simply belonging to a common homeland like Britain.

civitates Small territorial units within the Roman Empire, in Britain defined by existing tribal territory. Administration was usually located in the largest town, the *civitas*-capital.

comitatenses Mobile Roman field armies utilized in threatened provinces in the fourth and fifth centuries.

curiales and ***decuriones*** Both of these terms denote members of the *curia*, or town council, in the Roman provinces. These decurions tended to establish hereditary succession, hence the term 'curial families'.

Druid Member of the priest class in pagan Celtic societies. Highly esteemed, even respected, by some Greek writers for their learning, the Druids were guilty, nevertheless, of political intrigue and human sacrifice, and were thus persecuted by the Romans.

dux bellorum 'Leader of battles', a phrase used to describe Arthur in the *Historia Brittonum*.

foederati and ***laeti*** Official terms used to denote groups of barbarians hired to fight for Rome.

grail In general terms, a serving dish or cup, often ornate. Used by many medieval writers to refer specifically to a sacred vessel used by Jesus at the Last Supper, which later passed into the hands of Joseph of Arimathea and was eventually brought to Britain.

Hibernia Roman name for Ireland.

hillfort General term used by historians and archaeologists to describe defended hilltop settlements and other enclosed places of the Iron Age. Ubiquitous in Celtic-speaking lands, these settlements were eventually conquered by the Romans, but many in Britain were refortified in the **Brittonic Age**.

lai or **lay** A short song or tale performed by a medieval bard, especially in Brittany. By the twelfth century they had entered into French literature.

limes The Latin word for 'limit'; the borders or frontier of the Roman Empire.

Matter of Britain Used first in the twelfth century, *matière de Bretagne* denotes legendary material that originated in Britain and Brittany. Usually the subject-matter is Arthurian.

noblesse oblige The sense of obligation felt by the medieval European nobility to protect those below them in society.

Outremer Christian lands 'across the [Mediterranean] sea' in the Middle Ages, specifically the Crusader States of the Middle East.

Plantagenet The family of Geoffrey, Count of Anjou, whose son Henry became king of England in 1154.

possessores The general term for ***curiales*** and other landed aristocrats in the Roman provinces.

Saxons An historically attested tribe (or group of tribes) from northern Germany, some of whom participated as mercenaries and/or colonists in Britain. The term was used for centuries by Romans and Britons as a generic label for various Germanic peoples.

sub-Roman and **post-Roman Britain** Terms used, primarily by archaeologists, to describe Britain in the fifth and sixth centuries. However, sub-Roman often implies deterioration from Roman norms, and post-Roman has no obvious ending-point.

tyrannus 'Tyrant', used variously by Greek, Roman and Christian authors to denote usurpers, despots and sinful monarchs. It may, however, have been used colloquially in the **Brittonic Age** simply as a synonym for 'lord'.

vitae Shorthand for 'lives', that is, biographies of Christian saints. This literary genre, extremely popular throughout the Middle Ages, is called hagiography.

Gazetteer

The following is a brief gazetteer of sites in Britain that are associated with Arthur in history, myth and legend. It is representative rather than comprehensive. Included with each entry there is, where appropriate, a grid reference for locating the sites on *Ordnance Survey* maps.

Alnwick Castle, Northumberland (NU188136). One of two candidates (see **Bamburgh Castle**) for Lancelot's castle, Joyous Gard, offered by Malory.

Amesbury, Wiltshire (SU150417). In a story borrowed from the *Historia Brittonum*, Geoffrey of Monmouth describes a peace conference between Vortigern and Hengist during which the Saxons slew many British nobles. Geoffrey locates the conference at 'the Cloister of Ambrius', near Salisbury in Wiltshire. Malory relates a separate incident in which Guinevere retired to a nunnery at 'Almesbury' after Arthur fell at Camlann. At Amesbury, on the River Avon east of Salisbury, stands a Norman abbey church built on the site of a much earlier church or monastery.

Arthuret, Cumbria (NY404729). The Battle of Arthuret (in Welsh, Arderydd) was the cause of Myrddin's madness according to the Welsh poem 'Yr Afallennau' (The Apple Trees).

Arthur's Bed, Cornwall (SX240757). A granite monolith on Bodmin Moor which has a hollowed-out, coffin-shaped surface known as Arthur's Bed.

Arthur's O'en, Stirlingshire (NS879827). Arthur's O'en (that is, Oven) was a dome-shaped Roman building which once stood near the site of the Carron Ironworks. It is first mentioned in 1293 and an engraving was made of it in the eighteenth century, but nothing remains of it today.

Arthur's Quoit, Anglesey (SH432855 and SH501860), Caernarvonshire (SH230346 and SH499413), Merionethshire (SH588229), Pembrokeshire (SM725281, SN000360, and SN060394), and Carmarthenshire (SN729245). Arthur's Quoit (in Welsh, *Coetan Arthur*) is a name given to several ancient stone structures in Wales. Most are associated with megalithic burial chambers.

Arthur's Seat, Edinburgh (NT275729). The most famous Arthur's Seat is the picturesque mountain that rises above Holyrood Palace in Edinburgh. The mountain, which is now part of Holyrood Park, has several peaks which can be climbed for spectacular views of Edinburgh. Its association with King Arthur goes back to about the fifteenth century. Other Arthur's Seats are at Dumbarrow Hill, Angus (NO552479) and to the east of Liddesdale, Cumbria (NY495783).

Arthur's Stone, Herefordshire (SD3141). Several megaliths bear this name (see also **Arthur's Quoit**). Arthur's Stone is the name given locally to a megalithic burial site of c.3000 BC on a hill north of Dorstone. Dorstone is on the B4348 road, east of Hay-on-Wye.

Arthur's Stone, West Glamorgan (SS490905). Near Reynoldston, north of Cefn Bryn, is an ancient burial chamber known as Maen Ceti. The 25 ton capstone of this megalith is called Arthur's Stone and the king's ghost is said to emerge occasionally from beneath it. Arthur's Stone is north of the A4118 road.

Astolat (see **Guildford**)

Avalon (see **Glastonbury**)

Badbury Rings, Dorset (ST964030). One of the candidates for Gildas's Badon Hill. Visible today are the earthworks of the Iron Age hillfort, later the site of a Roman posting station.

Bamburgh Castle, Northumberland (NU183350). One of two candidates for Malory's Joyous Gard (see **Alnwick Castle**) and the site of an early Saxon fort.

Bath, Avon (ST751647). Geoffrey of Monmouth locates the Battle of Badon Hill in this Roman town.

Ben Arthur, Strathclyde (NN259058). A steep mountain 2 miles (3 km) west of the tip of Loch Long one of whose craggy promontories is known as Arthur's Seat.

Birdoswald, Cumbria (NY615663). Birdoswald is the site of the Roman fort, Banna, on Hadrian's Wall. It was once thought to have been called Camboglanna, and therefore some have linked it linguistically with Camlann, where Arthur's last battle took place. Recent excavations have revealed the reuse, in the fifth century, of two Roman granaries as feasting halls. Scholars are now convinced, however, that Camboglanna was in fact the Roman fort at **Castlesteads**.

Brecon Beacons, Powys (SO010214). According to Gerald of Wales, two of the peaks and the dip inbetween them form Arthur's Chair.

Brent Knoll, Somerset (ST341510). After Arthur knighted Ider, son of Nuth, he went to challenge three giants who lived on the Mount of Frogs, as Brent Knoll was once called. This isolated hill, close to the Bristol Channel, is 450 ft (140m) high and circled with Iron Age defences. Some have theorized that it, along with sites such as **Glastonbury Tor** and **South Cadbury**, may once have formed a chain of beacon signal stations in the sub-Roman period.

Caer Gai, Gwynedd (SH877315). This hillfort, north of Llanuwchllyn, once served as a base for Roman troops. Its name, which means 'the stronghold of Cai', refers to the Sir Kay of later romances. Today, some of the ramparts of the Roman fort are visible.

Caerleon, Gwent (ST339906). The place, according to Geoffrey of Monmouth, where Arthur held court. Before it was excavated, Caerleon's amphitheatre was covered by a grassy mound known locally as Arthur's Table.

Camelford, Cornwall (SX105837). This village is one contender for Camelot or, at least, a place where later writers imagined Arthur's fabled court to have been.

Camelot (see **Camelford**)

Camlann (see **Birdoswald** and **Castlesteads**)

Cardigan, Dyfed (SN1746). In Chrétien's *Erec and Enide*, and in other early romances, Arthur holds court in the Welsh city of Cardigan.

Carlisle, Cumbria (NY400560). A number of romances describe Arthur as holding court at Carduel, which is generally considered to mean Carlisle, formerly the Roman town of Luguvalium. In Malory's *Le Morte d'Arthur*, Guinevere is exposed and sentenced to death at Carlisle.

Carmarthen, Dyfed (SN417205). According to Geoffrey, Merlin was born here and the city was later named Kaermerdin (Merlin's fortress) after him. An oak tree growing in the centre of the town was called Merlin's Tree and was associated with this prophecy:

> When Myrddin's Tree shall tumble down,
> Then shall fall Carmarthen town.

Carn March Arthur, Gwynedd (SN651982). On a hill above the Dovey estuary is a rock indented with what is said to be the hoofprint of Arthur's horse (*march Arthur*, in Welsh).

Castle Dore, Cornwall (SX103548). This Iron Age hillfort is associated with the figures of King Mark and Tristan (the so-called **Tristan Stone** is located nearby). The archaeologist C.A. Ralegh Radford believed that within the circular earthen ramparts lay a fifth- or sixth-century settlement.

Castlesteads, Cumbria (NY355163). A small fort along Hadrian's Wall, with no visible remains today. Scholars now believe that this fort bore the name Camboglanna, which some have linked linguistically with Camlann, the site of Arthur's last battle. See also **Birdoswald**.

Catterick, North Yorkshire (SE220990). Both a Roman fort (Cataractonium) and an early Anglo-Saxon settlement have been discovered at Catterick. The Battle of Catraeth, the subject of the *Gododdin*, has been located here by some modern scholars.

Chalice Well, Glastonbury (ST5139). A spring once ran between **Glastonbury Tor** and Chalice Hill. What remains of the spring is a well that is now surrounded by gardens. A description in *Perlesvaus* of Lancelot visiting a spring near Avalon may refer to Chalice Well. Though monks were apparently using it c.1200, its claim to be the resting-place of the Holy Grail is quite modern.

Chester, Cheshire (SJ405663). A contender for the 'City of the Legion', the site of Arthur's ninth battle in the *Historia Brittonum*.

Craig Arthur, Denbighshire (SJ224470). Craig Arthur, or 'Arthur's Rock', is the end of a long rocky ridge near the hillfort Dinas Bran.

Dinas Emrys, Gwynedd (SH606492). The site of Vortigern's tower in both the *Historia Brittonum* and Geoffrey of Monmouth's *History*. Modern excavations have revealed a settlement dating from the fourth to the sixth centuries.

Dover, Kent (TR325419). The site of Arthur's return to fight Modred in Malory's *Le Morte d'Arthur* and of Gawain's death and interment. Dover was a Roman fort (Dubris) whose lighthouse still stands, nearly intact, next to a Saxon church within the walls of the medieval castle.

Dozmary Pool, Cornwall (SX195745). High on Bodmin Moor is Dozmary Pool, the alleged site of Excalibur's return.

Drumelzier, Borders (NT135343). Merlin's grave is said to be located here, according to this couplet attributed to Thomas the Rhymer (1220–97):

> When Tweed and Pausayl meet at Merlin's grave,
> Scotland and England shall one monarch have.

On the other side of the River Tweed is a spot called Merlindale.

Dumbarton Rock, Strathclyde (NS400745). Legendary birthplace of Modred, also called Arthur's Castle in a document dated 1367. The Celticist John Rhys has theorized that Dumbarton was **Astolat**. Modern excavations have revealed sub-Roman fortifications at Dumbarton and traces of Mediterranean imports.

Eildon Hills, Borders (NT548339). The Eildon Hills lie to the southeast of Melrose, in southern Scotland. According to one legend, Arthur and his knights lie sleeping in a hidden cavern beneath the hills.

Glastonbury Abbey, Somerset (ST500388). Glastonbury has many Arthurian associations. The Abbey, which may date back to early Christian times, was an important monastic centre in both Anglo-Saxon and Norman England. It was the site of an excavation, in 1191, during which its monks claimed to have found the bodies of both Arthur and Guinevere. Due to the elaborate tomb built to house their bones, and to a later legend that placed Joseph of Arimathea at Glastonbury, the Abbey became an even more famous destination for pilgrims, kings and tourists.

Glastonbury Tor, Somerset (ST512386). This hill rises 518 ft (158 m) above sea level, dominates the Glastonbury landscape and is visible for miles around. In prehistoric times it was probably surrounded by marshy water, giving it the appearance of an island and perhaps giving birth to the myth of the Isle of Avalon. Archaeological excavation has revealed traces of a sub-Roman settlement at the Tor, but of an unknown character. Modern visitors come seeking everything from druidic mazes to grails, but the only thing clearly visible today are the tower remains of the late medieval church of St Michael.

Gloucester, Gloucestershire (SO830190). This Roman site (the colony, Glevum) features as a powerful fortress in *Culhwch and Olwen*, while *Peredur* mentions the 'nine hags of Gloucester'.

Guildford, Surrey (TQ0448). Malory identifies Guildford as the location of **Astolat**, where the Fair Maid, Elaine, died of grief for loving Lancelot.

Killibury, Cornwall (SX018736). Kelliwic (Celliwig, in Welsh) is the site of Arthur's court in the Welsh Triads. Its location is unknown. Killibury is one contender: it is a small double-banked, concentric hillfort dating back to the Iron Age. Fragments of Mediterranean pottery found in the topsoil suggest occupation in the fifth or sixth century as well.

Liddington Castle, Wiltshire (SU208796). Another proposed candidate for Badon Hill, the site of Arthur's most famous battle. The 'Castle' refers to the earthen ramparts of an Iron Age hillfort.

Llongborth Site of a battle involving Arthur's warriors and Geraint, who was slain there, according to the Welsh poem *Geraint son of Erbin*. There are two chief contenders for this locale: Langport (ST422267), in Somerset, and the Roman fort of Portchester (SU625046), in Hampshire.

London In Layamon's *Brut* and in some of the early romances, Arthur holds court in the city of London. Malory relates the story of Guinevere trying to elude a pursuing Modred by fleeing to London and locking herself inside the Tower. Some of the Late Roman city wall survives and there is archaeological evidence that Britons and Saxons lived in and around the city in the fifth and sixth centuries, but London's political status in the post-Roman period is uncertain.

Lyonesse The legendary kingdom of Tristan, Galahalt and other Arthurian figures. Many have speculated that this was once what are now the Isles of Scilly. The sea has since separated the islands from each other and from Cornwall.

Maiden Castle, Dorset (SY6788). While the Castle of the Maidens figures in later Arthurian romance, it is unlikely that there is any direct connection to this important centre of the Celtic Iron Age. The circuit of its massive ramparts can still be traced today.

Merlin's Chair, Dyfed (SN4120). A few miles east of **Carmarthen** is Merlin's Hill, the summit of which resembles a chair. Merlin is said to be sleeping inside the hill and is also associated with a sacred tree within the city.

Merlin's Mound, Wiltshire (SU183686). About 5 miles (8 km) east of Avebury, within the grounds of Marlborough College, is a terraced earthwork known as Merlin's Mound, once thought to be his grave. Marlborough was Latinized as 'Merleburgia', and this may have prompted the connection with Merlin.

Merlin's Rock, Cornwall (SW470259). At the southern end of the quay in the village of Mousehole (pronounced 'Mouzel'), rising from the water, is Merlin's Rock. Here Merlin is said to have prophesied:

> There shall land on the Rock of Merlin
> Those who shall burn Paul, Penzance and Newlyn.

In 1595 four Spanish galleys fulfilled this 'prophecy'.

Moel Arthur, Clwyd (SJ145660). Moel Arthur, or 'Arthur's Hill', is an ancient hillfort in north Wales.

Orkney Islands In some later romances the Orkney Isles, off the north coast of Scotland, are home to the rebel king Lot and his sons, Gawain, Agravaine, Gaheris and Gareth.

Pen Arthur, Dyfed (SN717237). A hill in south Wales where, according to one legend, Arthur hurled a boulder from the summit into the River Sawdde a mile away (1.5 km). This hill may also be one of the places where Arthur and his men, in *Culhwch and Olwen*, fight the boar Twrch Trwyth.

Pendragon Castle, Cumbria (NY782026). Traditionally the fortress of Arthur's father, Uther Pendragon, 'the Castle of Pendragon' is, in *Le Morte d'Arthur*, given by Lancelot to the young knight Sir Cote Male Taile.

Pillar of Eliseg, Clwyd (SJ202445). The broken shaft of a stone cross which bears a (now illegible) Latin inscription mentioning the tyrant Vortigern.

St Govan's Chapel, Dyfed (SR967929). St Govan's Head is on the southwest coast of Wales, near the village of Bosherton, south of Pembroke. A stone chapel there is thought to have been the hermitage of St Govan, a sixth-century Irish monk. William of Malmesbury, writing in the twelfth century, claimed that Gawain's tomb had been found in Pembrokeshire and Govan's Chapel was thought to be the site. There is little evidence to support any older association with Gawain.

Samson, Isles of Scilly (SV8712). According to Chrétien, Tristan fought his duel with Morholt (Malory's Sir Marhaus) on the island of Samson. The island, named after the sixth-century Cornish saint, is now uninhabited.

Silchester, Hampshire (SU640625). According to Geoffrey of Monmouth, Arthur was crowned in this Roman city (Calleva Atrebatum). Extensive excavations have revealed the circuit of the city walls, what may be an early basilical church and evidence of continued occupation into the fifth and sixth centuries. There is a very small museum on the site, but most of Silchester's artifacts are at the nearby Reading Museum.

Slaughter Bridge, Cornwall (SX109855). Near **Camelford** there is an ancient granite bridge which crosses the River Camel. The area is associated both with Arthur's birth and with his death at the Battle of Camlann.

South Cadbury, Somerset (ST628252). The hill at South Cadbury, sometimes called Cadbury Castle, is over 500 ft (152 m) high, with five massive earthen ramparts enclosing a plateau of about 18 acres (7 hectares). The Tudor antiquarians Leland and Camden recorded local belief that the hill was none other than Arthur's Camelot. Large-scale excavations in the 1960s revealed sub-Roman occupation of an Iron Age hillfort which produced new ramparts, a gatehouse and several buildings on the plateau including a great feasting hall.

Stonehenge, Wiltshire (SU122422). This famous megalithic structure on Salisbury Plain owes its Arthurian connection to Geoffrey of Monmouth, who describes it as a British war memorial erected by Merlin.

Tintagel, Cornwall (SX0588). According to Geoffrey of Monmouth, Tintagel Castle was the site of Arthur's conception and birth. A Norman castle was later erected on the site of a sub-Roman settlement, the foundations of whose small buildings can still be seen. Once thought to have been a monastery, scholars now prefer to see Tintagel as a secular stronghold or trading centre. In the nearby parish churchyard, evidence of early Christian activity has been unearthed.

Tristan Stone, Cornwall (SX111522). Near the small port of Fowey stands a stone monolith with the inscription DRUSTANUS HIC IACIT CVNOMORI FILIVS (Here lies Drustanus, son of Cunomorus). Some have interpreted this as being a reference to Tristan and King Mark.

Wearyall Hill, Somerset (ST494383). A site in Glastonbury where, according to late medieval tradition, Joseph of Arimathea planted his staff and where the Holy Thorn now grows.

Winchester, Hampshire (SU478295). Winchester is the site of a Roman town (Venta Bulgarum), a fifth-century cemetery, the Anglo-Saxon capital city under Alfred the Great and the medieval cathedral city. Malory claimed that Winchester was the site of Arthur's famous court which the French writers called Camelot. The Round Table which hangs in the Great Hall of Winchester Castle was claimed, by Henry VIII and others, to have belonged to Arthur. It is most likely that this tabletop, 18 ft (5.5 m) in diameter, originated as a thirteenth-century pageantry device and was repainted in the Tudor period.

Further Reading

Periodicals

Arthurian Interpretations. Multidisciplinary journal of Arthurian studies published biannually by the English Department, Memphis State University, Tenn. 1968–1993.

Arthurian Literature. Annual publication from Boydell and Brewer, Woodbridge, Suffolk 1981–.

Arthurian Yearbook. Annual publication from Garland, New York 1991–93.

Arthuriana. Scholarly journal of the International Arthurian Society (North American Branch), B. Wheeler (ed.), 1994–. *Arthuriana* is the successor of both *Arthurian Interpretations* and *Quondam et Futurus*.

Avalon to Camelot. Arthurian magazine, F. Reeves Lambides, Evanston, Ill. 1983–85.

Bibliographic Bulletin of the International Arthurian Society/Bulletin Bibliographique dela Societé Internationale Arthurienne. Annual publication, 1949–.

Quondam et Futurus. Scholarly newsletter devoted to Arthurian and medieval topics, M. Leake Day (ed.), published quarterly, 1979–1990.

Bibliographies, Collections, Dictionaries and Encyclopedias

The Arthuriana/Camelot Project Bibliographies
www.lib.rochester.edu/camelot/acpbibs/bibhome.stm

Bibliography of Modern Arthurian Fiction
www.dragonfire.net/~DRAGONLORDS/bkarthur3.htm

Bruce, C. W., *The Arthurian Name Dictionary*, Garland, New York 1999.

Coe, J. B., *Arthurian Bibliography*
www.aber.ac.uk/~jbc97/Bibliography.html

Coe, J. B. and Young, S., *The Celtic Sources for the Arthurian Legend*. Llanerch, Lampeter, Wales 1995.

Coghlan, R., *The Illustrated Encyclopedia of Arthurian Legends*, Barnes and Noble, New York 1995.

Hamilton, A.C. et al. (eds), *The Spenser Encyclopedia*, Routledge, London 1990.

Ireland, S., *Roman Britain: A Sourcebook*, Routledge, London and New York, 1986.

Koch, J. T. (ed.), *The Celtic Heroic Age: Literary Sources*, Celtic Studies Publications, Malden, Mass., 1995 (2nd edn).

Lacy, N.J. and Ashe, G., *The Arthurian Handbook*, Garland, New York 1988.

Lacy, N. J., Ashe, G. and Mancoff, D.N., *The Arthurian Handbook*, Garland, New York 1997 (2nd edn).

Lacy, N. J. (ed), *The Arthurian Encyclopedia*, Garland, New York 1986.

———, *The New Arthurian Encyclopedia*, Garland, New York 1991.

Minary, R. and Moorman, C., *An Arthurian Dictionary*, Academy Chicago Publishers, Ill. 1990.

Nash-Williams, V.E., *The Early Christian Monuments of Wales*, University of Wales Press, Cardiff 1950.

Pickford, C. E. and Last, R., *The Arthurian Bibliography*, St Edmundsbury Press, Bury St Edmunds, Suffolk 1981.

Reiss, E., Reiss, L. Homer and Taylor, B. (eds), *Arthurian Legend and Literature: An Annotated Bibliography, vol. 1: The Middle Ages*, Garland, New York 1984.

White, R. (ed.), *King Arthur in Legend and History*, Routledge, New York 1998.

Williams, A., Smyth, A.P. and Kirby, D.P., *A Biographical Dictionary of Dark Age Britain: England, Scotland and Wales c.500–c.1050*, Seaby, London 1991.

Primary Sources (Historical)

Adomnán of Iona: Life of St Columba, trans. and intro. R. Sharpe, Penguin, New York 1995.

Ammianus Marcellinus (Loeb edn), 3 vols, trans. J. C. Rolfe, Harvard University Press, Cambridge, Mass. 1935–40.

Bede: The Ecclesiastical History of the English Peoples, ed. and trans. J. McClure and R. Collins, Oxford University Press, Oxford 1994.

Brut y Tywysogyon, or The Chronicle of the Princes, ed. and trans. T. Jones, University of Wales Press, Cardiff 1955.

Caesar: *The Gallic War*, trans. C. Hammond, Oxford University Press, Oxford 1996.

Claudian (Loeb edn), 2 vols, ed. and trans. M. Platnauer, Harvard University Press, Cambridge, Mass. 1922.

Constance de Lyon: Vie de Saint Germain d'Auxerre, Editions du Cerf, Paris 1965.

Constantius: *Vita Sancti Germani*, ed. W. Levison, in *Scriptores Rerum Merovingicarum*, vol. 7, *Monumenta Germaniae Historica*, ed. and French trans. R. Borius, Weidmann, Berlin 1920.
Geoffrey of Monmouth: The History of the Kings of Britain, trans. L. Thorpe, Penguin, New York 1966.
Gildas: The Ruin of Britain and Other Works, ed. and trans. M. Winterbottom, Rowman and Littlefield, Totowa, NJ 1978.
Nennius: British History and the Welsh Annals. ed. and trans. J. Morris, Phillimore, London 1980.
Notitia Dignitatum, ed. O. Seeck, Minerva, Frankfurt 1962.
Saint Patrick: His Writings and Muirchu's 'Life', ed. and trans. A.B.E. Hood, Phillimore, London and Chichester 1978.
Procopius: *Bellum Vandalicum* (Loeb edn), trans. H.B. Dewing, Harvard University Press, Cambridge, Mass. 1919.
Sidonius Appolinaris: Poems and Letters (Loeb edn), 2 vols, ed. and trans. W.B. Anderson, Harvard University Press, Cambridge, Mass. 1936.
Tacitus: *Agricola*, trans. H.W. Benario, University of Oklahoma Press, Norman, Okla. 1991 (revised edn).
———: *The Annals*, trans. A.J. Church and W.J. Brodribb, The Franklin Library, Franklin Center, Phil. 1982.
———: *Germania*. *Zosimus: New History*, trans. R.T. Ridley, Association for Byzantine Studies, Sydney 1982.

Literary Works

Aneirn: *Y Gododdin*, ed. and trans. A.O.H. Jarman, Gomer, Llandysul, Dyfed 1988.
———, *The 'Gododdin' of Aneirin: Text and Context from Dark-Age North Britain*, ed. and trans. J.T. Koch, University of Wales Press, Cardiff 1997.
Barthelme, D., *The King*, illus. B. Moser, Harper and Rowe, New York 1990.
Bédier: *The Romance of Tristan and Iseult*, trans. H. Belloc and P. Rosenfeld, Doubleday, New York 1955.
Berger, T., *Arthur Rex*, Laurel, 1985.
Béroul: *The Romance of Tristan*, trans. A.S. Fedrick, Penguin, New York 1970.
———: *The Romance of Tristran*, ed. and trans. N.J. Lacy, Garland, New York 1989.
The Breton Lays in Middle English, ed. T.C. Rumble, Wayne State University Press, Detroit 1965.
Camelot 3000, M.W. Barr, illus. B.Bolland, Warner Books, New York 1988.
Chrétien de Troyes: Arthurian Romances, trans. D.D.R. Owen, Everyman's Library, J.M. Dent & Sons, London 1987.
Christian, C., *The Pendragon*, Warner Books, New York 1978.
Culhwch and Olwen: An Edition and Study of the Oldest Arthurian Tale, ed. R. Bromwich and D.S. Evans, University of Wales Press, Cardiff 1992.
Sir Gawain and the Green Knight, trans. B. Stone Penguin, New York 1979.
Sir Gawain: Eleven Romances and Tales, ed. T. Hahn, TEAMS Middle English Texts Series, Medieval Institute Publications, Kalamazoo, Mich. 1995.
Geoffrey of Monmouth. *The History of the Kings of Britain*, trans. L. Thorpe, Penguin, New York 1966.
Godwin, P., *Firelord*, Bantam Books, New York 1980.
Gottfried von Strassburg: *Tristan*, trans. A.T. Hatto, Penguin, New York 1960.
Invitation to Camelot, ed. P. Godwin, Ace Books, New York 1988.
Karr, P.A., *The Idylls of the Queen*, Berkley Books, New York 1985.
King Arthur's Death ('Morte Arthure' and 'Le Morte Arthur'), trans. B. Stone, Penguin, New York 1988.
Laubenthal, S.A., *Excalibur*, Ballantine Books, New York 1973.
Lawhead, S., *Arthur*, Crossway Books, Westchester, Ill. 1989.
———, *Merlin*, Crossway Books, Westchester, Ill. 1988.
———, *Taliesin*, Crossway Books, Westchester, Ill. 1987.
The Lancelot-Grail Cycle, 5 vols, gen. ed. N.J. Lacy, Garland, New York 1993–96.
Layamon: *Lawman: Brut*, trans. R. Allen, Dent, London 1992.
The Mabinogi and Other Medieval Welsh Tales, ed. and trans. P.K. Ford, University of California Press, Berkeley 1977.
Malory, Sir Thomas: *Le Morte D'Arthur*, 2 vols, ed. J. Cowen, Penguin, New York 1969.
———: *Works*, ed. E. Vinaver, Oxford University Press, New York 1971. Revised version P.J.C. Field, 3 vols, Clarendon Press, Oxford 1990.
———: *Le Morte Darthur*, intro. Helen Moore, Wordsworth Classics, Ware, Hertfordshire 1996.
Newman, S., *Guinevere*, Futura, London 1984.
The Pendragon Chronicles, ed. M. Ashley, Wings Books, New York 1993.
Pyle, H., *The Story of King Arthur and his Knights*, Signet, New York 1986.
The Quest of the Holy Grail, trans. P.M. Matarasso, Penguin, New York 1969.
Steinbeck, J., *The Acts of King Arthur and His Noble Knights*, ed. C. Horton, Ballantine Books, New York 1976.
Stewart, M.,*The Crystal Cave*, Fawcett Crest, New York 1970.
———, *The Hollow Hills*, Fawcett Crest, New York 1973.
———, *The Last Enchantment*, Fawcett Crest, New York 1979.
———, *The Wicked Day*, Fawcett Crest, New York 1983.
Sutcliff, R., *Sword at Sunset*, Tor Books, New York 1987.
Taliesin: *The Poems of Taliesin*, ed. I. Williams, trans. J.E. Caerwyn Williams. Institute for Advanced Studies, Dublin 1968.
———: *Armes Prydein ('The Prophecy of Britain') from the Book of Taliesin*, ed. I. Williams, trans. R. Bromwich, Institute for Advanced Studies, Dublin 1972.
Tennyson, A., *'Idylls of the King' and a Selection of Poems*, Signet, New York 1961.
Trioedd Ynys Prydein: The Welsh Triads, ed. and trans. R. Bromwich, University of Wales Press, Cardiff 1961 (2nd edn 1978).
Twain, M., *A Connecticut Yankee in King Arthur's Court*, Signet, New York.
Wace and Layamon: *The Life of King Arthur*, trans. J.Weiss and R. Allen, Everyman Edition, Dent, London 1997.
White, T.H. *The Sword in the Stone*, Time-Life, New York 1958.
———, *The Once and Future King*, Berkley, New York 1971.
———, *The Book of Merlyn*, Berkley, New York 1983.
Williams, C., *'Taliessin Through Logres' and 'The Region of the Summer Stars'*, commentary C. Williams and C.S. Lewis, Eerdmans, Grand Rapids, Mich. 1974.
Wooley, P., *Child of the Northern Spring*, Pocket Books, New York, 1988.
———, *Queen of the Summer Stars*, Poseidon Press, New York 1990.
———, *Guinevere: The Legend in Autumn*, Pocket Books, New York 1991.
Yolen, J., *Merlin's Booke*, Ace Books, New York, 1986.

Chapter 1: Introduction

There are dozens of good general, introductory works on Arthur, and an equal number of little worth. The two best, for their scholarship (to which the present book is indebted) and broad scope, are N.J. Lacy (ed.), *The New Arthurian Encyclopedia* (Garland, New York 1991), and N.J. Lacy, G. Ashe and D.N. Mancoff, *The Arthurian Handbook*, (Garland, New York 1997, 2nd edn). The following are some other, more lavishly illustrated, recommendations:

Ashe, G., *King Arthur: The Dream of a Golden Age*, Thames and Hudson, London 1990.
Berthelot, A., *King Arthur: Chivalry and Legend*, trans. R. Sharman, Thames and Hudson, London 1997.
Coghlan, R., *The Illustrated Encyclopedia of Arthurian Legends*, Barnes and Noble, New York 1995.
Dunning, R.W., *Arthur: The King in the West*, St Martin's Press, New York 1995.

Chapter 2: Background

In recent years many general works on the Celts and the Druids have been published, again of varying quality, and a few significant scholarly works on British prehistory and the European Iron Age. Here are some noteworthy recent contributions:

Celts: Europe's People of Iron, Time-Life Books, Alexandria, Va. 1994.
Chadwick, N., *The Celts*, Penguin, New York 1971.
Collis, J., *The European Iron Age*, Batsford, London 1984.
Cunliffe, B., *Iron Age Communities in Britain*, Routledge, London 1991 (3rd edn).
———, *The Celtic World*, St Martin's, New York 1993.
———, *The Ancient Celts*, Oxford University Press, Oxford 1997.
Green, M.J., *The Celtic World*, Routledge, London, 1995.
———, *The World of the Druids*, Thames and Hudson, New York 1997 (pub. as *Exploring the World of the Druids*, Thames and Hudson, London 1997).
James, S., *The World of the Celts*, Thames and Hudson, New York 1993 (pub. as *Exploring the World of the Celts*, Thames and Hudson, London 1993).
———, *The Atlantic Celts: Ancient People or Modern Invention?* British Museum Press, London 1999.
Kruta, V. et al. (eds), *The Celts*, Rizzoli, New York 1999.
Piggott, S., *The Druids*, Thames and Hudson, New York 1985.
Powell, T.G.E., *The Celts*, Thames and Hudson, London 1980.
Rankin, H.D., *Celts and the Classical World*, Croom Helm, London 1987.

There is an enormous body of scholarship on Roman Britain. The following is a small selection from this corpus:

Clayton, Peter (ed.), *A Companion to Roman Britain*, Dorset Press, 1985.
Esmonde Cleary, A.S., *The Ending of Roman Britain*, Batsford, London 1989.
Frere, S., *Britannia: A History of Roman Britain*, Routledge and Kegan Paul, London 1987.
Johnson, S., *Later Roman Britain*, Paladin, London 1986.
Jones, M.E., *The End of Roman Britain*, Cornell University Press, Ithaca, NY 1996.
Millet, M., *The Romanization of Britain*, Cambridge University Press, Cambridge 1990.
Salway, P., *The Oxford Illustrated History of Roman Britain*, Oxford University Press, Oxford 1993.
Scullard, H.H., *Roman Britain: Outpost of the Empire*, Thames and Hudson, London 1979.
Thomas, C., *Christianity in Roman Britain to AD 500*, University of California Press, Berkeley, Calif. 1981.

Chapter 3: The Age of Arthur

Alcock, L., *Arthur's Britain*, Penguin, London and New York, 1971.
Alcock, L. et al., *Cadbury Castle, Somerset. The Early Medieval Archaeology*, University of Wales Press, Cardiff 1995.
Arnold, C.J., *Roman Britain to Anglo-Saxon England*, Indiana University Press, Bloomington, Indiana 1984.
Bannerman, J., *Studies in the History of Dalriada*, Scottish Academic Press, Edinburgh, 1974.
Bassett, S. (ed.), *The Origins of the Anglo-Saxon Kingdoms*. Leicester University Press, Leicester 1989.
Campbell, J. (ed.), *The Anglo-Saxons*, Cornell University Press, Ithaca, NY 1982.
Cummins, W.A., *The Age of the Picts*, Alan Sutton, Stroud, Gloucestershire 1995.
Dark, K.R., *Civitas to Kingdom: British Political Continuity 300–800*, Leicester University Press, Leicester 1993.
Foster, S.M., *Picts, Gaels and Scots*, Batsford/Historic Scotland, London 1996.
Henderson, I., *The Picts*, Praeger, New York 1967.
Higham, N.J., *Rome, Britain and the Anglo-Saxons*, Seaby, London 1992.
———, *The English Conquest: Gildas and Britain in the Fifth Century*, Manchester University Press, Manchester and New York 1994.
Hill, P., *Whithorn and St Ninian: The Excavations of a Monastic Town, 1984–91*. Alan Sutton, Stroud, Gloucestershire 1997.
Myres, J.N.L. *The English Settlements*, Clarendon Press, Oxford 1986.
Nicoll, E.H. (ed.), *A Pictish Panorama: The Story of the Picts and A Pictish Bibliography*, Pictish Arts Society, The Pinkfoot Press, Belgavies, Angus 1995.
Ó Cróinín, D., *Early Medieval Ireland, 400–1200*, Longman, London 1995.
Ritchie, A., *The Picts*, HMSO, Edinburgh 1989.
Snyder, C.A., *Sub-Roman Britain (AD 400–600): A Gazetteer of Sites*, British Archaeological Reports, Series No. 247, Tempvs Reparatvm, Oxford 1996.
———, *An Age of Tyrants: Britain and the Britons, AD 400–600*, Penn State University Press, Pa. 1998.
Thomas, C., *Christianity in Roman Britain to AD 500*, Batsford, London 1981.
———, *Celtic Britain*, Thames and Hudson, London 1986.
———, *Tintagel: Arthur and Archaeology*, English Heritage/Batsford, London 1993.
Thompson, E.A., 'Britain, AD 406–410' *Britannia* 8 (1977): 303–18.
———, *St Germanus of Auxerre and the End of Roman Britain*, Boydell, Woodbridge, Suffolk 1984.
Welch, M., *Discovering Anglo-Saxon England*, Penn State University Press, Pa. 1992.
Wilmott, T. et al., *Birdoswald: Excavations of a Roman Fort on Hadrian's Wall and its Successor Settlements: 1987–92*, English Heritage, London 1997.
Wilson, D.M. (ed.), *The Northern World: The History and Heritage of Northern Europe, AD 400–1100*, Harry N. Abrams, New York, 1980.
Wood, I., 'The End of Roman Britain: Continental Evidence and Parallels', in *Gildas: New Approaches*, M. Lapidge and D. Dumville (eds), pp. 1–25, Boydell, Woodbridge, Suffolk 1984.

Chapter 4: The Chronicles of the Britons

Dumville, D.N., *Histories and Pseudo-Histories of the Insular Middle Ages*, Variorum, Aldershot 1990.
Field, P.J.C., 'Nennius and His History', in *Studia Celtica* 30 (1996): pp. 159–65.
Hanning, R.W., *The Vision of History in Early Britain: From Gildas to Geoffrey of Monmouth*, Columbia University Press, New York 1966.
Hanson, R.P.C., *St Patrick: His Origins and Career*, Clarendon Press, Oxford 1968.
Howlett, D.R., *The Celtic Latin Tradition of Biblical Style*, Four Courts Press, Portland, Oreg. 1995.
Kerlouégan, F., *Le De Excidio Britanniae de Gildas: Les destinées de la culture latine dans l'île de Bretagne au VIème siècle*, Publications de la Sorbonne, Paris 1987.
Lapidge, M. and Dumville, D. (eds), *Gildas: New Approaches*, Boydell, Woodbridge, Suffolk 1984.
Thompson, E.A., *Who Was Saint Patrick?* St Martin's Press, New York 1985.

Chapter 5: The Legends of the Britons

For recent editions and translations of the texts, see **Literary Works**, above.

Archibald, E. and Edwards, A.S.G.(eds), *A Companion to Malory*, D.S. Brewer, Cambridge 1996.
Barron, W.R.J. (ed.), *The Arthur of the English*, University of Wales Press, Cardiff 1999.
Bromwich, R. et al., *The Arthur of the Welsh: The Arthurian Legend in Medieval Welsh Literature*, University of Wales Press, Cardiff 1991.
Coe, J.B. and Young, S., *The Celtic Sources for the Arthurian Legend* (texts with English translations), Llanerch, Lampeter, Wales 1995.
Field, P.J.C., *The Life and Times of Sir Thomas Malory*, D.S. Brewer, Cambridge 1993.
———, *Malory: Texts and Sources*, D.S. Brewer, Cambridge 1998.
Ford, P.K., *The Mabinogi and Other Medieval Welsh Tales*, University of California Press, Berkeley 1977.
Jarman, A.O.H., 'The Arthurian Allusions in the Book of Aneirin', in *Studia Celtica* 24/25 (1988/89): pp. 15–25.
Koch, J.T., *The 'Gododdin' of Aneirin: Text and Context from Dark-Age North Britain*, University of Wales Press, Cardiff 1997.
Lacy, N.J. (ed.), *Text and Intertext in Medieval Arthurian Literature*, Garland, New York 1996.
———, *Medieval Arthurian Literature: A Guide to Recent Research*, Garland, New York 1996.
Loomis, R.S. (ed.), *Arthurian Literature in the Middle Ages: A Collaborative History*, Clarendon Press, Oxford 1959.
Sullivan, C.W. III (ed.), *'The Mabinogi': A Book of Essays*, Garland, New York 1996.

Chapter 6: Monarchy, Chivalry and the Return of Arthur

Dean, C., *Arthur of England: English Attitudes to King Arthur and the Knights of the Round Table in the Middle Ages and the Renaissance*, University of Toronto Press, Toronto 1987.
Field, P.J.C., 'Shakespeare's King Arthur', in *The Welsh Connection*, W.M. Tydeman (ed.), Gomer, Llandyssul 1986.
———, *The Life and Times of Sir Thomas Malory*, D.S. Brewer, Cambridge 1993.
Girouard, M., *The Return to Camelot: Chivalry and the English Gentleman*, Yale University Press, New Haven 1981.
Haskins, C.H., 'Henry II as Patron of Literature', in *Essays in Medieval History*, Books for Libraries Press, New York 1967.
Knight, S., *Arthurian Literature and Society*, St Martin's Press, New York 1983.
Mancoff, D.N., *The Arthurian Revival in Victorian Art*, Garland, New York 1990.
———, *The Return of King Arthur: The Legend Through Victorian Eyes*, Harry N. Abrams, New York 1995.
Mancoff, D.N. (ed.), *The Arthurian Revival: Essays on Form, Tradition, and Transformation*, Garland, New York 1992.
Spisak, J.W. (ed.), *Studies in Malory*, Medieval Institute Publications, Kalamazoo, Mich. 1985.
Wood, Christopher, *The Pre-Raphaelites*, Wiedenfeld and Nicolson, London 1981.

Chapter 7: The Quest for Camelot.

Ashe, G., *Avalonian Quest*, Fontana, London 1984.
——— (ed.), *The Quest for Arthur's Britain*, Paladin, London 1971.
———, 'The Origins of the Arthurian Legends', in *Arthuriana* 5, no. 3 (Fall 1995): pp. 1–24.
Bachrach, B.S., 'The Questions of King Arthur's Existence and of Romano-British Naval Operations', in *Haskins Society Journal* 2 (1991): pp. 13–28.
Barber, R., *The Figure of Arthur*, Longman, London 1972.
Bromwich, R., 'Concepts of Arthur', in *Studia Celtica* 10/11 (1975/76): pp. 163–81. (The northern Arthur theory.)
Chambers, E.K., *Arthur of Britain*, October House, New York 1967. First published 1927.

Collingwood, R.G. and Myres, J.N.L., *Roman Britain and the English Settlements*, Clarendon Press, Oxford 1936.
Dumville, D.N., 'Sub-Roman Britain: History and Legend' in *History* 62 (1977): pp. 173–92.
Green, T., 'The Historicity and Historicisation of Arthur', at **www.users.globalnet.co.uk/~tomgreen/arthur.htm** (first appeared March 1998).
———, 'Myrddin/Merlin', at **www.users.globalnet.co.uk/~tomgreen/myrddin.htm** (first appeared May 1998).
Jarman, A.O.H., 'Early Stages in the Development of the Myrddin Legend', in *Astudiaethau ar yr Hengerdd*, R. Bromwich and Jones, R. (eds), pp. 326–49, Gwasg Prifysgol Cymru, Cardiff 1978.
———, 'The Merlin Legend and the Welsh Tradition of Prophecy', in *The Arthur of the Welsh*, pp. 118–1991, University of Wales Press, Cardiff, 1991.
Loomis, R.S., *The Grail: From Celtic Myth to Christian Symbol*, Columbia University Press, New York 1963.
———, *Celtic Myth and Arthurian Romance*, Haskell House, New York 1967.
Malone, K., 'Artorius', in *Modern Philology* 22 (1925): pp. 367–74.
Nickel, H., 'The Dawn of Chivalry', in *Metropolitan Museum of Art Bulletin* 32 (1975): pp. 150–52.
Padel, O.J., 'The Nature of Arthur' in CMCS 27 (Summer 1994): pp. 1–31.
Parins, M.J., 'Looking for Arthur', in *King Arthur: A Casebook*, E. Donald Kennedy (ed.), pp. 3–28, Garland, New York 1996.
Snyder, C.A., 'Once and Future Kings: Political Prophecy in the Medieval Celtic Fringe', (forthcoming).
Weston, J.L., *From Ritual to Romance*, Princeton University Press, NJ 1993.

The following works advocate a particular theory for an historical Arthur, Merlin or Grail. The level of scholarship represented varies greatly.

Ashe, G., 'A Certain Very Ancient Book', in *Speculum* 56 (1981): pp. 301–23.
———, *The Discovery of King Arthur*, Doubleday, New York 1985.
Baigent, M., Leigh, R., and Lincoln, H., *Holy Blood, Holy Grail*, Delacorte Press, New York 1982.
Barber, C. and Pykitt, D., *Journey to Avalon: The Final Discovery of King Arthur*, Samuel Weiser, York Beach, Me. 1997.
Blackett, A.T. and Wilson, A., *Arthur King of Glamorgan and Gwent*, M.T. Byrd and Co., Cardiff 1981.
Darrah, J., *The Real Camelot: Paganism and the Arthurian Romances*, Thames and Hudson, New York 1981.
The Heroic Age 1 (Summer 1999), at **members.aol.com/heroicage1/Issue1/hatoc.htm**. This special issue is devoted to the historical Arthur debate and includes articles about Artuir of Dalriada and Lucius Artorius Castus.
Holmes, M., *King Arthur: A Military History*, Blandford, London 1996.
Littleton, C.S. and Thomas, A.C., 'The Sarmatian Connection: New Light on the Origin of the Arthurian and Holy Grail Legends', in *The Journal of American Folklore* 91 (1978): pp. 512–27.
Littleton, C.S. and Malcor, L.A., *From Scythia to Camelot*, Garland, New York 1994.
Markale, J., *King of the Celts: Arthurian Legends and Celtic Tradition*, trans. C. Hauch, Inner Traditions, Rochester, Vt. 1994.
Millar, R., *Will the Real King Arthur Please Stand Up?*, Cassell, London 1978.
Phillips, G. and Keatman, M., *King Arthur: The True Story*, Random House, London 1993.
Reno, F.D., *The Historic King Arthur: Authenticating the Celtic Hero of Post-Roman Britain*, McFarland, Jefferson, NC, 1996.
Tolstoy, N., '*Merlinus Redivivus*', in *Studia Celtica* 18/19 (1983/84): pp. 11–29.
———, *The Quest for Merlin*, Little, Brown and Co., Boston 1985.
Turner, P.F.J., *The REAL King Arthur, A History of Post-Roman Britannia, AD 410–AD 597*, SKS Publishing, Houston 1993.
Wilson, A. and Blackett, B., *Artorius Rex Discovered*, M.T. Byrd and Co., Cardiff 1985.

Chapter 8: Conclusion.

Harty, K.J., *The Reel Middle Ages*, McFarland and Co., Jefferson, NC 1999.
Lupack, A. and Lupack, B.T., *King Arthur in America*, D.S. Brewer, Cambridge 1999.
Mancoff, D.N. (ed.), *The Arthurian Revival: Essays on Form, Tradition, and Transformation*, Garland, New York 1992.
Ward, B.J. 'King Arthur in Traditional Music', in *Keystone Folklore* 2 (1984): pp. 23–33.

Gazetteer

Anderton, B., *Guide to Ancient Britain*, Foulsham, London 1991.
Ashe, G., *A Guidebook to Arthurian Britain*, The Aquarian Press, Wellingborough, Northamptonshire 1983.
———, *The Landscape of King Arthur*, photographs S. McBride, Webb and Bower, Exeter 1987.
Fairbairn, N. and Cyprien, M., *A Traveller's Guide to the Kingdoms of Arthur*, Historical Times, Harrisburg 1983.
Snyder, C.A., *Sub-Roman Britain (AD 400–600): A Gazetteer of Sites*, British Archaeological Reports, Series No. 247, Tempvs Reparatvm, Oxford 1996.
———, 'A Gazetteer of Sub-Roman Britain (AD 400–600): The British Sites', *Internet Archaeology* 3, at **intarch.ac.uk/**, 1997.

INTERNET RESOURCES

ArthurNet (Arthurian discussion list)
web.clas.ufl.edu/users/jshoaf/Arthurnet.htm
The *Camelot Courier* on-line
(a collection of references to Arthuriana in popular culture)
www.english.udel.edu/rewa/
The *Charrette* Project (a scholarly, multi-media electronic archive containing the medieval manuscript tradition of Chrétien's *Le Chevalier de la Charrette*)
www.princeton.edu/~lancelot/
Doherty, J.J., 'A Handlist of Arthurian Science Fiction and Fantasy, 1980–89'
www.lib.rochester.edu/camelot/acpbibs/doherty.htm
Doherty, J.J., Arthurian Resources on the Internet
jan.ucc.nau.edu/~jjd23/arthur/
Field, P.J.C., 'Historical Arthur Bibliography'
www.lib.rochester.edu/camelot/acpbibs/hisarth.htm
Green, T., 'Arthurian Resources'
www.users.globalnet.co.uk/~tomgreen/Arthuriana.htm
Harty, K.J. 'Arthurian Film Bibliography'
www.lib.rochester.edu/camelot/acpbibs/harty.htm
The Heroic Age: A Journal of Early Medieval Northwest Europe
members.aol.com/heroicage1/homepage.html
The International Marie de France Society
saturn.vcu.edu/~cmarecha/
The Internet Medieval Sourcebook
www.fordham.edu/halsall/sbook.html
Labyrinth's Arthurian Links
data.georgetown.edu/labyrinth/arthurian/
Reel, J.V., Jr., 'Arthurian Musical Theatre: A Listing'
www.lib.rochester.edu/camelot/acpbibs/reel.htm
Salda, M.N., 'Arthurian Animation Bibliography'
www.lib.rochester.edu/camelot/acpbibs/toonbib.htm
Snyder, C.A., 'Arthuriana Chronology', *Arthuriana* (1999)
dc.smu.edu/Arthuriana/
———, 'A Gazetteer of Arthurian Sites', *Arthuriana* (1999)
dc.smu.edu/Arthuriana/
———, 'Sub-Roman Britain,' in *ORB Encyclopedia* (April 1996), C. Schriber et al. (eds)
orb.rhodes.edu/encyclop/early/origins/rom_celt/subroman.html
Stewart, A., 'Camelot in Four Colors: A Survey of the Arthurian Legend in Comics'
camelot4colors.tripod.com/
TEAMS Middle English Texts On-line
www.lib.rochester.edu/camelot/teams/tmsmenu.htm
Torregrossa, M., '*Camelot 3000* and Beyond: An Annotated Listing of Arthurian Comic Books Published in the United States c.1980–1998'
www.lib.rochester.edu/camelot/acpbibs/comicbib.htm

Acknowledgments

Chapter 1: Introduction
p. 7 'brief, shining moment', A.J. Lerner, lyric from the musical *Camelot*.
p. 16 'was received into the prince's . . .' Roger Ascham, from W.H. Schofield, *Chivalryin English Literature* (Harvard University Press, Cambridge, Mass. 1912), p. 79.
p. 18 A version of the Timeline previously appeared on the *Arthuriana* webpage **(dc.smu.edu/Arthuriana)** 1999.

Chapter 2: Background
p. 23 'The Celts live beyond . . .' from A. de Sélincourt, ed. and trans., *Herodotus: The Histories* (Penguin, New York 1972), p. 142.
p. 23 Chart of the Celtic languages based on Foster, *Picts, Gaels and Scots*, p. 23.
p. 26 'So the Romans slaughtered . . .' from Winterbottom, ed. and trans., *Gildas*, p. 18.
p. 27 'did what they were told by the Romans . . .' from Millet, *The Romanization of Britain*, p. *xv*.
p. 27 'never advanced to exalted . . .' from M.E. Jones, 'The Failure of Romanization in Celtic Britain', in *Proceedings of the Harvard Celtic Colloquium 7* (1987), p. 134.
p. 31 'were no longer principally economic', and the paradigm of Late Roman urban restructuring, from Millet, *The Romanization of Britain*, p. 221.

Chapter 3: The Age of Arthur
Some of the material in this chapter appeared previously in C.A. Snyder, *An Age of Tyrants: Britain and the Britons*, AD *400-600*.
pp. 36–37 Quotations about the British usurpers and revolts are from Ridley, trans., *Zosimus*, Book 6.
pp. 37 'the Romans were no longer able . . .' from Dewing, trans., Procopius's *Bellum Vandalicum*, 3.2.38.
p. 45 'the last classically inspired . . .' from G. Webster, *The Cornovii* (Duckworth, London 1975).

Chapter 4: The Chronicles of the Britons
pp. 68–71 Excerpts from Gildas are from Winterbottom, ed. and trans., *Gildas*.
pp. 72–73 and 76–77 Excerpts from the *Annales Cambriae* and the *Historia Brittonum* are from Morris, ed. and trans., *Nennius*.
pp. 80–85 Excerpts from Geoffrey of Monmouth's works are from Thorpe, trans., *Geoffrey of Monmouth*.

Chapter 5: The Legends of the Britons
p. 94 Text of *Y Gododdin* from Coe and Young, *The Celtic Sources for the Arthurian Legend*, p. 154.
p. 95 'a fourth and exceptional . . .' from B. Roberts, 'Culhwch ac Olwen, the Triads, Saints' Lives', in *The Arthur of the Welsh*, R. Bromwich et al. (eds), pp. 73–95.
p. 97 Excerpt from *Culhwch and Olwen* from Ford, ed. and trans., *The Mabinogi*, p. 135.
p. 116 Excerpts from Gottfried von Strassburg are from Hatto, trans., *Tristan*.
p. 118 'What place is there . . .' Alanus de Insulis, from Geoffrey Ashe, ed., *The Quest for Arthur's Britain*, 8.
p. 121 Excerpt from Chaucer's 'The Franklin's Tale', from T.C. Rumble, ed., *The Breton Lays in Middle English*, p. 229.
p. 123 Excerpt from *Sir Gawain and the Green Knight*, Stone, trans., p.26.
p. 125 'The Death of Lancelot' excerpt is from Malory, *Le Morte Darthur*, intro. H. Moore, pp. 802–3.

Chapter 6: Monarchy, Chivalry and the Return of Arthur
p. 130 'the hope of his people', from E.K. Chambers, *Arthur of Britain*, p. 112.
p. 133 'that there might once more . . .' from D. William, 'The Family of Henry VII', in *History Today* 4 (1954), p. 84.
p.133 The phrase '*Arturius Redivivus*' was used by John Leland; 'Arthur magnified' is from S.L. Jansen, 'Prophecy, Propaganda, and Henry VIII: Arthurian Tradition in the Sixteenth Century', in *King Arthur Through the Ages*, V.M. Lagorio and M.L. Day (eds), (Garland, New York 1990), p. 278.
p. 135 'the Worshipfull Societe . . .' from C.B. Millican, 'Spenser and the Arthurian Legend', *The Review of English Studies* 6, no. 22 (April 1930), p. 3.
p. 136 'by raising the popular material . . .' from G. Teskey, 'Arthur in The Faerie Queene', in *The Spenser Encyclopedia* (University of Toronto Press, Toronto 1992), p. 69.

Chapter 7: The Quest for Camelot
p. 148 'the last Roman emperor . . .' from J. Morris, *The Age of Arthur* (Scribner's, New York 1973), p.141.
p. 148 'The fact of the matter . . .' from D. Dumville, 'Sub-Roman Britain: History and Legend', *History* 62 (1977): pp. 173–192 (188).
p. 151 Quotations from R.S. Loomis, *Celtic Myth and Arthurian Romance*, pp. 350 and 353.
p. 151 Quotations from J. Darrah, *The Real Camelot: Paganism and the Arthurian Romances*, p. 7.
p. 151 Quotations from O.J. Padel, 'The Nature of Arthur', CMCS 27 (Summer 1994): pp. 1–31.
pp. 154–57 All quotations can be found in C.A. Snyder, 'Once and Future Kings: Political Prophecy in the Medieval Celtic Fringe' (forthcoming).
p. 161 'The Otherworld is . . .' from J. Weston, *From Ritual to Romance*, p. 186.

Gazetteer
A version of the Gazetteer previously appeared on the *Arthuriana* webpage **(dc.smu.edu/Arthuriana)** *Arthuriana*, 1999.

Illustration credits
t=top, a=above, b=below, c=centre, l=left, r=right

The drawings on the following pages are by Samuel Valentino: 10l, 11r, 15, 16tl, 18–19, 23, 24b, 28b, 38–39, 40tl, 42tl, 42cl, 43bl, 45tr, 49a, 49b, 52a, 52b, 53a, 55a, 56tr, 58, 63, 89, 96, 116, 130, 151, 155b, 168l.

The photographs on the following pages are by Christopher Snyder: 16l, 29, 31a, 41b, 42br, 44a, 44-45, 45cr, 68b, 161tl, 176b.

6–7 Bibliothèque nationale de France, Paris, MS Fr 112. 8l The Royal Photographic Society Collection, Bath, England. Website **www.rps.org**. 8r Photo Hulton Getty, London. 9l Bodleian Library, University of Oxford, MS Douce 383, f. 12v. 9r BFI Films: Stills, Posters and Designs. 10tr Drawing by Trevor Stubley. Courtesy of the artist. 10–11b Birmingham Museums & Art Gallery. 11a Photo © The SKYSCAN Photolibrary. 12a © British Museum 2000. 12b © British Museum 2000. 13a Drawing by Caroline Fleming. From *Sutton Hoo: Burial Ground of Kings* by Martin Carver (British Museum Press, London 1998). 13b Photo Janet & Colin Bord/Fortean Picture Library. 14tl Bibliothèque nationale de France, Paris MS Fr. 95, f.159v. 14tr *Britannia* webpage. **www.britannia.com/history/h12.html**. 14b Photo Paul Broadhurst/Fortean Picture Library. 16l Collection Powys Council. 16b From *Lancelot du Lac* (printed by Jean Dupre, Paris, 1488). 16tr BFI Films: Stills, Posters and Designs. 17 Illustration from Thomas Malory's *La Mort d'Arthur*, London, 1894. 20–21 Photo The British Tourist Authority. 22a Photo Christopher Chippindale. 22b By permission of the British Library, MS Egerton 3028 f.30r. 24a © British Museum 2000. 25a © British Museum 2000. 25b Courtesy of Peter Connolly. 26l © British Museum 2000. 27a Photographed by Cambridge University Aerial Photography Unit. 27b Photo Peter Chèze-Brown. 28a Photo Roman Baths Museum, Bath. 30a Photo German Archaeological Institute, Rome. 30b Page from 5th century *Notitia Dignitatum*. Bodleian Library, University of Oxford. 31b © British Museum 2000. 32–33 By permission of the British Library, MS Royal 20 A II , f. 3R. 34–35 © Crown Copyright NMR. 36 © British Museum 2000. 37a Monza, Cathedral Treasury. Photo Hirmer. 37b By permission of the British Library, MS Eg 3628. 38 Photo National Museum of Ireland, Dublin. 39 By permission of the British Library, Cotton Tibernius Cii, f. 5v. 40bl Manx National Heritage. 40br © English Heritage Photo Library/Jonathan Bailey. 42bl Photo Peter Chèze-Brown. 43tl Photo Associated Press, 1967. 43tr Reproduced by kind permission of Prof. Leslie Alcock. 46a Bodleian Library, University of Oxford. 46b Front of cross slab,

Glamis, Angus, 8th century. Crown Copyright: Reproduced by Permission of Historic Scotland. 47b Photos Worthing Museum and Art Gallery. 50 Drawing by Peter Froste. Courtesy of Colchester Archaeological Trust Ltd. 51 © British Museum 2000. 53b © British Museum 2000. 54bl Drawing by Anthony Barton. 54br Drawing by Simon James. 55b Photo Peter Chèze-Brown. 56c © British Museum 2000. 56bl Crown Copyright: Royal Commission on the Ancient and Historical Monuments of Scotland. 56br © The Trustees of the National Museums of Scotland 2000. 57bl Drawing by Stephen Conlin from Mallory 'Navan Fort', 1985. 57br Crown Copyright. 59a The Board of Trinity College, Dublin. 59b Photo © Mick Sharp. 61a © Danish National Museum, Copenhagen. 61b © British Museum 2000. 62a Drawing by Peter Dunn. © English Heritage Photo Library. 62b Ashmolean Musem, Oxford. 64–65 Illustration by Gustav Doré to Tennyson's *Idylls of the King*, 1868. 66–67 By permission of the British Library, MS Cotton Vitellius A vi. 69 Photo © Cambridge University Aerial Photography Unit. 70 Photo © Jean Williamson/Mick Sharp. 72 By permission of the British Library. 73a Lambeth Palace Library, MS. 6, f. 66v. 73b Photo Fortean Picture Library. 74–75 Mary Evans Picture Library/Arthur Rackham Collection. Reproduced by kind permission of the artist's family. 76bl Bodleian Library, University of Oxford, MS. Bodl. Rolls 3. 76tr © British Museum 2000, Ms. Harley 3859, f. 187. 77 Photo Scala. 78–79 Bibliothèque nationale de France, Paris, MS. Fr. 343, f.3. 80 Bibliothèque Municipale, Douai. 81 Copyright Brussels, Royal Library of Belgium, MS. 9243, f.36v. 82 By permission of the British Library, MS Add 10,294, f.94. 83 By permission of the British Library, MS. Add. 10, 292, f. 97v. 84l Bradford Art Galleries and Museums, West Yorkshire, UK/Bridgeman Art Library. 84r Lambeth Palace Library, MS.6, f.62v. 85 Birmingham Museums & Art Gallery. 86–87 The Hague, Koninklijke Bibliotheek, KA 20, f. 163v. 88a The De Morgan Foundation. 88b By permission of the British Library, MS Egerton 3028. 90–91 Illustration by Gustav Doré to Tennyson's *Idylls of the King*, 1868. 92 National Museum of Wales, Cardiff. 93 Birmingham Museums & Art Gallery. 94 Cardiff MS 1 (2.81), reproduced by kind permission of Cardiff County Library Service and the National Library of Wales, Aberystwyth. 95 The Royal Photographic Society Collection, Bath, England. Website **www.rps.org**. 97 © Alan Lee. 98 Cardiff MS 1 (2.81), reproduced by kind permission of Cardiff County Library Service and the National Library of Wales, Aberystwyth. 99 Bibliothèque nationale de France, Paris. 100 Photo Martin Hürlimann. 101 Russell-Cotes Art Gallery and Museum, Bournemouth, UK/Bridgeman Art Library. 102–103 Photo Christie's Images, London. 104 From Thomas Malory *The Birth, Life and Acts of King Arthur* (NY, EP Dutton, 1927). 105 Mary Evans Picture Library/Arthur Rackham Collection. Reproduced by kind permission of the artist's family. 106 Bibliothèque nationale de France, Paris, Fr 120, f. 590 v. 107a Bibliothèque nationale de France, Paris, MS Fr. 122, f.1. 107b Musée du Louvre, Paris. 108–109 National Museum of American Art, Washington DC/Art Resource, NY. 110 Bibliothèque nationale de France, Paris. MS Fr 12577. 111 Walker Art Gallery, Liverpool. 112 By permission of the British Library, Add 10, 294 f.66v. 113a Bibliothèque nationale de France, Paris, MS Fr. 343, f. 18. 113b Fogg Art Museum, Bequest of Grenville L. Winthrop, Harvard University Art Museums, USA /Bridgeman Art Library. 114–115 Bibliothèque nationale de France, Fr 112, f.239. 117a City Art Centre, City of Edinburgh Museums and Galleries. © Estate of John Duncan 2000. All rights reserved DACS. 117b © British Museum 2000. 118a Bibliothèque nationale de France, Paris, MS Fr99, f.561r. 118b Photo © Doug Corrance/Still Moving Picture Co. 119a Photo Bildarchiv Foto Marburg. 119bl The Arni Magnusson Institute, Flateyjarbok, GKS 1005 f. Photo © Stofnun Árna Magnússonar. 119br Prince Charles Bridge, built c.1357. Prague. 120a Photo Alinari. 120bl By permission of the British Library, Ms. Add. 7169, f. 11. 120br Photo Instituto Amatller De Arte Hispanico, Madrid. 121a Wife of Bath from Chaucer's *Canterbury Tales*, Caxton's edition, c.1484. 121b © British Museum 2000, MS Add. 5141, f.1. 122 Reproduced with permission of the Palace of Westminster (WOA 3152). 123 By permission of The British Library, MS. Cott Nero A X, f.94v. 124a By courtesy of the National Portrait Gallery, London. 124b Caxton's trademark and initials. 125 Reproduced by courtesy of the Director and University Librarian, The John Rylands University Library of Manchester. 126–127 Victoria and Albert Museum, London. 128tr Photo Scala. 128cl Photo Eileen Tweedy. 128b Fr 22495, f.69v, Bibliothèque Nationale Paris, France/Bridgeman Art Library. 129r From William Camden's *Britannia* (1607 edition). 129l Drawing by Judith Dobie. © English Heritage Photo Library. 131 Bodleian Library, University of Oxford. MS Douce 383, f.16. 132 Bibliothèque nationale de France. 133a The Royal Collection © 2000, Her Majesty Queen Elizabeth II. 133b Victoria and Albert Museum, London. 134a Reproduced by kind permission of Hampshire County Council. 134b Sketches of Cadbury 'Camelot' from Musgraves *Antiquitates Britanno-Belgicae*, 1719. 135a Christopher Wood Gallery, London, UK/Bridgeman Art Library. 135b National Maritime Museum, Greenwich. 136tl The Red Cross Knight from Edmund Spenser's *The Faerie Queen*. Woodcut, 1590. 136tr Courtesy of The Marquess of Salisbury. 136b Title page of Edmund Spenser's *The Faerie Queen*, 1590. 137a Reproduced by permission of Dumfries and Galloway Council/National Trust for Scotland. 137b From *Cleave's Gazette of Variety*, 14 September, 1839. By permission of the British Library. 138l The Royal Photographic Society Collection, Bath, England. Website **www.rps.org**. 138r The Royal Collection © 2000, Her Majesty Queen Elizabeth II. 139a Reproduced with permission of the Palace of Westminster (WOA S114). 139b Reproduced with permission of the Palace of Westminster. 140–141 Tate Gallery, London 2000. 142bl © Manchester City Art Galleries. 142tr Photos R. Wagner Archive, Bayreuth. 142br Richard Wagner Museum, Bayreuth. 143a Tate Gallery, London 2000. 143b Photo The Mark Twain House, Hartford, CT. 144–145 South Cadbury. Photo Tony McGrath. Courtesy The Observer Picture Desk. 146a By permission of the British Library. MS Roy. 20.A.II, f. 4r. 146b Editions Gallimard. 147 Photo Janet & Colin Bord/Fortean Picture Library. 148 Musée de Bretagne, Rennes. 149 Historisches Museum, Bern. 150 Photo © Grosvenor Museum, Chester. 152–153 Mary Evans Picture Library/Arthur Rackham Collection. Reproduced by kind permission of the artist's family. 154tl Bodleian Library, University of Oxford. MS Douce 178. 154bl National Museum of Wales, Cardiff. 155a Photo Janet & Colin Bord/Fortean Picture Library. 156a Lambeth Palace Library, MS6, f.43v. 156b By permission of the British Library, MS. Roy. 20.A.II, f. 3v. 157a Drawing by Louis Rhead. 157b Photo *Western Mail and Echo*, Cardiff. 158a Photo National Museum of Ireland, Dublin. 158b MS Arsenal 5218, Bibliothèque de l'Arsenal, Paris. 159a John Matthews Collection. 159b Photo Boston Public Library. 160a By permission of the British Library, MS Add. 10, 292, f.74. 160b Photo © Cambridge University Aerial Photography Unit. 161bl Photo Reece Winstone. 161br William Morris Gallery, Walthamstow, London. 162–163 Glasgow Museums: Art Gallery & Museum, Kelvingrove. 164–165 Courtesy of Python (Monty) Pictures Ltd. Photo Ronald Grant Archive. 166 Cover illustration by Brad Bradlt. 167l George Allen & Unwin Ltd. 167r Drawing by T.H. White for *The Sword in the Stone* (Published by Wm. Collins). 168r Camelot 3000 ™ and © 2000 DC Comics. All rights reserved. Used with permission. 169a © Walt Disney Co. Photo The Ronald Grant Archive. 169bl Photo The Ronald Grant Archive. 169br Photo Photofest, New York. 170l BFI Films: Stills, Posters and Designs. 170–171 BFI Films: Stills, Posters and Designs. 171tr Photo The Ronald Grant Archive. 172l Photo © Clive Barda/Performing Arts Library, London. 172r Photo Martin Gwynedd. 173a Photo Pierre Petit and Trinquant, Paris 1860. Richard Wagner Museum, Bayreuth. 173b Bildarchiv-Bayreuther Festspiele. Photo Lauterwasser. 174a BFI Films: Stills, Posters and Designs. 174b Homepage of 'The Camelot Project' at the University of Rochester, created by Alan Lupack and Barbara Tepa Lupack. 175a Photo courtesy of John F. Kennedy Library, Boston. 175b From James M. Ward, and Robert J. Kuntz, *Deities and Demigods* (AD&D), Lake Geneva, WI, 1980. 176a Photo Janet & Colin Bord/Fortean Picture Library. 177 Mary Evans Picture Library.

Index

Page numbers in *italic* refer to illustrations and captions. There may also be textual references on these pages.